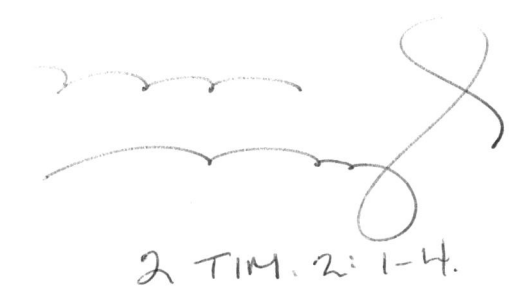

LET THE
WARRIORS ARISE

2 TIM. 2: 1-4.

LET THE WARRIORS ARISE

TAKE UP YOUR IDENTITY AND DESTINY IN CHRIST

DONALD BOYD

© Copyright 2017 – Donald Boyd
All rights reserved.

This book may not be copied or reprinted for commercial gain or profit.

Unless otherwise indicated Scripture quotations are from the

New Living Translation of the Bible.
2nd Edition Tyndale Publishers, Inc., Carol Stream, Illinois, 1996, 2004,
Tyndale Charitable Trust, Scripture quotations marked NLT are taken
from the *Holy Bible,* New Living Translation. Copyright © 1996, 2004.
Used by permission of Tyndale House Publishers, Inc.,
Carol Stream, Illinios. All rights reserved.

Cover Artwork: Rachael Rector

ISBN-13: 978-1976236259
ISBN-10: 1976236258

DEDICATION

First and foremost, this book is dedicated
to the glory of God, my Saviour, Jesus Christ.
I owe everything to Him and pray that He will be exalted
by all who read it.

I also dedicate "Let the Warriors Arise"
to my darling wife, Sharon.
Thank you for your prayers, friendship and strength.

Last, but not least, I offer my work as a legacy
to my son, Andrew, and daughter, Heather,
and to their respective families, to whom I must confess
that I have inadequately portrayed the heart of the Father.
May the next generations go above and beyond
in the things pertaining to the Faith.

ACKNOWLEDGEMENTS

Although it seems trite, I want to start by thanking God for His grace and favour in my life. Without Christ, I have no idea where I'd be today. It is His goodness and His good pleasure that have inspired this book.

I am also grateful for the godly heritage received from my parents, particularly my mom. Her example of unwavering faith in God and her many, many prayers for her sons served as a strong foundation for my life of faith.

I owe a huge debt of gratitude to my wife and companion, Sharon, who has endured my 'stuff' as I've struggled to embrace transformation in my own life. I am grateful for her patience and the balance she has brought into my life. Opposites do attract – but they also bring much needed balance. Her partnership in ministry has enabled me to go far above and beyond what I could have done on my own. I should also acknowledge my son, Andrew, and daughter, Heather, who saw too much of their 'old man's old man,' and love me just the same.

Many thanks also go to a variety friends who have walked with me, both in this endeavour and in ministry. I owe a huge debt of gratitude to Donna Parachin, Steve Chua, Nicola Tayebwa, Carol Miller, Mike and Becky Chaille, Martin Frankenna, and many others. Their ministry in my life was a huge learning curve for which I am very grateful. Particular blessings go to my very dear friends, Paul and Angie Wagler, of Arise Now Ministries, www.arisenow.ca, who have encouraged and coached me in the writing, editing, cover design, and publishing of this book; to James McDowell, who spent many hours reviewing the manuscript; and to the artist, Rachael Rector, who serves with LIVING WALK – a ministry of SOS Canada, https://www.livingwalk.ca, and who created the artwork for the front cover. Their encouragement and expertise are deeply appreciated!

I am reminded of the Apostle Paul's words to the Corinthians, *"I planted the seed in your hearts, and Apollos watered it, but it was God who made it grow. It's not important who does the planting, or who does the watering. What's important is that God makes the seed grow. The one who plants and the one who waters work together with the same purpose"* (1 Corinthians 3:6-8a). My name may be on the front of this book; but, in a variety of ways, many have contributed to it.

Unless otherwise specified, Biblical quotes have been taken from the Holy Bible, New Living Translation.

ENDORSEMENTS

Having known and walked with Don Boyd for over 15 years, we count him one of our dear friends. Don is an ardent follower of Jesus Christ; and his is not an ordinary life, but one of unusual experiences, of significant loss, and of great recovery.

We commend to you, both Don and his first book, "Let the Warriors Arise." This is 'Christianity 101'— a must read for all who desire to follow Jesus well. Don teaches us how to align ourselves with the purposes and plans of God for our lives by taking us on a journey of transformation and helping us to understand the image in which we were created, how it was lost, and how God wants to transform us back into that image. This is also a book about recovering and discovering our spiritual identity.

It's time to "Let the Warriors Arise," so that each one of us can take the ground we are called to take and to walk in all that God has designed for us!

Paul and Angie Wagler,
Authors, speakers, founders of Arise Now — a ministry to encourage and equip! — www.arisenow.ca www.facebook.com/arisenow.ca

"Don Boyd writes with the authority of a pastor who has 'been there, done that,' and the empathy of a fellow pilgrim on the road less travelled. He knows and understands 'the human condition.' This read is a good one."

Rev. James Cantelon
Founder & President — WOW, Working for Orphans & Widows/A ministry of Visionledd — www.wowmission.com

TABLE OF CONTENTS

Preface		13
Introduction		17
Chapter 1	Life as it was Meant to Be	21
Chapter 2	This is Going to Be Bad; Really, Really Bad	33
Chapter 3	Amazing Grace; How Sweet the Sound!	53
Chapter 4	Let's Begin Again	75
Chapter 5	Of Course, You Know; This Means War	93
Chapter 6	Plunging Headlong Into Battle	105
Chapter 7	In the M*A*S*H Unit	125
Chapter 8	Identity Issues - Yours, Mine and Ours	141
Chapter 9	Follow the Leader; It's Not Just a Kids' Game	161
Chapter 10	No Man is an Island	181
Chapter 11	Walking in Freedom in the Here and Now	201
Chapter 12	Finally Home	231
Conclusion		241
Footnotes		243

PREFACE

In the Bible, the Book of Judges tells us the amazing life-story of a common, ordinary man named Gideon. He was a nobody from an unimportant clan and a nondescript heritage. Furthermore, his people were oppressed by the enemy; and Gideon was scratching out a living, hiding from the foe. He had no idea what God had in store for him or his people. Without warning, an angel of God appeared, addressing Gideon with a shocking rhema (personal prophetic) word, "Hail, Mighty Man of Valour!" Gideon probably looked around for someone else and thought, "Who? Me?"

Nonetheless, once Gideon embraced his spiritual identity and began following the orders he had received from the Lord, he went on to accomplish great things and to experience many amazing adventures as he freed Israel from their oppressors and restored the worship of his God. What if Gideon hadn't learned who he was or what his commission might be? His miserable life wouldn't have changed; he and his people would have lived out their days in misery and oppression. But that's not how the story ended.

What about you and me? Regardless of whether you're just exploring Christianity and wondering what this faith is all about, or a new believer – someone who has recently begun to follow Jesus – or someone who's been around the faith for quite a while, we'd all do well to wonder, "What identity and destiny does God have for me? Do I have an adventure to experience and a commission to fulfill?" It is amazing how many people don't realize all that God has for them. That leaves us with some very important questions; "How do I find out what my destiny is?" and "How do I get there?" to name a few.

Or is Christianity just about 'when we all get to Heaven…'? While it is true that God wants each of His children to spend eternity with Him, the Christian life is less about getting us to our final destination and more about us becoming the people we were made to be. Romans 8:29 tells us that God's ultimate goal and perpetual activity is to conform His sons and daughters into the image of Christ. He invites each of us to participate with Him in that life-transforming process and to join Him on the journey into our identity and destiny.

I appreciate the story about a man who was watching a silversmith at his trade. The crafts-man would heat up the raw silver and then skim off the impurities, only to repeat the process over and over again. Eventually, the visitor asked the smith how he knew the silver was finally pure. His answer? "When I can see my face looking back at me." What a great picture! God is at work in our lives until He sees Himself in us!

It's a life-long process that will last until we stand in Eternity and see our Saviour face to face. Then, and only then, will the transformation be complete! As 1 John 3:2 puts it, *"…He has not yet shown us what we will be like when Christ appears. But we do know that we will be like Him, for we will see Him as He really is."* While that's great news, the end-product of the transformation process is also hard to imagine. I wonder if a caterpillar has any concept of what a butterfly actually is or what life on the other side of the chrysalis is like!

Between the reality of 'now' and the eventuality of 'then,' what do we do with our lives? Ask a person what his or her destiny is, chances are, they'll automatically talk about some activity. In reality, pursuing our destiny is more about becoming the right person, than finding the right activity. Oddly enough, becoming the person God intends you and me to be will lead us into a cause that is worth living and dying for and the purpose for which we were created. Not only that, embracing the transformation process enables us to give expression to the new life – the life of God – that resides deep within each believer.

PREFACE

Let's face it; God is a warrior; He bares His strong right arm and fights for His people. Not only that, just as He called Gideon, He calls us to become spiritual warriors and to join Him in setting the captives free. Moving us from hiding cowards to Mighty Men of Valour is a journey on which God takes each of His children.

This book is offered as a guide to the transformation process. On this journey, we'll find twelve stops along the route, each one with its own central theme and challenge. They're presented in the hope that the larger picture, as well as the twelve vignettes, will explain what God might be up to in your life and inspire you to work with Him in that great enterprise. My prayer is that you will gain understanding and vision. Beyond that, I trust that you will be encouraged, exhorted, and comforted, and that you, Mighty Warrior, will arise!

Lastly, let me say that, although I am making progress, I'm still in process. I've learned a lot; but the more I know, the more I understand how little I know. Even toward the end of his life, the Apostle Paul had to admit that he had not yet arrived.

So, let me invite you, as one traveller in process to another, to come along to discover what God is accomplishing in our lives. Who knows? It might just be one wild adventure!

INTRODUCTION

In the Spring of 1997, I found myself battered, beaten and broken. Although I'd been a Christian for almost forty years and had been in ministry for more than twenty, I was exhausted, discouraged, and defeated as I laid on a gurney in the emergency ward, wondering if I'd ever see my wife and children again. As the Apostle Paul said, when explaining the reality of his recent experiences, *"We were crushed and overwhelmed beyond our ability to endure, and we thought we would never live through it"* (2 Corinthians 1:8b). At that point, I told my wife, "I don't know who I am, and I don't know who God is…" It was the worst season of my life.

In the midst of all that, God was very gracious. In answer to prayer, He healed me in a miraculous and instantaneous way. That experience gave me my life back and restored my physical health. More importantly, I met God in an entirely new manner. I had never known the love of the Father in a personal way before; but, since that experience, I no longer need to wonder who God is or if He loves me.

Not only that, but I believe God told me in very specific terms who I am in Him – what my spiritual identity is: a spiritual warrior. In one evening, God answered both of my questions; "Who is God?" and "Who am I?" He is so good and kind! I had experienced God's love in a very profound way; and I learned who I am in Him. But God wasn't finished with me yet. He also implanted in my spirit what I see as 'my commission.' Somehow, in the midst of all of that, something was placed deep into the core of my being; it is one little line, spoken by Jesus, and reflects the heart of the Father so well.

In Luke 4, Jesus was reading from Isaiah 61 and telling the crowd that He was the fulfillment of Isaiah's prophecy. It is a pretty famous portion of Scripture; *"The Spirit of the Lord is upon Me, for He has anointed Me to bring Good News to the poor. He has sent Me to proclaim **that captives will be released**, that the blind will see, that the oppressed will be set free, and that the time of the Lord's favor has come"* (Emphasis mine). In my encounter with the living God, it came across this way: *"to set the captives free."*

Although we might not know it, we ALL have a spiritual identity, a commission, and a destiny in God. Those always reflect the heart of the Father. After all, we have been made in the image of God and to represent Him here on Planet Earth.

The Father's desire to set the captives free has been wonderfully portrayed for us in the story of the Exodus. That book of the Bible recounts God's powerful plan to free His Chosen People from bondage in Egypt, how He led them patiently and faithfully through the wilderness, and then enabled them to possess the land and the destiny that He had promised to His children. This is more than an accurate, historical account of God's activity on behalf of those He loved; it is an allegorical illustration of what He wants to do for each of us – to free us from slavery to sin, to transform our lives back into His image, and to release us into the destiny that He has for you and me.

In the Exodus story, we find that obtaining such liberty and blessing required a two-fold approach. God was willing to do what only He could do. After all, God is a loving and passionate father; and, like any good father, He will do pretty much anything for the good of His children, even if it means taking on the persona of a Mighty Warrior. What father, seeing His children being oppressed and abused, wouldn't be moved to action – even violent action – in order to rescue them?

Moving three million people from Egypt to Israel also took the cooperative and obedient efforts of His people. In the same way,

INTRODUCTION

walking in freedom, identity, transformation, and blessing requires that we do our part to cooperate with what God wants to do in us, for us, and through us.

That trek from Egypt to Israel was really only a few day's journey, but it took the Israelites more than forty years because God's people didn't 'get with the program.' Their unbelief and resultant lack of obedience slowed the process down. Although they knew their final destination, the Israelites didn't know HOW God would do what He said He would do. Perhaps this lack of vision led to lack of faith, and lack of faith led to a lack in obedience. The result? A whole generation never entered their destiny in the Promised Land.

This book is not really about THEIR journey; it is about OURS! It is offered in an attempt to explain how Father God works in the lives of His children and walks with them on their journey to freedom and blessing. Perhaps it will help you to 'get with the program' and to embrace what God is doing in your life.

Using the 'warrior' analogy, we could see it as an over-view of the battle strategy already launched on our behalf from the war-room of Heaven. If we understand the war, maybe we'll be better prepared for battle. After all, the Israelites had to fight many a battle in order to possess what God had promised. In the same way, we are called to fight for the freedom that is only found in God's plan for our lives.

Jeremiah 29:11 is a well-known and very inspiring verse: *"For I know the plans I have for you,' says the Lord. 'They are plans for good and not for disaster, to give you a future and a hope.'"* The question is, "How can we align ourselves with what God is doing and enter into the things He has for us?" When we come to understand what God is doing, it becomes possible for us to co-operate with Him in the effort.

This information is more than just theory; I've lived it, am still in the process, and have seen others embrace the same understanding. While I'm still on my journey – I haven't arrived yet, by any means - I am no longer where I used to be, and I'm not who I used to be.

19

Although I never want to go back to those difficult days of 1997, I am so grateful that God not only took me *to* them, He took me *through* them. Just as the Israelites had to leave the wilderness and cross over the Jordan River to enter the Promised Land, I've found that life is SO much better on this side of Jordan!

I've learned so much in the process and want to share it with you. My word of encouragement: "If God can do it for me; He can do it for you, too." Here's my invitation for you to come along on the journey of transformation and to embrace some important insight and vision. Whether you're exploring Christianity, a new believer, or have been a follower of Jesus for a while now, I hope you'll enjoy the journey and that by the time you finish the book, you'll say, "Well, that explains a lot!"

CHAPTER 1

LIFE AS IT WAS MEANT TO BE
(Before the war...)

***Genesis 1:31** "Then God looked over all He had made, and He saw that it was very good!"*

Many people know the 'first rule of real estate:' "Location, location, location!" The value of the property you're buying varies greatly depending on its location. For example, the house you might buy in Kitchener, Ontario would be less than half the price you'd pay in Vancouver, British Columbia for the same thing. A house next to a factory or beside a graveyard won't fetch the same price as an identical structure in a beautiful, gated community.

What is the location for our stories, yours and mine? In order to comprehend that, we'll need to get a good understanding of the larger picture of human experience according to the Bible. Where else would our story begin but at the beginning, in Genesis?

There are times to take the language and terminology of the Bible literally; there are times to take it figuratively. For example, the Bible speaks of Jesus as the "Lamb of God." This does not mean the Jesus is a young sheep with four legs, curly hair, and the potential to make a good meal. We understand that this reference is a metaphor and indicates that Jesus would be God's ultimate sacrifice for sin (Anything that is not in line with the moral character and will of God). Normally, though, we let the text say what it means and mean what it says; we assume that God wants to communicate with His people and so speaks clearly and literally.

The problem with this is that a literal understanding of some Bible passages presents quite a challenge to our human intellect. Occasionally, a literal interpretation of a passage can create a conflict between what the Bible seems to say and the information we've learned through scientific investigation. For example, the first book in the Bible, Genesis, speaks of a creation that took six days to accomplish. Taking the Creation Narrative literally presents quite a contrast to the millions and millions of years that the theory of evolution espouses. Both positions – creation and evolution – require faith – even blind faith – to believe. Some Christians hold to one theory, and others embrace the alternative.

Whether a person takes the Book of Genesis literally or allegorically, there is much to be learned about God's original intent and design for us humans. From our vantage point in the present, as we look back at the reality of human history, with all its joys and sorrows, accomplishments or failures, and with our moral uprightness or depravity, we are forced to wonder, "God, what were You thinking?" As my daughter, Heather, sadly comments, "Our world is so broken…"

This makes it difficult for us to grasp what a whole or healthy world would have been like. All we really know is that it was different from what we see today. Certainly, the effects of sin and abuse have changed the natural world around us, and we assume that the change has not been for the better. I suspect that, like looking at a long-abandoned homestead with a dilapidated house, barn and out-buildings, we find it hard to imagine what the place looked like when it was newly settled.

A quick overview of the early chapters of Genesis shows us a very different world from the one in which we live – one big land mass surrounded by water, no rain, no sin, no fear, no shame, no sickness or death, a talking animal, and two unique people who apparently knew God and walked and talked with Him face to face. It is no surprise that we call it, "Paradise!" While the secular world depicts our earliest ancestors as bulky, hairy, knuckle-draggers, recently emerged from some primordial swamp as the result of time and chance, the Bible gives us a very different perspective.

As you listen to what Genesis 1:26a and 27 say about mankind, keep in mind that often the first time we read about something in Scripture gives particular insight into that thing, person or event. *"Then God said, 'Let Us make human beings in Our image, to be like Us…' So, God created human beings in His own image. In the image of God, He created them; male and female He created them."*

These verses contain two deep truths or principle concepts: creation and image. God created man. The verb indicates a conscious, intentional decision to make something. Mankind was no accident, but the product of an intentional, pre-determined act of God. He chose to make us, and He intelligently and intentionally designed how He wanted to make us. Scripture uses the imagery of a potter throwing some vessel on the wheel to portray how God works with His people. Isaiah 64:8 reads, *"And yet, O Lord, You are our Father. We are the clay, and You are the potter. We all are formed by Your hand."*

The second concept from Genesis 1 is the intent or purpose for which mankind was created. In Genesis 1:26,27, we repeatedly see the terms, 'like' and 'image.' 'Like' is the Hebrew word 'demuth' and is pretty much directly translated 'likeness' and is "an attempt to explain something by referring to something else that it is like."[1] 'Image' (Hebrew: tzelem) means 'representation.'[2] If we assume that this indicates that mankind is a physical replica of God, we may end up doing what is mentioned in Romans 1:23, *"…and instead of worshiping the glorious, ever-living God, they worshiped idols made to look like mere people and birds and animals and reptiles…"*

A better understanding of Genesis 1:26 would be to see these verses addressing God's intent in creating man. We were to be His representatives on the Earth. Let's allow the context and what else is in the passage to bring clarity. The last half of Verse 26 adds, *"…They will reign over the fish in the sea, the birds in the sky, the livestock, all the wild animals on the Earth, and the small animals that scurry along* the ground." Verse 28 extends the idea, *"Then God blessed them and said, 'Be fruitful and multiply. Fill the Earth and govern it. Reign over the fish in the sea, the birds in the sky, and all the animals that scurry along the ground.'"* 'Govern' (Hebrew: kabash) means 'to subdue or dominate or tread down.'[3] In other words, man was given dominion – the authority and power to rule over the animals and the rest of creation. 'Reign' backs up this idea; the Hebrew word, 'radah' means 'to rule, have dominion, reign.'[4] Unfortunately, we tend to assume that reigning or having dominion suggests some form of hard-hearted despot, using and abusing his realm without restraint or accountability. Thankfully, God is not like that; it's not His nature. As His representatives, Adam and Eve tended and cared for the garden; they didn't abuse it. Such a thing wasn't in their nature either! Perhaps they 'reigned' and 'had dominion' by caring for and ordering their world in a way that God, who loves His creation, would have wanted them to do.

Inherent in the idea of being in the image of God is the concept that we were created to represent Him by reigning over the Earth and all that is in it. In Canada, we have a Governor-General who represents either the King or Queen of England in our country. While some people regard this as little more than a social hangover from colonial days, the Governor-General still authoritatively represents, acts on behalf of, and speaks for the Queen. Similarly, we have men and women who are political ambassadors. They have been chosen to represent the people of Canada in whatever country they have been granted authority. They speak on behalf of our country and are backed up by all the resources of the Canadian government. The only reason for an ambassador to be in a foreign land is to represent his or her country in that nation. In the same way, mankind was created to represent, to speak for, and to act on behalf of God. Not only that, God was prepared to back us up as we acted in His name.

Adam and Eve had both authority and power to act on God's behalf. It is important to have both authority and power! 'Authority' carries the idea of being legitimately entrusted with the legal right to act. 'Power' suggests the physical strength to enforce what authority demands.

CHAPTER 1 – LIFE AS IT WAS MEANT TO BE

Authority without power is just so much hot air; power without authority is abusive. One lone policeman can theoretically command a driver to stop his car 'in the name of the law' by simply raising his hand in such a way to communicate that the traffic should come to a halt. He does not have the physical power to make the driver stop; if he attempted to do so, he'd just get run over! The humans were given both authority and power to represent God on the Earth.

In any functional organizational structure, authority and responsibility always go hand in hand. Responsibility without authority is overwhelmingly frustrating. In some senses, authority is just a tool you use to accomplish your responsibility. Without it, you're accountable to get a project accomplished but have no legitimate way to make anything happen. Imagine being a painter and responsible to paint the inside of a house, but the home owner provides you with no tools, no brushes or rollers, no ladders, and no paint. Not only that, the doors are locked; and you have no key. That's frustration!

On the other hand, authority without responsibility is meddlesome abuse. Too often, we meet people who are more than willing to pontificate into areas in which they have no authority. They have no trouble giving their 'two cent's worth,' (a surprisingly accurate evaluation) about a situation, even though it is technically none of their business. Oddly enough, they expect those legitimately involved to follow their leading! That is a dysfunctional system!

A second administrative principle also comes into play. You cannot give away or entrust to someone what you, yourself, do not have. I can only give you as much money as I have in my bank account. The Governor of Alabama cannot appoint someone as President of the United States. In other words, it takes a 'greater authority' to invest into a 'lesser authority.' When God entrusted Adam and Eve with the responsibility to rule or have dominion over all the Earth, He did so, as the greater authority investing lesser authority into His creation. In our culture, the word, 'dominate,' has taken on a negative, evil connotation. In actuality, it simply means to rule with legitimate, granted authority. Adam and Eve were charged with the responsibility to 'have dominion' over the Earth and all that was in it. The bottom line is simply this; God created us to represent Him by acting as His ambassadors, to rule and reign on His behalf and in His authority. Having said that, we need to appreciate that, like any good administrator, God never commands us to do something or entrusts us with responsibility unless He also provides the authority and resources to do it.

Herein lies a great paradox. Having entrusted mankind with responsibility, authority, and the necessary resources, He turns Adam and Eve loose to function independently, with a simple, "You go do it!" (A liberal paraphrase!). At the same time, God expects us to be completely reliant on Him. While teaching the disciples about their dependence on Him with the metaphor of the vine and branches, didn't Jesus say, *"...apart from Me you can do nothing"*? (John 15:5). While both concepts – free-will independence and complete reliance – seem to be in direct contradiction to each other, they are both true at the same time.

Why did God do this? While we don't have a specific answer, we know that there was agreement between the persons of God. Notice that Genesis 1:26 says, *"Let Us make human beings in **Our** image, to be like **Us**"* (Emphasis mine). God, in a wisdom that far exceeds our own, agreed to entrust us with His image, the authority and awesome responsibility to represent Him, and the independence and free-will to act on our own.

The idea that people are the image-bearers of God, demands that we ask a question, "What is God like?" Immediately, we recognize that God is not some vague force in the universe, but that He has (They – Father, Son and Holy Spirit – have) intelligence, creativity, and will – the building blocks of personality - as well as the strength and resources to carry out His plans.

He is also a God of created order and beauty. As God began His work on the Six Days of Creation, the Earth was *"formless and empty,*

CHAPTER 1 – LIFE AS IT WAS MEANT TO BE

and darkness covered the deep waters" (Genesis 1:1). By the time He had finished His work, we see order, beauty, and efficiency. Everything had its place and was in its place; chaos had been tamed. We also see efficiency; although many things seem very fanciful and imaginative, each detail was purposeful and fulfilled a specific task. Each evening, God evaluated His handiwork and found that it was "good" or "very good."

Frequently, other passages in the Bible use a particular word to describe God; He is said to be 'holy.' In Isaiah 6, we read of the angels crying, *"Holy, holy, holy, is the Lord of Hosts!"* But what does 'holy' mean? At the root of all it implies, lies the thought that the holy thing is 'separate, distinct, different.'[5] My suspicion is that, while God, the Creator, was always distinct and different from His creation, Adam and Eve, in their originally created states, were not all that different from God in regard to their character. They were like Him in their personality, perspective, and purpose. Perhaps this is why we see God's desire for authentic relationship with His creation and all peoples.

As we understand the purpose for which mankind was created, we also can learn how we came to be. During those first six days of creation in the Genesis narrative, God spoke everything into being. *"God said, 'Let there be...'"* Genesis, Chapter 2, seems to build on Chapter 1 and adds further detail to the story. There, we find details that demonstrate a human's physical and spiritual uniqueness. *"Then the Lord God formed the man from the dust of the ground. He breathed the breath of life into the man's nostrils, and the man became a living person,"* (Vs. 7). The expression "breath of life" and "living person" bear investigation. 'Breath' (Hebrew: neshawmah) can be translated 'puff of air, spirit, a living soul, blast, wind, of vital breath, divine inspiration, intellect, or animal spirit.'[6] This breath is described by the phrase 'of life.' 'Life' comes from the Hebrew word, 'chay,' and means pretty much what it says, 'alive, fresh, strong, life, etc.'[7] God's breath was fresh and alive, and He blew it into the dusty sculpture's nostrils (Literally 'nose, nostrils, face').[8] The result was something that had not been done before. Man became a "living person." That

27

Hebrew word, 'nephesh,' indicates a breathing creature, literally, but also carries the idea of an entity with desires, pleasures and will.[9] It might be appropriate to think of it this way. The sculpted dust, filled with the living breath (spirit?) of God became a living human being. Genesis 2:19 says that God 'formed' the animals from the dust of the ground as well. It is the same Hebrew word (yatzar – to form, fashion, frame, constitute),[10] but there is no mention of God breathing into them His own breath or spirit. Human beings were physically sculpted by the hand of God and invested with the breath and spirit of God. *"Then God looked over all He had made, and He saw that it was very good!"* (Genesis 1:31).

I recently heard something that just might have some application here. Apparently, if your dog is not minding you, if he is not obeying, or if he is distracted, you should grab him by the muzzle and breathe your breath into his nostrils. Because dogs are so scent attentive, this refocuses his thinking and attention back to you. This might seem to be nothing more than an insulting comparison, so take it for whatever it might be worth. The Bible tells us that God breathed His breath into the nostrils of the newly formed man. Could it be that the man came alive and was focused on Creator God at the same moment? Physically speaking, if someone is blowing up your nose, the first thing you see and attend to would be that person's face. I wonder if Adam found his life and was immediately focused on God, all at the same time. It seems to me that the less focused on God we become, the more death-prone we are and the farther we get from His original intent.

Summarizing what we discover in the Genesis account, we find that we humans are a unique combination of the material (dust) and the immaterial (living breath of God); and the result is a living creature with values and desires and the ability to choose and function independently. Adam and Eve were not unthinking robots or Zombie-like creatures waiting for some external force to stimulate them into mind-less action. Just as God obviously has character, intellect, values, choice, and a will of His own; mankind was created as His

CHAPTER 1 – LIFE AS IT WAS MEANT TO BE

representatives, and we inherited the same nature and functions as our Father, Creator and Potter.

In 1 Thessalonians 5:23, Paul prayed for the church this way; *"Now may the God of peace make you holy in every way, and may your whole spirit and soul and body be kept blameless until our Lord Jesus Christ comes again."* This tells us that people have three distinct parts; their physical body, their spirit or life, and their soul. We understand 'soul' to indicate a person's personality; their mind or intellect, their emotions and values; and their will and the ability to make choices.

Most importantly, God also created us for relationship. Remember, it was not good for man to be alone, so God came up with the idea of Eve! Evidence suggests that Adam and Eve were far from barely coherent individuals, but were, in fact, highly developed and intelligent. Genesis 1:19 tells us that Adam named or classified all the various types of animals. Wow! What a task!

That process was part of God's plan to provide Adam with a suitable helper – someone to come along side and with whom he could relate and both offer and receive support. As the animals were paraded in front of Adam so he could name them, no suitable partner was found; and so it was that God created Eve. We know that Eve was not some after-thought, the remedial solution to an unforeseen problem. Even before God began creation, He intended to make humans, both male and female (Genesis 1:27).

Such a partner was necessary for us to fulfill the second part of our mandate; to be fruitful and fill the Earth (Genesis 1:28). Apparently only two representatives would not be sufficient; more were needed. Adam and Eve, the representatives of God, were to create other images and so on and so on. They also were to be the accurate representations of the character and will of God, extending His kingdom and dominion over the Earth.

We can understand it this way. Every human is essentially a spirit-being, living in a physical body that expresses our personality; our mind, emotions and will. We were designed for destiny and purpose - to represent God on the Earth – and came equipped with all that was necessary to fulfil the mandate to fill the Earth, subdue it, and reign over it – to extend the will and ways of God over the face of the Earth.

Not only that, but Adam and Eve, having been created in God's image, were also in personal relationship with Him and with one another. In Genesis 3, we read that God's presence would come and manifest itself in the garden where Adam and Eve were living. They could hear the sound of God's presence there as He walked in the cool of the day. Verse 8 speaks of God walking in the garden. With that, comes the idea of His abiding or ongoing presence there. The word translated 'walking,' is the Hebrew word, 'Halak' and means 'to walk abroad, on, to and fro, up and down' and carries the idea of 'to go on habitually or up and down.'[11] Imagine that; God's presence being habitually and physically manifested in the natural realm. I wonder what sound He made!

The humans apparently walked and talked with God on a regular, habitual basis. Who knows for sure what the topics of conversation were, but it doesn't take a lot of imagination to figure out that it would be about the business of the kingdom, the affairs of state, and the relational aspects between the Creator and the Created. Adam and Eve were in perfect relationship with each other and with God; they drew their life and revelation from their mutual relationship with God. They lived in the spiritual realm receiving life, affection, and revelation from God, while dwelling in the natural world and expressing what was spiritual into the natural.

Although it may be difficult for us to imagine, Adam and Eve not only enjoyed unbroken fellowship with God on a daily basis, they lived in complete unity and harmony with each other. In the original creation, where sin (anything that was not in line with the will, values, and character of God) was still a foreign concept, neither

CHAPTER 1 – LIFE AS IT WAS MEANT TO BE

Adam nor Eve had any notion of emotional wounded-ness. They had no emotional 'buttons' and no experience of selfishness, guilt, shame, or any other negative emotion. Genesis 2:25 says, *"Now the man and his wife were both naked, but they felt no shame."*

While it is possible that this statement should only be taken literally – that she was so beautiful and he was so handsome that they had no hesitation be to seen in all their naked glory, it is likely also reasonable to see what else may be implied here. Having been made in the likeness of God and having never sinned, the two would have no experience with any negative emotion, including that haunting sense of inadequacy, or the fear of not being 'good enough.' Imagine being fully alive, always feeling competent and acceptable, and always sensing, "I am what I am; and what I am is 'very good'!"

Up to this point, Adam and Eve only lived in complete peace and security; there was nothing evil or sinister to attack them. As one reads the Genesis account, it appears that there was no danger – no sickness or disease, and no death. Fear was a foreign concept. Some Bible scholars speculate that the animals all appear to have been herbivores at this point. If that were the case, there would be neither hunter nor the hunted.

What a fabulous existence! Adam and Eve knew nothing but happiness and bliss. They knew who their God was and that He was good; they knew who they were and that they were good. They had no doubt about their God-given purpose or destiny. They lived in a beautiful garden where every need was met and where no threats to their idyllic life ever entered into their experience. Infused with the Spirit of God, Adam and Eve were accurate but finite images or representations of the Creator, living in a sinless world. They were at peace with God, with each other, and with the world. It was Paradise, and it was perfect!

But then something changed, and not for the better!

SOMETHING TO THINK ABOUT...

1. On a scale from zero to ten, with zero representing 'complete failure' and ten representing 'perfectly,' how well does mankind represent God today?

2. On a scale from zero to ten, with zero representing 'complete failure' and ten representing 'perfectly,' how well does your life represent God?

3. What can you do about that?

4. So why are you here? What is your purpose and destiny?

5. The world in which we live is pretty different from the Paradise of Eden. If you could restore all things, where would you start? What would you do first to 'fix' our broken world? Think about the implications such a change would make. For example, if your answer would be to do away with death, the globe would soon be over-populated and resources would become so diminished that the whole system would break down. Where would you start?

SOMETHING TO DO...

Are you ready to embrace the purpose for which you were made? If so, why not commit yourself to that task? You might pray something like this: "Heavenly Father, I know that all of us – me included – were made to be Your representation here on Earth. We were to be like You and to do things Your way. I admit that I haven't done a very good job of that. Please forgive me and teach me to do a better job. Amen."

CHAPTER 2

THIS IS GOING TO BE BAD; REALLY, REALLY BAD
(Under Attack)

***Romans 3:23** "For everyone has sinned; we all fall short of God's glorious standard."*

Such idyllic paradise was not to last long.

Whether one takes the Genesis story literally or figuratively, two themes appear in the interaction between God and people. First, they were His images and acted as His agents on the Earth; to rule and reign in His name. They conducted business FOR Him. Secondly, God desired that they walk in fellowship. They lived WITH Him. So it is, that we find God pursuing that relationship by coming on a daily basis to presence Himself in face-to-face conversation with Adam and Eve (Genesis 3:8).

Real relationship demands choice, and true loyalty requires an alternative. If man had no option but to be loyal, his allegiance could never be tested, tried, or proven. Similarly, we do not enjoy a relationship that is void of desire. When one person chooses, of his or her own free will, to be in a relationship, it is much more satisfying than if they are in the relationship just because they must be there. For example, a marriage is much more fulfilling and rewarding if both parties want to be in it and when no one feels stuck in the arrangement.

Assuming rightly that it was God who originated the idea of optional relationship, we understand that, with that option, came the possibility in any relationship that our beloved may choose to opt out of the relationship for another. At the same time, unchallenged loyalty is no loyalty at all; an alternative is required for authentic allegiance to exist.

One simple and easy answer, when one struggles with the problem of evil, would be to remove the possibility for disobedience. How many people have wondered, "Why doesn't God just take away our free will and make everyone obey Him?" Wouldn't that solve all the problems in the world today? Sure, it would! But forced obedience negates true relationship.

I remember when, in one such philosophical discussion with my teen-age son, I asked him if he would rather have a relationship with his computer or a robot that would always do exactly as he commanded, or be in a relationship with his girl-friend, who might someday choose to disagree with him or, even worse, to leave the relationship altogether and 'dump' him for another. His choice was clear; he'd rather live with the risk and have a girl-friend.

How would we expect God to be less committed to relationship with His creation? Could He have been satisfied with robots that would always choose His bidding? Apparently not. Even in His sovereignty and foreknowledge, God chose that we might have free will and, with it, the potential for disobedience and to break His heart.

What would be the test of that loyalty and relationship? To our knowledge, everything in the Garden of Eden was wonderful and permissible; except for one thing. In the middle of all that God had established in the garden, grew two trees; the Tree of Life and the Tree of the Knowledge of Good and Evil. Contrary to popular rumour, these were not apple trees. Their very names indicate their complete uniqueness. Genesis 2:8 tells us that God planted a variety of trees, all of which were beautiful and produced delicious fruit. In Verses 15 and 16, God allowed the forefathers to eat freely of any tree, except the Tree of the Knowledge of Good and Evil.

CHAPTER 2 – THIS IS GOING TO BE BAD...

And therein was the test, the option that would either prove man's loyalty to God or find that loyalty wanting. It seemed like a small thing – one tree among possibly hundreds or more; surely, Adam and Eve could do without that one tree. Unless there were some external, sinister influence...

Inasmuch as God created all that we see and know ex nihilo (Latin: out of nothing), He did not do so in a spiritual void. There was some "pre-history history" setting the stage for World History – a backstory to the play of Human History. A new face was to appear on stage, and so entered the serpent.

Although a complete detailing of the person and work of Satan is beyond the scope of this book, there are a few details that directly come into play at this point. Biblical revelation tells us that Satan was once one of three arch-angels, along with Michael and Gabriel. At one point, he had been the worship leader in Heaven's throne room (See Ezekiel 28). Even his physical being, as much as angels seem to have physical presence, was composed of a variety of odd musical instruments; and he was a thing of great beauty. Although it is hard for us to imagine, given our vantage point in time and space, Satan, in a fit of self-appreciation, decided that he should rule all of Heaven and creation, and rose up in rebellion against God. (See Isaiah 14). In that rebellion, many scholars believe that he led one-third of the angels in a civil war up-rising as a vain and failing attempt to dethrone God and establish his own throne over all (See Revelation 12:4,9).

There, we see that Satan and the angels who rebelled with him were 'cast down to the Earth,' which explains his presence here, along with his (un)faithful, fallen angels, now manifesting as the demonic horde. Oddly enough, we learn from Job that Satan continues to have access to the throne room of God (Job 1), and brings accusation against believers today. Jesus ever lives to make intercession on our behalf (Hebrews 7:25). In this verse, Jesus is technically acting as our defence lawyer in the courtroom of Heaven. It only makes sense that, if we need a defense attorney, there must also be a prosecuting attorney, namely the accuser of the brethren, Satan (Revelation 12:10).

It would appear that, Satan, although banished from the Heavenly presence of God after his failed attempt to usurp the throne, continues to wage war against the Kingdom of God and tries to establish his own kingdom here on Earth.

And so, Genesis introduces a new face into the picture; a serpent who enters the Garden. The account in Genesis 3 again causes us to wonder about the kind of world in which they lived. In our world, if any animal came up and began a conversation in a language that we could understand, it would be shocking. FREAKY!!!!!, in fact. Apparently, this event didn't even phase Eve; she just took it all in stride. Perhaps she didn't even 'bat an eye.'

Before we begin railing on Eve, let's remember a couple of factors. Up to this point, Eve lived in this seemingly perfect world where there was no known danger, no suffering, no pain, and no death. Neither had there been any sinful deceit; and Eve was innocent and, as might well be expected, naïve.

I wonder how Adam and Eve understood the impact of God's words, *"If you eat its fruit,* (the fruit from the Tree of the Knowledge of Good and Evil) *you are sure to die."* As far as we know, they had had no experience with this foreign concept of death. Although it is an argument from silence, no animal appears to have been killed or died in their presence.

To this point, 'sin' was also a foreign concept. One working definition of 'sin' is 'anything contrary to the moral character and will of God.' As God's created and empowered agents, Adam and Eve had no experience in this field; and, until temptation arrived on their doorstep, they had no reason to be on their guard against it.

And so it was that Eve was drawn into a fateful conversation with a 'serpent.' Many theologians tend to assume that the serpent was some physical manifestation or personification of Satan. That discourse is found in Genesis, Chapter 3. Today, Satan is often pleased to attack the very notion of God; but on that day, such philosophical debate would have been useless. Eve had spoken with God face to face; there would be no convincing her that He did not exist.

The Serpent did not attack the idea of God directly, but launched a three-pronged assault – one attack on the revelation of God and one against the representation of God. In the process, he also came against the nature and character of the Creator. The three concepts were so interwoven into the conversation that we might miss their full impact unless we unpack what he was saying.

In Genesis 3:1, we see that the serpent was the 'shrewdest' of all the animals. Other versions use the term 'subtle' (KJV), or 'crafty' (NASB); and the Hebrew word, 'arum,' means "cunning, crafty, prudent, subtle"[1]. In other words, with ill motives, he uses arguments that sound logical, but are actually meant to deceive.

First, he called the revelation of God into question by asking, *"Did God really say…?"* At this point, the content did not seem to matter; what was important was to know if God actually said it or not. With the question also came that first seed of doubt. If one isn't thoroughly aware of what God has communicated or revealed, that person can easily be fooled into doubting, not just if what God said was true, but if He had even said it at all.

Doesn't that sound familiar in today's culture? If the idea of a Creator God is acknowledged at all, His Word is certainly under attack. Sometimes scientific theory is taught as absolute and unquestionable truth while, at the same time, Biblical revelation has been relegated to unsophisticated and superstitious myth. I mean, really, how do we know that God actually said that? And there is the doubt – implanted into many an unsuspecting young mind, once raised in the faith, but now impregnated with questions about the trustworthiness of revelation.

Notice that the question itself was not without guile. Satan asked, *"Did God really say…"* but added just a slight misquote of what he already knew fully well that God had, indeed, said. In Genesis 2:16, 17, we read, *"But the Lord God warned him, 'You may freely eat the fruit of every tree in the garden except the tree of the knowledge of good and evil. If you eat its fruit, you are sure to die.'"* Notice how the serpent changed what God had said to the complete opposite: *"Did God really say you must not eat the fruit from any of the trees in the garden?"*

You'd think that this contradiction would have been a 'red flag' or a warning sign for Eve; "There's something wrong about this guy..." Perhaps Eve was just so innocent and guileless that she naturally assumed that Satan was merely mistaken or misunderstood, and not intentionally deceptive in his line of questioning. After all, hadn't he come asking questions and seeking some truth? On the other hand, maybe Eve didn't think about it much, if at all.

She responded with the right answer – almost. Eve seems to practically quote verbatim God's ban on the fruit of the one tree, but then she adds an interesting piece of information. *"'Of course we may eat fruit from the trees in the garden,' the woman replied. 'It's only the fruit from the tree in the middle of the garden that we are not allowed to eat. God said, 'You must not eat it or even touch it;* (Where'd that come from?) *if you do, you will die'"* (Genesis 3:2,3).

We know that Eve added to what God had said in Genesis 2:16,17, but we do not know why she did it. It is possible that, at a time apart from God speaking the original ban on eating the fruit, He also told them that even touching the tree or its fruit would prove fatal. This line of thinking, however, is pure conjecture. The other option is that, for some unknown reason, Eve intentionally or accidentally exaggerated the ban, adding her own ideas to what God had said. Human nature being what it is, it isn't hard to imagine that someone might toss in a new idea here or there. The Ten Commandments eventually became literally hundreds of rules and regulations in the minds of the religious Jews. Either Eve spoke the truth, or falsehood and error just made its first appearance on the human stage. I suppose it doesn't really matter; Satan was not to be stopped so easily.

CHAPTER 2 – THIS IS GOING TO BE BAD...

Changing tactics, Satan, went from merely questioning God's word, as if that wasn't bad enough, to directly and openly contradicting it. Genesis 3:4 records his contrary word to the woman, *"You won't die!"*

And so, it was that Eve found herself in the throes of her first moral dilemma. God said one thing, but He apparently was not around to defend His word; and the serpent said the complete opposite, challenging what she believed. Choices, choices! What to do?

I suppose that there were a few options. She might have waited until later to ask God about it in their daily face-to-face chat. Adam might have been able to confirm the correct answer. Immediately, there was one way to find out who was telling the truth. Logically, she'd have to eat the fruit. If she died, God would be the truth-teller; and the serpent would be exposed either as the deceived, at best, or the deceiver, at worst, or maybe both. If she ate and lived, it would prove that God was in the wrong and this serpent was in the right. But, what a gamble!

If directly contradicting or replacing the word – the revelation – wasn't working, perhaps attacking the character and the motives of the Reveal-er would help. Verse 5 tells us about Satan's next volley: *"God knows that your eyes will be opened as soon as you eat it, and you will be like God, knowing both good and evil."*

This 'line' was just full of information or, rather, misinformation. Effectively, it called God's character and motives into question. At the same time, it also said a lot about Eve.

If Eve's eyes would be opened on the day that she ate the fruit, the obvious implication is that her eyes were still closed. What does that say about Eve? That she's blind and doesn't even know it. Obviously, Eve was not physically blind; that would have been a statement too easy to disprove. Satan was referring, not to physical eyes, but to either intellectual or spiritual sight.

Even today, when we refer to someone who is blind in the non-physical sense, we're saying that they are somehow stupid or too dull to realize the truth. Even "blind-faith" speaks of accepting something without adequate proof of its truthfulness. To the intellectual mind, this sounds a lot like "kissing your brains good-bye;" so that faith is seen as a pursuit for the weak-minded and gullible.

Little wonder! 2 Corinthians 4:4 says that *"Satan, who is the god of this world, has blinded the minds of those who don't believe. They are unable to see the glorious light of the Good News. They don't understand this message about the glory of Christ, who is the exact likeness of God."* How ironic that the one who blinds people's minds implied that Eve was also blind and that it was God who intended to keep her that way!

Not only was Eve learning that she was somehow blind and didn't know it; she was also, shall we say, ignorant, unlearned, uneducated, and naïve. According to Satan, God's second objection to mankind partaking of the fruit was that He did not want them to know 'good and evil.' Perhaps Eve had begun to believe that such understanding would be a good, beneficial, and positive thing that God was, for one reason or another, unwilling to share with the humans. It seems that it didn't occur to Eve to question if such knowledge would actually be a good thing. Apparently, God was holding out on her, and whatever it was that was being withheld, she now wanted it!

I believe that there was a positively logical reason why a loving and benevolent God would not want to share this seemingly wonderful knowledge with Adam and Eve. It would be bad for them! Like a good father, He was protecting His children from that which would only prove harmful. Why do good parents withhold the sugar-highs of too much candy from their children? Because it would be bad for them! Why don't loving moms and dads let the toddlers play on the highway? Because it would not be safe, and it would not be good.

I think it would be safe to say that God knew that knowledge of evil – especially experiential knowledge – would be harmful. What loving parent thinks, "I hope my kid learns early-on what an evil and dangerous place this world is; it'll be good for him!"? If God made His creation, "good" or "very good," why would He want Adam and Eve to know evil? He wouldn't! In fact, I believe that God never wanted humans to have experiential knowledge of evil. But, remember; free-will choice required legitimate options.

As the serpent presented the 'facts,' he added a third element to his argument; Eve was supposedly NOT like God. Forget the fact that she had been created in the image of God and, therefore, served as His representation; if she ate, she would 'become like God,' according to the enemy of our souls. The serpent's logical implication was that Eve was not like God, but she could be! And why wouldn't a 'loving God' want her to be like Him?

This was the 'thin edge of the wedge' that Satan used to cause division between Eve and her God. God was holding-out on her. He was intentionally keeping her defective, deficient, blind, ignorant, and ungodly! What kind of God was that? Who would want to know and serve, much less bear the image of a God who would utter false threats to keep her suppressed and to deny her all the supposed benefits that 'sight,' 'knowledge,' and 'godliness' had to offer? Talk about defamation of God's character! And it worked so well. The implication was clear: God must be a bad god.

God wasn't the only one who got 'slammed' in this brief exchange. Apparently, something was desperately 'wrong' with Eve. In the length of time it took the serpent to utter one sentence, to her own mind, Eve was transformed into a blind, ignorant, and ungodly creature. Her obedience to the serpent's promptings suggests that this is what she had come to believe. Satan knows the Word and will twist and use its principles against us, if we allow him to do so. As Proverbs 23:7 says, *"For as he thinks within himself, so he is."* (NASB). In other words, what we believe about ourselves determines what we become. It is one of those inexplicable truisms, a life-principle that we can't seem to escape. Satan convinced Eve that she was blind, unlearned and un-godly. She had big problems and needed to do something to fix herself. Of course, Satan had a plan – an easy, no-fail, guaranteed way to fix everything that was wrong with her – just eat the fruit!

Amazingly, his same tactics still work today. In well over a decade of practising inner-healing and pastoral prayer ministry, I have yet to meet a single person who does not struggle with self-worth issues to some degree or another or anyone who is truly content with who they are. Everyone, and I do mean everyone, is naturally plagued with some level of self-doubt, rejection, and a nagging feeling or fear of worthlessness or failure.

Eve was also victimized by the lies of the enemy. Believing his lies and deception, she became vulnerable prey for his schemes. She could 'fix' herself by doing things his way – by eating the forbidden fruit. The 'cure' was easy, available, and, according to its purveyor, without negative consequences. It was a perfect plan; or was it?

In Genesis 3:6, we find the following: *"The woman was convinced. She saw that the tree was beautiful and its fruit looked delicious, and she wanted the wisdom it would give her. So, she took some of the fruit and ate it. Then she gave some to her husband, who was with her, and he ate it, too."* Not only was Eve led astray by the serpent's seductive offer, the desires of her own body began to betray her. Unrestrained, her desire for good food and the visual appeal of the fruit itself only added to the tempting situation. This all sounds vaguely familiar. 1 John 2:16 reads, *"For the world offers only a craving for physical pleasure, a craving for everything we see, and pride in our achievements and possessions. These are not from the Father, but are from this world."* Eve had fallen prey to all three. Legitimate need for nutrition easily can become food-lust; visual appeal causes the lust of the eyes; and Eve's desire for sight, knowledge and false godliness, led to giving in to Satan's temptation.

And so, she ate. At this point, Adam re-joined Eve, learned of his wife's disobedience; and, worse than falling to Satan's deception, seemed to make a deliberate choice to disobey. They ate; and, together, they

CHAPTER 2 – THIS IS GOING TO BE BAD...

suffered the consequences. Verse 7 tells us, *"At that moment their eyes were opened, and they suddenly felt shame at their nakedness. So they sewed fig leaves together to cover themselves."* The thing that was supposed to be their cure-all turned out to be their un-doing. Talk about disappointment!

It was highly unlikely that Eve's indiscretion and Adam's disobedient choice to eat was a conscious decision. Apparently, neither of them had thought the scenario through to its ultimate end; nevertheless, those consequences remained. As far as we know, neither of them logically thought things over and concluded, "Ok, then; it's settled. We're going to stop following the Creator and give ourselves to the serpent." God's immutable system was in place; disobedience was about to reap the consequences.

How many children, when 'in trouble,' try to buy some grace from a displeased parent by pleading, "But it was an accident! I didn't mean to do it!"? That usually doesn't work, does it? In some stores that display delicate items, you might see a sign that reads, "It's pretty to look at; it's nice to hold: but if you break it, it's sold!" Intent is not the issue; action is. Few fourteen-year old girls make a conscious choice to get pregnant, but some do. No drunk drivers decide, "I know, I think I'll go drive in my car, get into an accident and kill someone;" but the courts still find them, "Guilty, as charged!" In the same way, lack of intent or any shortage of discretion on Adam and Eve's part did not mitigate the results of their actions. They had been warned beforehand, and now it was time to 'face the music.'

How do we understand God's statement, *"If you eat its fruit, you are sure to die"*? The New American Standard Bible gives us more insight regarding the timing of such a death; *"in the day you eat of it, you shall surely die."* Knowing that Adam and Eve did not physically die within the prescribed 24 hours, we must either conclude that God is a liar and Satan told the truth, or come to a different understanding.

Minimally, we realize that Adam and Eve went from enjoying perfect health and life – conceivably with the ability to live forever in their sinless and perfect state, to being creatures rushing headlong toward the grave.

Actually, Adam and Eve did not shrivel up and die on THE DAY that they ate the forbidden fruit; they didn't drop dead immediately. Certainly, though, their bodies began the long and slow process of decay and eventual death. In fact, Genesis 5:5 tells us that, *"Adam lived 930 years, and then he died."* And that only includes the years after his disobedience! (See Genesis 5:3,4). Nevertheless, it is safe to say that, on the day of 'The Fall,' Adam and Eve immediately began the death process.

Emotionally, they also suffered the consequences of their sin. Some time must have passed between their creation and their departure from the revealed will of God. During those blissful days, they had known only peace and happiness. No negative emotion had scarred their personalities. They had been fully alive, enjoying only positive, healthy and life-giving emotions, and living in harmonious relationship with God and each other – until the serpent came along, and they began listening to his treacherous voice. Until then, the only 'threat' they'd ever known had come from God Himself – *"If you eat this fruit, you will die."* Perhaps it was more of a wise and loving warning, than an ominous threat.

Before the fruit was hardly digested in their stomachs, a flood of foreign and negative emotions came bubbling up within the man and woman. 'Foreign' seems to be an appropriate term; not only were these emotions from uncharted and unfamiliar territory, their labels were in an unknown language. What was 'guilt,' 'fear,' 'shame,' 'unacceptability,' 'blame,' or 'breakdown of relationship'? In God's created order, all of these things were unknown to Adam and Eve; but, suddenly, they were very real concepts with meaning that quickly became familiar through personal experience. Here are some examples:

In Genesis 2:25, we read, *"Now the man and his wife were both naked, but they felt no shame."* Apparently, there was no hint of the two not

CHAPTER 2 – THIS IS GOING TO BE BAD...

being acceptable physically; they could appear before each other and even God, without any hint of self-consciousness and without any fear of being found wanting. Such uninhibited freedom! Seven short verses later, in Genesis 3:7, a lot had changed! *"At that moment their eyes were opened, and they suddenly felt shame at their nakedness. So they sewed fig leaves together to cover themselves."* In that brief interval, they quickly learned that either whatever they were was 'not good enough' or that appearing in an uncovered state was somehow suddenly 'improper;' that certain parts of their bodies 'ought' to be covered; hence the fig leaves.

As the story unfolds in Genesis 3, their physical nakedness was not only an issue of shame but of fear – to the extent that they tried to hide from God. In Adam's words, *"I heard You walking in the garden, so I hid. I was afraid because I was naked"* (Genesis 3:10). Adam no longer joyfully awaited the physical return of the Creator to walk and fellowship with them in the natural realm; His presence had been turned into an occasion for shame and fear.

Amos 3:3 asks an applicable question at this point, *"Can two people walk together without agreeing on the direction?"* The word translated here as 'direction" is the Hebrew word, (yawad) means "to be met together by appointment;"[2] it is also translated, as the KJV puts it, *'be agreed.'* In Genesis 3, it would seem that, as God and Adam and Eve were no longer 'walking together' in unbroken and open fellowship, they were no longer 'agreed.' Their appointment had been missed!

Actually, this is exactly what happened. As long as Adam and Eve received and heeded the revelation given to them by God, they agreed with God, and their fellowship was sweet and unbroken emotionally. When mankind chose to follow the leading and clues of the Enemy rather than obediently honouring the will and command of God, their fellowship with God became broken.

Just as their physical bodies died that day, in the sense that they started the death process, so Adam and Eve's emotional state became wounded. Rather than enjoying full emotional health, they began to suffer new agonies of emotional damage.

This damage was not just between mankind and his Maker, but also between Man and Woman. When God asked what they had done, Eve blamed the Serpent, as if to say, "It isn't my fault; don't blame me. The Serpent tricked me; I'm just an innocent party here." (See Genesis 3:13 for a more literal translation). Adam was quick to follow suit. *"The man replied, 'It was the woman You gave me who gave me the fruit, and I ate it.'"* In other words, "Hey, God; don't blame me. SHE gave me the fruit; it is HER fault, and YOU gave her to me, so in a sense, it is YOUR fault; but don't blame me!"

Imagine the new, strange distance between the Creator and the Created as well as between marriage partners! Finding themselves naked and therefore somehow shameful, they had distanced themselves from each other with fig leaves and from God by hiding among the trees. The guilty pair had begun pointing fingers in each other's direction. Apparently, Adam had not yet learned that blaming your wife only makes her angry and rarely, if ever, solves anything! Obviously, God was displeased with the situation; but we can only imagine the burning anger and resentment that might have surfaced between the people.

Taking all these factors into consideration, it isn't a huge stretch for us to come to the conclusion that Adam and Eve were also experiencing a form of emotional distress that would eventually lead to emotional death.

Most importantly and fundamentally, I believe that it was spiritual death that was indicated here. While Adam and Eve did begin the death process on the day that they ate the forbidden fruit, they did not experience actual physical death immediately. The aging process began; sickness, disease and a difficult life-style would eventually take their toll; but they did not drop dead in one day.

Similarly, their personalities, (their mind, emotions and will), while damaged, were still fairly functional. They could think (Yikes! I'm naked, and that's not good!), feel (I am ashamed and afraid), and

CHAPTER 2 – THIS IS GOING TO BE BAD...

choose (Let's make aprons and hide in the trees!). But they were introduced into a whole new realm of negative emotions, which, rather than being life-giving and encouraging, worked in exactly the opposite direction, with broken relationships, guilt, shame, and fear.

If they didn't immediately 'die' in the physical or emotional sense, what had God meant? It must have been their human spirits that were to experience such a death. As was mentioned earlier; Adam and Eve had been created in sweet harmony with their Creator and in complete obedience to His will. Being 'agreed,' they had walked together with their God. Once that agreement ended, so did their fellowship.

Until "The Fall," Adam and Eve were in a right relationship with God; they had received His breath during the creation process; they received revelation from Him and knew His heart and His will; their very life came from Him. But, with the decision to obey Satan and, therefore to disobey God, all of that ended. It appears, that, once man has life, his spirit lives forever – hence the concept of an eternity in either Heaven or Hell – but, in the sense that spiritual death took place when they ate the fruit, Adam and Eve died spiritually. If one lives apart from God in this life; he or she will certainly live without Him in the next.

This does not mean that their spirits stopped functioning or no longer existed. It does indicate that their relationship with God was broken, their ability to hear and obey God was at least damaged, and they lost the anointing of God's spirit to enable them to live both with Him and for Him. Adam and Eve had, for the first time, become independent from and different from God and could no longer be accurate representations of the Creator. Being different, they became 'un-holy.' They were 'broken' spiritually and separated from God. Such a tragic loss! And for what? To embrace the deceptive plan of the enemy in an attempt to 'fix' that which was not broken.

Not only did they lose their standing and relationship with God, they 'gained' something in a negative way. Romans 6 gives us an immutable law or principle. In Verse 16, Paul asks this question, *"Don't you realize that you become the slave of whatever you choose to obey? You can be a slave to sin, which leads to death, or you can choose to obey God, which leads to righteous living."* By rejecting the lordship of God in their lives in order to wilfully embrace the suggestions and treachery of the Enemy, they 'gained' a new master. They became slaves of the serpent whom they obeyed.

It wasn't as if their spirits had died and stopped working; their spirits still worked; but they had turned their attention and their allegiance from God to Satan. In their obedience to Satan, they had enslaved themselves to the one whom they obeyed; and, now, they were under his dominion. Colossians 1:13 speaks of the *'kingdom of darkness'* into which all men are born. Romans 5 adds a variety of perspectives: *"For the sin of this one man, Adam, brought death to many"* (Vs. 15); *"For Adam's sin led to condemnation..."* (Vs. 16b).

What was left? Fallen and condemned people and a fallen and cursed world – both under the thumb of a new ruler. No wonder the Bible refers to us as "slaves to sin!"

To make matters worse, with our relationship with God broken, our spirits are dead inside of us. God's revelation is still available, although to a somewhat limited degree, as 1 Corinthians 2:14 tells us that, *"... people who aren't spiritual can't receive these truths from God's Spirit. It all sounds foolish to them; and they can't understand it, for only those who are spiritual can understand what the Spirit means."* The word translated 'understand,' in the NASB or 'discerned' in the KJV, means 'to judge closely, examine.'[3] In other words, those who are not in relationship with God through Christ CANNOT understand God – it is beyond their capacity.

Humans were not the only ones to be impacted by this degenerative transformation process. In Genesis 3, we find a whole litany of curses pronounced on Adam, on Eve, on the ground, and on the serpent. I believe that passage is often misinterpreted. Rather than assuming that these are the plans of an angry and vengeful God, railing against those who were not obedient or loyal to Him, what we really have is, for lack of a better term, a "disappointed and broken-hearted" God, listing all the negative consequences that resulted from their disobedience. Although this interpretation takes a different slant on things, its ramifications are profound. There is a huge difference between a loving parent teaching a child, "You touched the hot stove and now your fingers are burned," and an angry parent snarling, "Because you touched the hot stove, I'm going to burn your fingers!" The first interpretation reflects the heart of a God who still loves His creation; the second negates the God who still *"so loved the world that He gave..."* Either way one chooses to understand the various curses, the effect is the same – a fallen and seriously broken world inhabited by dead men walking.

The effects of the curses were both external (what was happening around Adam and Eve), as well as internal (what was going on inside Adam and Eve).

In Luke 6:40, Jesus gave us another immutable life principle: *"Students are not greater than their teacher. But the student who is fully trained will become like the teacher."* This truism has far-reaching effects for us today. When we align ourselves under the influence of a teacher, pastor, or some other authority, the expected result will be that we become like that person. Sometimes, that's a scary thought! Similarly, when Adam and Eve came under the tutelage of Satan and followed his directives, they began the degenerative transformation process of being transformed into the image of their new teacher, Satan.

We can see this principle working itself out in Jesus' interaction with those around Him. In John 8:44, Jesus said to the Jews who claimed to be right with God solely because their fore-father was Abraham, *"For you are the children of your father the devil, and you love to do the evil things he does. He was a murderer from the beginning. He has always hated the truth, because there is no truth in him. When he lies, it is consistent with his character; for he is a liar and the father of lies."* This tells us that, even though these were the "Chosen People," they were, by nature, desire, action, and word, like Satan. That must have been a shocking indictment for those with whom Jesus was speaking. Talk about a slap in the face!

Even Jesus' own disciples were not free from the effects of this principle. When Jesus began to tell them about His journey toward Jerusalem and crucifixion, Peter protested against the idea. Jesus was able to accurately discern what was in Peter's heart at that moment and was quick and brutally honest as He addressed what was wrong. *"Jesus turned to Peter and said, 'Get away from Me, Satan! You are a dangerous trap to Me. You are seeing things merely from a human point of view, not from God's'"* (Matthew 16:23). Ouch! This was not a personal attack against one of Jesus' closest friends. While God always loves the sinner, He addresses the sin.

Little wonder that Romans 5:12 summarizes our plight this way, *"Therefore, just as through one man (Adam) sin entered into the world, and death through sin, and so death spread to all men, because all sinned."*

I have heard a wonderful teaching by a scientist who is a Christian; but, unfortunately, I don't remember his name. He was saying that, scientifically speaking, there is no such thing as cold. What we experience as 'cold' is actually a lack of heat. Similarly, there is no technical entity known as darkness; there is only a lack of light. We have 'light rays' but not 'dark rays.' In the same way, when we remove God from the picture, all the goodness, beauty and order that is inherent in His character is also retracted from the scene. Remove love and you get hatred. Remove health and you reap sickness and death. In their obedience to Satan, Adam and Eve betrayed their loyalty to the Creator; and they not only lost all the blessing that came with the reign of God in their lives, they stepped into the Kingdom of Darkness, a kingdom bereft of the life of God.

It was bad; very, very bad. Thankfully, that isn't the end of our story...

CHAPTER 2 – THIS IS GOING TO BE BAD...

SOMETHING TO THINK ABOUT...

1. No one is completely good, and no one is completely evil. Think of the most evil person you know. Is there anything 'good' about that person? Is there any remaining vestige of the image of God in him or her?

2. Think about yourself. Name 3 ways in which you are, at least to some extent, like God. Name 3 ways in which you are still not so much like Him.

3. In any area that you are NOT like God, who are you like?

4. If we all became completely like Satan, what would our world and your life be like?

5. Why do you suppose God didn't just scrap the whole project and destroy His creation, including the treacherous human beings?

SOMETHING TO DO...

Conviction is the work of God's spirit in our lives – He points out to us the ways that we are not like God so that we can correct that behaviour. You might pray and ask the Father to convict you of a particular way that you are not like Him. When He shows or tells you something specific; ask Him to help you change in that area.

CHAPTER 3

AMAZING GRACE; HOW SWEET THE SOUND!
(Rally the troops!)

***Romans 6:23** "For the wages of sin is death, but the free gift of God is eternal life through Christ Jesus our Lord."*

If you and I were God, and thankfully, we are not; we might have done as many budding artists do – looked at our creation, decided it was 'not right,' scrunched it up in a ball, and tossed it into the garbage. Like a potter, hunched over his wheel, when the pot he is casting crumples in his hand, we might have been totally justified in squashing the whole thing and starting all over again, perhaps more than a bit disgusted that things hadn't turned out better than they had.

Thankfully, though, God is not us; nor is He like us. We know that *"God is love"* (I John 4: 8 & 16), and that *"He cannot deny who He is"* (2 Timothy 2:13). In other words, God is always true to His character and to His nature; and everything He does is completely consistent with, and in alignment with who He is. Regardless of how 'wrong' things had gotten here on Planet Earth, God was still unchanging God, still on the throne, and still loved His creation. As the book of Psalms puts it so eloquently, "Selah!" ("Think about it!") It truly is "Amazing Grace!"

Even when God's patience appears to have worn thin and He *"...was sorry He had ever made them and put them on the Earth. It broke His heart"* (Genesis 6:6), God was not without mercy. True, God's sorrow moved Him to cleanse the Earth by means of the "Great Flood;"

but, even in that scenario, we find His overriding grace for Noah and his family. Such grace was pictured for us, as we understand that the physical ark – that place of safety and mercy in the midst of unprecedented storm – was also representative of God's grace and mercy, manifested in Jesus Christ.

We might well wonder why God would care for mankind, particularly when, in Heaven's eyes, we had become the *"enemies of God"* (Romans 5:10b). In his rebellion, Satan became the enemy of God; and in our rebellion, we joined the rebel army and became the enemies of God ourselves. Yet, miraculously, marvellously, we are still the objects of God's affection. In this light, we can understand that all of written revelation, the Bible, is the story of God's unfailing love for His creation and His relentless efforts to draw us back to relationship with Himself.

Perhaps, one of the reasons for such grace is that, having been created in God's image, we still bear, to some greater or lesser degree, a remnant of that likeness. It is a basic life principle that what we see in others, particularly our authorities, we attribute, rightly or wrongly, to Father God. How many sons and daughters, looking at their earthly fathers, have concluded that the Heavenly Father is the same? Paul hints at this same idea when he chides the 'professing' but unbelieving and ungodly Jewish leaders by saying that, *"The Gentiles blaspheme the name of God because of you"* (Romans 2:24). For some reason, when people look at those who profess godliness but do not exhibit it, they blaspheme (speak badly of and blame) God. In other words, they assume that the same characteristics that can be found in His people are also found in God. No wonder we read, *"For everyone has sinned; we all fall short of God's glorious standard"* (Romans 3:23). The KJV uses the term "glory." It is not that we have NO glory; but that our glory does not do God, whom we continue to represent, justice. None of us is an accurate depiction of God. Perhaps it is that residue of God's glory in us, no matter how small, that causes God to love us. Perhaps we'll never really know.

CHAPTER 3 - AMAZING GRACE...

As amazing as God's love might be, His redemptive plan is equally beyond full comprehension. Early in Scripture, we find that God, both in his foreknowledge of "The Fall" and after that tragic event, continued to love mankind and to call people into right relationship with Himself.

As early as Genesis 6:18, God began to reveal the concept of 'covenant.' At its heart, a covenant is a statement of the working relationship between two or more parties. This first mention of covenant is a working arrangement between Sovereign God and His companion, Noah. Genesis 6:9 casually mentions that Noah walked with God – an expression indicating the agreement and companionship between Creator and Creature. In other words, they were in some degree of relationship and fellowship with each other. That relationship, in all likelihood, was the underlying motivation that caused God to enter into covenant with Noah. By the way, did you notice that, even though God, who knows everything, including Adam and Eve's disloyalty, still came to have fellowship with them? Even in their sin, God continued to love them and to want relationship with them. In Genesis 6:18, God graciously offered Noah His hand in a formalized agreement that would not only provide safety and protection for Noah and his family, but would also preserve the human race, as God prepared to come against the evil of the day.

A few chapters later, God approached another person who, for whatever reason, caught His attention. This covenant was offered to a man who very well may have been a "pagan." Abram was a descendant of Noah's, ten generations removed, mind you. Other than that, there may have been little to commend Abram to the Lord. He had been raised in the pagan and ungodly culture of Ur of the Chaldeans; but sometime after Abram was old enough to have a nephew and a wife, his father, Terah, moved the family from Ur to the city of Haran, in the land of Canaan. We can only speculate the motive for such a move. Was it simply a relocation to facilitate economic growth? Had the Spirit of God led him, even as a pagan, to relocate? We aren't told.

We do know this: God promised, many years later, in Deuteronomy 5:10, that He would show *"... unfailing love for a thousand generations on those who love Me and obey My commands."* It is possible that the accompanying generational curse – to visit the iniquity of those who hate God to the third and forth generation – and this generational blessing – to a thousand generations of those who love and obey Him – came into play in Abram's life? Assuming that it is true that Noah both loved and obeyed God, we find the blessing of relationship extended to Abram, only the tenth generation removed from a patriarch who at least obeyed God and probably also loved Him.

Regardless of the spiritual state Abram was in, God's visitation and revelation to him was about to change his life – and the lives of countless descendants – in a way that Abram could scarcely understand.

In Genesis 12, God began calling, not just an individual into relationship with Himself; He started offering relationship to a whole nation. There, we find God, in His sovereignty, offering to raise up, out of one old man and his barren, aged wife, an entire nation. Listen to the exciting promise of God, *"Leave your native country, your relatives, and your father's family, and go to the land that I will show you. I will make you into a great nation. I will bless you and make you famous, and you will be a blessing to others. I will bless those who bless you and curse those who treat you with contempt. All the families on earth will be blessed through you"* (Genesis 12:1b–3). Wow! Imagine receiving such a promise! How wonderful and how unbelievable at the same time! Looking, by sight, Abram realized that both he and his wife were well past childbearing years. Having a child at their age? Impossible!

How was it that Abram received such a promise? By faith. Listen to the testimony of God regarding Abram: *"Abraham believed God, and God counted him as righteous because of his faith... Even when there was no reason for hope, Abraham kept hoping—believing that he would become the father of many nations ... And Abraham's faith did not weaken, even though, at about 100 years of age, he figured his body was as good as dead—and so was Sarah's womb. Abraham never wavered in believing God's promise. In fact, his faith grew stronger, and in this he brought glory to God. He was fully convinced that God is able to do whatever He promises. And because of Abraham's faith, God counted him as righteous"* (Romans 4:3b, 18–22). In the economy of God, faith is what is required, both to receive what God has promised, and as the key to receiving righteousness in the eyes of the Lord.

This wonderful invitation to come into relationship and fellowship with the living God was extended over and over again throughout human history. It was repeated, in whole or in part to Abram, renamed "Abraham" in Genesis 13:14–17; 15:4–21; 17:1–8; and 22:17,18. It was extended to Moses in legal terms (Exodus 19,20). God covenanted with David (2 Samuel 7:8–17), promising that his descendant would continuously and eternally be installed on David's throne. The remainder of the Old Testament is the account of God working out His covenant with His people, regardless of how well or how poorly they walked in covenant relationship with their God. It also is the account of God preparing His people and the entire world for a new and better covenant.

As wonderful as these promises were, the best was yet to come. God would not be satisfied with just the one nation, Israel. He had compassion for all peoples and wanted all nations to be in relationship with Himself. In Revelation 5, a new song was being sung to the Lord Jesus. There we read, *"You are worthy to take the scroll and break its seals and open it. For You were slaughtered, and your blood has ransomed people for God from every tribe and language and people and nation…"* Why would Christ do such a thing?

The best answer is found in a verse that is so familiar, we may have lost sight of its full impact. *"For this is how God loved the world: He gave His one and only Son, so that everyone who believes in Him will not perish but have eternal life"* (John 3:16). In this verse, we return to the same two themes: God's love and our required response of belief or faith. Even though man has turned his back and has taken his allegiance away from God to serve another; even though we are broken and poor images of the Creator, HE STILL LOVES US!

This unfailing love of the Father stands in direct contrast to a picture of God that is all too familiar for many "Christians." How many of us grew up under this false impression? God is a very old and angry man, sitting behind the bench of the courtroom of Heaven with a scowl on His face, anger in His heart, and a heavy gavel in His hand. He's ready to bring it down with a bang, pronouncing judgement, condemnation, and punishment against anyone who dares to step out of line. How different that is from the God who loved so much that He'd send His own Son to die in our place!

That verse, John 3:16, is found in the context of a discussion between Jesus, the Son that Verse 16 talks about, and a Pharisee, named Nicodemus. Apparently, Nicodemus had some questions that he wanted to discuss with Jesus, but was afraid of what the 'others' might think, so he came to Jesus under the cover of darkness.

Before Nicodemus got around to asking any of his questions – he was still complimenting Jesus on His miraculous abilities and revealing a level of faith by admitting his own conviction that Jesus had come from God – Jesus stopped him in his tracks and cut right to the heart of the matter. *"...I tell you the truth, unless you are born again, you cannot see the Kingdom of God"* (John 3:3).

That must have been quite a "shocker" for Nicodemus who, typically, might have looked confidently to his Jewish roots. Weren't they the people of God? Or what about all the religious activity and piety inherent in being a Pharisee? Wouldn't that count for something? Surely, if anyone could deserve to be in the kingdom of God, it would be a Pharisee!

Apparently not! Jesus required only one thing: being 'born again.' Since that original conversation, the term, 'born again,' has come to mean many things to many people. The question is, "What did it mean to Jesus?"

In the initial reading, it seems that Nicodemus was inclined to take the saying literally and questioned Jesus about the unpleasant and impossible concept of re-entering his mother's womb as a full-grown adult, only to, once again, pass through the birth canal into life in this world. Surely a literal interpretation would necessitate that no one would see the Kingdom. Perhaps Nicodemus was admitting that he knew they weren't talking about physical rebirth and was asking for an alternative interpretation.

Jesus' answer clarified that He was not speaking of a literal, physical re-birth, but of a spiritual one. In Verse 5, Christ added, *"I assure you, no one can enter the Kingdom of God without being born of water and the Spirit."* There seems to be a degree of Hebrew parallelism in the passage. *"Born again"* equates to being *"born of water and the Spirit,"* while *"see the kingdom of God"* has been restated as *"enter the kingdom."* Still more light is given in Verse 6, *"Humans can reproduce only human life, but the Holy Spirit gives birth to spiritual life."*

We can understand this verse to mean that there is a physical birth and there is a spiritual birth as well. The use of the term 'reborn' or 'born again' seems to indicate that unless one is born physically and then born spiritually (a second birth chronologically), the person cannot see or enter the kingdom of God. This is not just a matter of chronology, where 'second' would only mean that some form of spiritual birth takes place some time after the person is physically born into this world. Obviously, if you'd never been born physically, you couldn't be born spiritually sometime later. There must be a deeper understanding.

In one sense, God 'birthed' mankind when He breathed into Adam's nostrils the breath of life and Adam became a 'living creature.' The giving of physical life requires the giving of spiritual life. In human experience, the seed and the ovum unite to become a zygote and foetus; and there is the implanting of human life at the moment of conception. This is one of the greatest arguments for the protection of the unborn. Life entered the womb at conception; a grand and noble, living being; tiny, helpless, still unformed, but life, none the less.

But what about this idea of 're-birth' or 'second birth'?

Inasmuch as mankind was originally born spiritually alive – living in right relationship and fellowship with God; Adam and Eve fell into sin too soon, and 'died' spiritually. In this sense, the concept of 'second birth' suggests that it is possible for a human's 'dead' spirit to be regenerated, and for God's life to again enter the living dead man.

Later, John testified, *"Everyone who believes that Jesus is the Christ has become a child of God ..."* (1 John 5:1) and, *"Whoever has the Son* (Jesus) *has life ..."* (1 John 5:12a). In these two verses, we find the keys to being 'born again' and spiritual life. The first is found in believing that Jesus is the Christ; the second involves 'having the Son.'

But what does it mean to believe in something? There are different levels of belief. The first and most basic level is to give cognisant consent. In other words, a person believes in a basic truth. For example, I could say that I believe in grass or dirt. In so doing, I am only saying that I acknowledge that it exists; "Yes, there is such a thing as grass." Many people believe that Jesus existed; they've heard of Him, read about Him, etc.; but that is the extent of their relationship. "Jesus was some guy that existed a long time ago; He was a real person." This is intellectual awareness and acceptance of the fact that Jesus lived. Is that enough? James said, *"Even the demons believe..."* (James 2:19). That kind of belief does not seem to have done the demonic 'believers' much good! This kind of belief only serves to stimulate the brain.

A second level of 'believe' is what one might call, "moral approval." Such a 'believer' might believe in some kind of a cause or moral principle. For example, "I believe in fairness," or "I believe that feeding starving children is a good thing." This kind of Christian 'belief' might be summed up as both an intellectual acceptance of Jesus' existence and the moral principles of His teachings as being good ideas. After all, "Jesus was a nice guy; how can you argue with Jesus?" This kind of belief both activates brain activity and may also provide some form of warm, emotional affirmation. It makes us feel good.

Surely that should be enough. Just one problem! Jesus said, *"But I warn you—unless your righteousness is better than the righteousness of the teachers of religious law and the Pharisees, you will never enter the Kingdom of Heaven!"* (Matthew 5:20). Do warm, fuzzy thoughts about Jesus provide us with any kind of righteousness? I think not!

The last level of belief is to make a strong commitment to an idea or cause, so that your life is committed to it and transformed by it. If I truly believe in Jesus, I am committed to Him, to His ways, and to His character. And I trust Him.

Looking at this in another way, at one point I 'knew' the woman who is now my wife in the sense that I knew about her. Perhaps someone had referenced her in a conversation or shown me a picture. The conversation would sound something like this, "Hey, Don, do you know Sharon Hill?" "Oh yeah, she's that girl in the picture you showed me." Later on, someone actually introduced us, and the way I knew Sharon had just taken a huge step forward. We'd met each other, spent some time together; and I got to know Sharon. But there was only a level of actually knowing Sharon, and I'm not talking physically here, that I could only experience by committing my life to her and asking her to be my bride and my life-partner. Even since then, I've gotten to know her a lot better!

So it is, with knowing or 'having' the Son. We learn that He existed; we get to know about Him, perhaps through someone's witness or a Bible study; but we really don't 'know' or 'have' Him, until we give ourselves to Him in a life commitment to be His followers and to walk in obedient fellowship with Him. Just as in marriage, a man doesn't have a wife until he commits to her and covenants with her. Similarly, we don't have Jesus until we commit to Him and covenant with Him.

If God's purpose was to bring man back into living relationship and fellowship with Himself, and it was, then which of the 3 'believes' 'knows,' or 'haves' would accomplish God's plan? Wouldn't it be the third – the "I am committed to relationship with God by believing in and being committed to Jesus Christ in a covenant relationship"?

In Verse 13 of 1 John 5, we find these words of assurance; *"I have written this to you who believe in the name of the Son of God, so that you may **know** you have eternal life"* (Emphasis mine). God doesn't want us to guess that we have eternal life; He doesn't want us to hope that we do. He wants us to KNOW and have assurance that if we BELIEVE, then we HAVE both the Son and the eternal life He died to provide. That takes us back to Paul's testimony about Abram… *"And because of Abraham's faith, God counted him as righteous"* (Romans 4:22). Going back to the concept of marriage, when one is asked the question, "Are you married?" there should be no doubt about it. "I hope so," or "I think so," is inadequate. Only a 'yes-or-no' answer is acceptable. God wants us to KNOW! How do you know? Because you entered into a specific covenant relationship with another person. How do I know that I'm married to Sharon? Because we entered into covenant relationship and gave ourselves to each other! Remember the words, "I, Donald, do take you, Sharon..."?

So 'faith' or 'believing' plays a major, major role spiritually. But faith in what? Today's North American culture would have us believe that it doesn't really matter what you believe in, just as long as you are sincere. The philosophers and thinkers of our day have decided that pluralism and tolerance are the supreme virtues of our society. Everyone can believe whatever they want and still be 'right' in their belief system. Based on the 'absolute truth' that there is no such thing as absolute truth, this way of thinking assumes that everything must be true philosophically. Anyone who would dare to disagree with this idea is automatically labelled 'intolerant.' Who do you think you are, saying, "I'm right, and you're wrong!"?

A number of problems come out of such thinking. If there is no absolute truth, then nothing can be true; and if nothing is true, then everything is meaningless. Conversely, if everything is true, then nothing can be false, either by deception or by error. Ultimately, it really wouldn't matter what anyone believes. Under that system, either everyone is right or everyone is wrong. Except for one immutable law; the law of tolerance. The one thing our society cannot and will not tolerate is intolerance! Anyone who claims to have 'the truth,' and particularly a Bible-believing Christian, is quickly labelled and condemned as 'small minded,' 'superstitious,' and 'arrogantly intolerant'!

If we accept the premise that it doesn't really matter what 'truth' we put our trust in, then we are free to make 'God' in our own image; He (or She) can be whatever we imagine Him, or Her, to be! Very convenient! That way, we never need to be accountable or responsible to a 'higher power.'

In stark and railing contrast to prevailing 21st century thought, we find the words of Jesus in John 14:6: *"I am the way and the truth and the life."* Notice the use of the definite article, "the." Jesus is not claiming to be one way among many, nor to be one truth among a host of truths. He's not even one life among many. He claims to be THE way, THE truth and THE life. If He is (and I believe that He is) these three things, Jesus is exclusive, not inclusive; and He's the only hope for our fallen, broken world. Although it was not Jesus' intent to do so, the last half of this saying seems to add insult to injury; *"NO ONE can come to the Father except through Me"* (Emphasis mine).

That puts us in a dilemma. What do we do with these words? As Josh McDowell put it so succinctly in his book by the name, "Liar, Lunatic, or Lord," one possibility is that Jesus was intentionally lying and making an outrageous claim that He knew was not true, but one that would somehow expand His ministry and influence. Or perhaps Jesus was just some crazy ego-maniac who was so insane that He believed He was God. (That does happen – mentally ill people sometimes claim to be God!) The third possible conclusion is that what Jesus said was correct and that He is uniquely and gloriously Lord.

Previously, 1 John 5:12a was mentioned; now it is time for part b. *"Whoever does not have God's Son does not have life."* That's pretty exclusive too! Either we believe what God has said in His Word, or we don't.

But what does it mean to believe that Jesus was the Christ? "The Christ" means, "the Anointed One," a Jewish term reserved exclusively for the Messiah. From Heaven's vantage point, the Messiah was the Son of God who would come to the world and save the people from their sins and from the punishment for sin. From a much narrower and Earth-bound understanding, the Jews believed that the Messiah would come to free them from their human oppressors through some miraculous political intervention and re-establish the Nation of Israel, righting all injustices, and freeing the nation politically. But when the Coming King came as a helpless baby in a borrowed manger, those with human eyes rejected the One whom God had sent. John 1:11 puts it this way; *"He came to His own people, and even they rejected Him."* Fortunately, Verses 12, and 13 draw to a very different conclusion, *"But to all who believed Him and accepted Him, He gave the right to become children of God. They are reborn— not with a physical birth resulting from human passion or plan, but a birth that comes from God."* We find ourselves right back at the original premise. God seeks to draw us into relationship, and what closer relationship can there be than Father to children? How was this possible? By belief; by faith; by receiving Him. The result, not surprisingly, was birth, not physical birth, but spiritual – not through human effort or will, but by the will of God.

Another familiar passage puts it this way; *"God saved you by His grace when you believed. And you can't take credit for this; it is a gift from God. Salvation is not a reward for the good things we have done..."* (Ephesians 2:8,9). Even the faith that leads to salvation is a gift from God, not something we generate within ourselves, and certainly not the result of a compilation of various forms of religious deeds or good works. Just to make God's position even clearer, it adds, *"...so none of us can boast about it."* It is all of God; grace, faith, salvation – the whole 'kit and caboodle,' as they used to say. No wonder we can't boast; all the glory goes to God!

This 'faith-thing' stands in stark contrast to the plan of Satan: that humans, in their own strength and effort, can somehow fix themselves. In the garden, Satan convinced Eve, who was in the image of God, that she was broken and needed fixing. According to the Deceiver, Eve, fortunately, had within her own human potential the ability to fix what was apparently so wrong with her; "Just do something; eat the fruit!" (See Genesis 3).

Religion, in contrast to faith, always wants to add in some vestige of human virtue – something that we must DO, beyond simply having faith – to commend us to God. Faith is necessary, but what about all those rules? What about the "do's and don't's" that we were taught about in Sunday School? Don't they count for something? Isn't it up to us to maintain fellowship with God by our good behaviour? Don't we need to pray, read the Bible, and give our money and time? And what about that pesky on-going struggle with temptation? Surely, if we cross the line too many times, we can never cross back again can we? Can't we lose our salvation?

Let me answer those questions with a few of my own. First of all, "Was Jesus' death on the cross an adequate payment for all our sin?" That wasn't just an accident, you know. Matthew 20:28 and Mark 10:45 speak to the intentionality of the cross, *"...For even the Son of Man came not to be served but to serve others and to give His life as a ransom for many."* It was God's intention to provide the RANSOM for our lives. We know that, *"For the wages of sin is death, but the gift of God is eternal life through Christ Jesus our Lord"* (Romans 6:23). Sin demands death; and Christ died in our place, paying the penalty for our sin, so that we might live. Again, "Selah!" Just how much of that ransom did Jesus pay? All of it, or just a part?

Even if it were up to us, and it isn't, what could we pay? Throughout the Old Testament Scriptures we find that every sacrifice had to be perfect; *"without spot or blemish."* What could we offer as a payment for our sin, especially when Scripture makes it clear that, *"We are all infected and impure with sin. When we display our righteous deeds, they are nothing but filthy rags. Like autumn leaves, we wither and fall, and our sins sweep us away like the wind"* (Isaiah 64:6). No wonder Paul says that we were *"helpless"* (Romans 5:6).

Among the Sayings from the Cross, we find Jesus' words, "It is finished" (John 19:30). He was saying that the FULL payment for our sins was now complete; nothing further could be added. The perfect Son of God had given up His life in full payment for sin. It's done! Hallelujah!

James 2:10 adds to the argument against 'salvation by works,' when he says, *"For the person who keeps all of the laws except one is as guilty as a person who has broken all of God's laws."* If a person thinks he can work his way into God's good graces, there is only one standard: 100% pass or fail. Either you're perfect (and nobody is) or you're not.

Although there is not time here for a full study of the Book of Galatians at this point, we can further note that Paul stood adamantly opposed to any idea of adding religious merit to faith and the work of the cross. The letter to the Galatian church was, in its entirety, a warning against adding human merit or effort – even the Old Testament rules and regulations – to what Christ had done. Paul clearly drew a dividing line between those who were 'saved by faith,' and those who trusted in their works, particularly additional works. In the later half of Chapter 4, Paul allegorically distinguished between faith and works; between the Children of the free woman (i.e. Isaac) and the Children of slavery (i.e. Ishmael), with the first representing faith and the second the result of human effort. His conclusion, (See Vs. 30) was that the child of the bondwoman would not share in the inheritance with the son of promise.

This is all found in the larger context of the Book of Galatians, where Paul is writing to contradict the teaching of the Jews that the Christians also had to keep the Old Testament laws, including circumcision, to be saved. Paul makes a marvellous argument for salvation by faith alone, and even goes so far as to say this in Galatians 5: 2–4, *"...If you are counting on circumcision to make you right with God* (by adding your own righteousness to that which Christ provides), *then Christ will be of no benefit to you. For if you are trying to make yourselves right with God by keeping the law, you have been cut off from Christ!*

You have fallen away from God's grace." In other words, a person can only choose one covenant at a time; Old or New; works or faith; Law or Christ: You can't have both. If you choose works (and, thereby, your own righteousness), Christ will be of no benefit to you. We stand in our own human righteousness or in Christ's, but not both!

Remember how Ephesians says that salvation and faith are gifts? When a gift is offered to you, how do you 'get' it? By receiving it or taking it to yourself. You don't pay for the gift or offer to earn it through some system of merit; if you have to buy it in service or finances, it isn't a gift; it is just a purchase. In the same way, we can have the Son and the salvation that He offers freely, just by asking for it; by taking and accepting the gift.

Romans 10:9-11 says this: *"…if you openly declare that Jesus is Lord and believe in your heart that God raised Him from the dead, you will be saved. For it is by believing in your heart that you are made right with God, and it is by openly declaring your faith that you are saved. As the Scriptures tell us, 'Anyone who trusts in Him will never be disgraced.'"*

Although it might appear that the 'work' of confession has been added to the element of faith, ultimately what is confessed is of greater importance. In fact, Jesus really gave a definite answer to the 'works' question. *"Jesus told them, 'This is the only work God wants from you: Believe in the one He has sent'"* (John 6:29). Our only work is to believe and to commit. I know that I believe because I have committed myself to the cause of Christ and say so.

Commitment to Christ is often lacking, particularly in the North American church these days. Too often, a 'soft-sell' Christianity is made available. After all, we don't want to offend anyone with all this talk about sin or blood or sacrifice, not to mention punishment and Hell! We can 'win' more people if we just make the whole thing more palatable! I understand that those who preach such a 'gospel' have a heart that is eager to see people come into some form of relationship, in the hope that, as that relationship grows, a deeper, more mature level of commitment will also develop. Undoubtedly, some people have come into full faith under this method; but, unfortunately, others have been lulled into a false assurance that a shallow form of commitment is adequate.

On the other hand, we know that many people look back to some form of conversion experience when they said a prayer, 'went forward' at a church service, 'walked the aisle,' or said 'the sinner's prayer' in response to some form of evangelistic appeal. Many of us started our Christian experience in just such a manner; thank God. The problem arises when ALL the person can say is something along these lines: "I went forward in 1979; it really hasn't changed my life much; I'm pretty much the same now as I was before that. But they told me I was 'saved,' so I expect to go to Heaven when I die." Talk about 'false assurance!'

Is God somehow fooled by the 'commitment' of someone who only wants a fire-escape from Hell but isn't interested in a life-style that honours Him? I don't think so! Perhaps the 'blame' should be placed at the feet of the 'evangelist' (someone who is supposed to tell the 'good news') who is satisfied with making converts (someone who professes a change of allegiance) or profess-ors (speak of commitment but don't live it out) rather than disciples (students who are committed to follow the teacher; to learn from him and become like him). The "Great Commission" (Jesus' final instructions to His followers before returning to God in Heaven) says that we are to *"... make disciples,"* not just converts or profess-ors. The outworking of *"making disciples"* is found in *"baptizing them"* (public declaration of their decision and commitment to follow Jesus) and *"teach(ing) them to obey all the commands I have given you"* (See Matthew 28:19,20).

Let me put it this way; you know that someone's confession is genuine if you see them publically owning their commitment to Christ and then growing in their obedience to become like Him and to do what He would do. As James puts it, *"...I will show you my faith by my good deeds"* (James 2:18b).

I appreciate how Paul commended the early Thessalonian believers in 1 Thessalonians 1:9b *"...you turned away from idols to serve the living and true God."* How did Paul know that their faith was genuine? Because their lives changed; they broke their allegiance to whatever faith system they'd had previously, and embraced faith in God alone and began to serve Him.

Were they 'working their way' or 'keeping their salvation' by working? Not at all. Surely, if a person genuinely appreciates the glory and majesty and beauty of the one true God and accepts His gracious offer of forgiveness, salvation, and right relationship with Him through Jesus, that person will be thankful enough and love Jesus enough to live for Him and in such a way that pleases Him. I don't live a godly life-style so that I might be accepted by God; I try to live a godly life-style because I have already been accepted and I'm grateful. If we believe, we're thankful. If we're thankful, we want to please Him.

In summary, let's look at three or four diagrams. In the first one, we see man, made up of body (the physical part), soul (personality – mind, emotions, and will) and spirit (eternal, life-giving part). In creation, all three parts were made by God and in His image (like Him). Nothing separated man from God, and they lived in relationship and harmony. God's life was in man, and man received wisdom and revelation from God. In this diagram, the body attends to, and interacts with, the Natural Realm; and the human spirit attends to God and the godly forces in the Spiritual Realm. The Soul interacts with information from the natural and revelation from the spiritual.

DIAGRAM #1 [1]

Earth ⟷ Body ⟷ Soul ⟷ Spirit ⟷ God and angels
(Natural Realm)   (Spiritual Realm)

In Diagram #2, we see our 'natural state' after man fell into sin. The body is still living, but subject to stress, illness, degeneration, and, eventually, death. The soul is still functioning but plagued with all kinds of negative experiences, thoughts, and emotions – things that we were never intended to experience. Man's spirit, now separated and cut off from the life and revelation of God and effectively 'dead,' can no longer pass along revelation from God, but looks to other 'spiritual' forces and natural resources for information and 'guidance.' In this diagram, the dying body continues to attend to a cursed natural realm; and the human spirit attends, primarily, not to God's revelation, but to the evil forces in the spiritual realm, and so lives, by and large, completely without God. Man's soul attends to the natural information gathered by the body and to any (mis) information received from the spiritual realm.

DIAGRAM #2

Earth ↔ Body ↔ Soul ↔ Spirit ↔ Satan and demons
                                                                              God and angels
(Natural Realm)   (Spiritual Realm)

Thankfully, there is one more diagram (or maybe two). This is a picture of a true Christian – someone who has been born again. Here, the body continues to look to the natural Earth and life in the natural realm. The human spirit, having been born again by faith in Christ can again attend to God's revelation and has the life of God and relationship with Him miraculously restored. The soul can now walk, once again, in light of God's revelation as it re-learns how to attend to the life of God. Notice the additional element: God's Holy Spirit, living, not somewhere in outer space, but right inside of us. (More about that in Chapter 4.)

DIAGRAM #3

Earth ↔ Body ↔ Soul ↔ Spirit ↔ God and angels

(Natural Realm)　　　　　　　　Holy Spirit　　(Spiritual Realm)

If there were a fourth diagram, it would represent us in eternity, forever with the Lord. It will look like this:

DIAGRAM #4

New Earth & Heavens ↔ Body ↔ Soul ↔ Spirit ↔ God and angels

(Restored Natural Realm)　(Resurrected)　(Healed)　(Perfected)　(Spiritual Realm)
　　　　　　　　　　　　　　　　　　Holy Spirit

As you may have noticed in Diagram #3, there is a new element: God's Holy Spirit, dwelling in us. Listen to 1 Corinthians 3:16, *"Don't you realize that all of you together are the temple of God and that the Spirit of God lives in you?"* Paul repeats the same idea in 1 Corinthians 6:19, *"Don't you realize that your body is the temple of the Holy Spirit, who lives in you and was given to you by God? You do not belong to yourself..."* God lives IN believers! Now that's an incredible thought! Somehow the majestic, all-powerful God, who holds the universe together, also lives in you and me. Talk about mystery!

This verse tells us that we are His temple. In the Old Testament, God 'lived' in two places here on Earth. The first was the tabernacle in the wilderness. It was a special tent, intended, much like we'd use a tent today, as a mobile dwelling place as we move from place to place. God dwelt there, in one location, and on a temporary basis.

Once the Hebrews arrived in and possessed the Promised Land, a 'permanent' dwelling place for God was erected – a building called the Temple. If you wanted to be with God, you had to go where He was – to the Tabernacle or to the Temple. Even then, only the priests could enter into the very presence of God.

But the New Testament paints a very different picture! God no longer lives in a tent or a building, but in His children. We don't have to go somewhere to be with Him (despite what your mother told you about going to church). He lives in us! You can't get any closer relationship than that! WOW!

Another amazing thing happened, although we hardly recognized it at the time. Colossians 1:13 says, *"For He has rescued us from the kingdom of darkness and transferred us into the Kingdom of His dear Son..."*

When we came to Christ and trusted Him as our saviour, we gave Him our allegiance and loyalty. In that sense, we have a new King. This verse tells us that, before we were in Christ, we lived under the domain of spiritual darkness. We were living in darkness and under the rule of Satan. True, not many of us actually went before whatever throne Satan has, to cower at his feet, although some have worshipped him in that way; but we were under his influence and rule in our lives. Christ died to redeem us (buy us back) from Satan's rule in our lives. In other words, He paid the price to free us from Satan and translated (carried us across) into His own kingdom – which is a much better place to be. We have a new kingdom and a new King; His name is Jesus!

If that were true in the natural realm, we'd be so grateful. Imagine growing up and spending your whole life a nation ruled by an evil and iron-fisted, despotic dictator and then miraculously being set free from that nation and brought into a new country; one ruled, not by a malevolent dictator, but by a loving, generous, and gracious King. Talk about culture shock! How sad it would be to be in that new land but to continue living as if you were still under the dictates of the evil ruler! Think of all the wonderful things you'd miss! Let's make that a better deal; let's make it permanent.

CHAPTER 3 – AMAZING GRACE...

Ephesians 4:30 says this, *"And do not bring sorrow to God's Holy Spirit by the way you live. Remember, He has identified you as His own, guaranteeing that you will be saved on the day of redemption."* That term 'identified' is literally the Greek word, 'sphragidzo'. It carries the following meanings: a) security and permanency; b) formal ratification; c) secrecy and security; and d) ownership and security.[2] This tells us that, when God placed His identifying mark (Holy Spirit) on us, He was claiming us permanently as His own, providing us with assurance and security, in a formal agreement.

A similar thought is found in 2 Corinthians 1:22, where Paul talks about the Holy Spirit being the first 'instalment' that guarantees everything He has promised us. This Greek word, 'arrabon', carries this connotation: "Originally, earnest-money deposited by the purchaser and forfeited if the purchase was not completed… In general usage, it came to denote a pledge or earnest of any sort. In the NT, it is used only of that which is assured by God to believers; it is said of the Holy Spirit as the Divine pledge of all their future blessedness… particularly of their eternal inheritance. In modern Greek, an 'arrabona', is an engagement ring." [3]

Why does anyone provide a down-payment? Isn't it to signify his full intention and ability to complete the deal? If I wanted to buy a house, I'd write up a purchase agreement and provide the vendor with a down-payment or deposit. In our day and age, that deposit is sometimes 10% or more of the purchase price. On a $300,000 home that would be a deposit of $30,000. I can't afford to forfeit $30,000, so you know I'd be serious about making an offer on a house and that I'd be sure that I could complete the deal, rather than lose all that money. Why give an engagement ring if you don't fully intend to get married?

In the same way, the Holy Spirit is God's 'deposit' on our lives. God gave the Holy Spirit to prove both His sincerity and His ability to close the deal. We may have been *"redeemed… with precious blood… the blood of Christ"* (1 Peter 1:18,19), and *"have been bought with a price"* (1 Corinthians 6:20), but we are sealed and secured by the Holy Spirit. That's exactly the only reason Jesus went to the cross. It was God's plan to buy us for Himself. God can and will fully redeem us! Hallelujah!

SOMETHING TO THINK ABOUT…

1. Sometimes, we hear about being 'saved.' This means that God has rescued us from the effects of sin. We talk about 'salvation,' which refers to this whole plan by which God wants to restore our relationship with Him and forgive (by paying for) our sins – so we have no outstanding debts with him. Have you been saved?

2. If salvation is a gift, have you received that gift? How do you know?

3. Which level of faith in Jesus do you have = Level 1 – awareness of the facts; Level 2 – moral agreement and philosophical support; or Level 3 – personal commitment to the cause?

4. How do you react to Jesus' claim that no one can go to the Father, except through Him? Do you agree or disagree? Why?

5. In Thessalonians, Paul speaks of the believers who turned from serving idols and false gods to serve the true and living God. If you have trusted in Christ as your saviour, from what did you turn away?

SOMETHING TO DO…

If you have already accepted Christ as your Saviour, write out a prayer, thanking Him for what He has done for you. Writing it out gives you opportunity to be more intentional in what you want to say.

If you haven't committed your life to Christ, what's holding you back? Why not write out a prayer, asking God to clarify what needs to be dealt with?

Perhaps you're ready to make that commitment now. If so, just thank Jesus for dying for you and paying for your sins. Ask Him for the gift of salvation and forgiveness. Tell Him that you want to receive Him and give your life to Him. If you do that, be sure to tell a Christian so they can rejoice with you and help you get grounded in your faith. They'll be thrilled!

CHAPTER 4

LET'S BEGIN AGAIN
(Enlisting in the army...)

2 Corinthians 5:17 "This means that anyone who belongs to Christ has become a new person. The old life is gone; a new life has begun!"

I was considering choosing a different title for this chapter; "This Changes Everything...," but that would not exactly be true. Let me explain:

Let's talk about your typical person; we'll call him "Joe." Where are we in Joe's journey? Joe grew up in your typical, middle-class family. You know the type; mom, dad, one boy, one girl, a dog, and a hamster, living in suburbia in a raised ranch with a double car garage... Joe was neither unusually spiritual and holy, nor was he exceptionally evil. He was just a regular guy, trying to find his way in the world. His was not a particularly religious family; they attended church fairly regularly; every Christmas and every Easter, in fact; well, almost...

Joe was doing 'fine' in everyone else's eyes – he had everything 'together,' as they say. He was good looking, had a job that paid well, and was dating a sweet co-ed he'd met in college. Everything was going great – except for one thing – an emptiness, an inner void, if you will. Somehow, life just didn't seem complete; 'something' was definitely missing. (But what?) In the quieter moments of life, when Joe slowed down enough to listen to his own thoughts, he knew that there had to be more to life than 'this.' There were other dis-quieting questions that echoed in the back of his consciousness as well. "Why am I here?" "Why is any of this here?" "Is this all there is to life? Just to grow up, get an education, find a job, get married, raise a family, retire, and wait to die? Was that the meaning of life?" "Then what?" (That was the most disturbing question of all!) Although Joe didn't come up with any profound answers, life went on. Joe was happy, or, at least, happy enough.

Then, one day, while working out at the gym, Joe met Ray – another young fellow about Joe's age. They 'happened' to be working out side-by-side on the exercise machines and had a chance for brief conversations between sets. There was nothing outstanding about Ray, except he seemed happy, genuinely happy, and had a very positive out-look on life. As time progressed and they kept running into each other at the 'Y,' they became friends; and the chats became talks; and the talks became conversations.

Joe was surprised to find out that Ray was religious. Actually, that's putting it mildly; Ray was a Youth Pastor, whatever that was. Nevertheless, he intrigued Joe; and a friendship began to form. That's when the conversation began to take on a deeper meaning. Ray kept talking about a variety of things, and, without knowing it, started to speak into the very questions that plagued Joe's mind in the small hours of the night. He even talked about being 'born-again.' Although it didn't make a lot of sense to Joe early on in their friendship, a conviction began to form in Joe's mind – he HAD to find out about this Jesus who seemed to be so real to Ray.

One thing led to another, and eventually Ray posed a question; no, not *a* question, but *the* question that would change Joe's life – and his eternity, forever. Did Joe want to accept Jesus as his saviour? In that moment, it all seemed so clear; and Joe not only took the payment of Jesus' death as his own, he also decided to give his life to Christ – to live his life in a way that would honour Christ and demonstrate his gratitude for what Jesus had done for him.

TA DA!!!! End of story, right? Well, actually, that's just the beginning. Transformation is a long process, after all. Not everything changed overnight, but life was somehow different to say the least. This change in Joe began in that brief moment, when he prayed, "Jesus, thank You for dying to pay the penalty for my sin. You gave Your life for me; so, I am giving my life to You. Help me to live for You and to please You. Thank You." How long did that take? A few seconds. But the impact would be eternal!

So, what did happen? A number of things... If you read the Introduction to this book, you may remember the Key Verses that were mentioned there. It sums up all that this Christian life is supposed to be about. Let's look at it again, first from the Bible, and then in 'everyday' words. Romans 8:28–30 reads: *"And we know that God causes everything to work together for the good of those who love God and are called according to His purpose for them. For God knew His people in advance, and He chose them to become like His Son, so that His Son would be the firstborn among many brothers and sisters. And having chosen them, He called them to come to Him. And having called them, He gave them right standing with Himself. And having given them right standing, He gave them His glory."*

There are a lot of different concepts there. Other versions use fancier terminology with words such as 'foreknew', 'predestined', 'justified', and 'glorified'. What is God saying? Let me put it this way...

Remember how we said that God wants relationship with mankind and that He continues to love us even when we are disloyal and disobey Him? He still invites us into relationship with Him. He can do this because His Son, Jesus, gave His life to pay the penalty for our sin. Yes, God – the righteous judge - not only found and pronounced us, "Guilty!" and sentenced us to death; He turned around and paid the death sentence by dying in our place so that we could go free. That's how much He loves us. Amazing, isn't it?

1. The word, 'foreknew' (knew in advance) is one of those concepts that we have difficulty understanding. Literally, it means to 'know before' but it's meaning is deeper than that. It also implies that He chose us to know Him. This is only half of a paradox – two truths that seem to be complete opposites but are both true at the same

time. Actually, there are a variety of paradoxes in the Bible. God is one God but Three Persons – Father, Son and Holy Spirit – all at the same time. Both are true; but the limited human mind, especially those with Western thought patterns, find it difficult to reconcile. By faith we have to believe both.

While we know that God chooses us (Jesus told His followers in John 15:16, *"You did not choose Me, I chose you..."*, He also holds us accountable to choose Him. We have the opportunity to respond positively to God's invitation. God gave us free will – we get to choose – but we also read, *"He* (the Lord) *does not want anyone to be destroyed, but wants everyone to repent"* (2 Peter 3:9). Yet we know that people do choose to reject Christ and His offer of salvation. How do we make sense of this? By faith; by choosing to believe both and trusting that God can work it out.

2. These verses say that God 'calls' us to Himself. In other words, God works in us, giving us a desire to know Him and getting us ready to commit ourselves to following Jesus. Remember Joe's nagging questions? That was God at work!

3. This may be an over-simplification, but when God works in your life in that way, it is because He 'predestines' us. In other words, He has a plan and a destiny for your life; He wants you to walk it out and to find great fulfillment in being what He made you to be and in doing what He is calling you to do. He is at work behind the scenes in your life and in mine, transforming us, directing us, and leading us through life into what He has for us.

Jeremiah 29:11 says, *"'For I know the plans I have for you,' says the LORD. 'They are plans for good and not for disaster, to give you a future and a hope.'"* Life just doesn't get any better than that!

4. While the NLT says that God gives a 'right standing' with Himself, other versions use the word, 'justifies.' In theological terms ('Theology' just means 'the study about God.'), the doctrine (teaching) of 'justification' is very significant. Remember back to the days of

creation? God's purpose was to make humans in His own image – that we should be like Him and be accurate representatives of His character and will on the Earth. Sin made us different from God, so that we aren't good or accurate representatives. How many kids have looked at their own parents and instinctively said, "If that's what God is like, I want no part of Him!"? Why? Because there is something innate within us that recognizes that people, especially authorities, are supposed to show us what God is like.

Jesus declared something remarkable about Himself. In John 1:18, He said this, *"No one has ever seen God. But the unique One, who is Himself God, is near to the Father's heart. He has revealed God to us."* What was Jesus getting at? He was saying that, although regular humans haven't even seen God as He truly is, Jesus had shown us what God is like. The word, translated here as "revealed" is a Greek word that means "to explain fully." It is the word that those who study God and His Word know as 'exegesis,' which literally means to study a passage of Scripture and pull out all the truths that are contained in it. In that sense, Jesus, being the exact representation (that perfect image) of God, has not just told us what God is like, He demonstrated God to us. Let's put it this way. If you want to know what God is like, look at Jesus. He perfectly represents the Father.

A few years ago, a Christian novel came out; some loved it; some didn't. It's an allegory or parable – a natural story designed to teach spiritual truth. "The Shack" was written by William P. Young as an attempt to explain his spiritual journey to his own children. As he wrote, he had no idea that it would become a 'best-seller.' Some people had HUGE issues with some of the details in the book. Others looked past the specifics and took great pleasure and comfort in its over-all message.

In the story, the central character, Mack, was having a conversation with God. During that time, God said something that I think is profound. Mack says to Papa (God, the Father), "I always liked Jesus better than You. He seemed so gracious and You seemed so…" To that

Papa replied, "Mean? Sad, isn't it? He came to show people who I am, and most folks only believe it about Him. They still play us off like good cop/bad cop most of the time, especially the religious folk…"[1]

Jesus shows us what God is like. Being God, He is 'godly.' In Romans 8:30, we read that the ones God called He also 'justified,' but what does that mean? There is a lot of truth wrapped up in that one word. "Justification" in the Bible, comes from the Greek word that literally means 'to make the same.' It is an accounting term. When you 'justify' your own bookkeeping to the bank statement, you make sure that the two records say the same thing. If they don't, someone has made a mistake; and you either change your records or convince the bank to change theirs. (Good luck with that one!) When God justifies us, He makes us 'the same as' Jesus. He doesn't bring Jesus down to our level; He raises us up to His. In other words, He restores us to our original image.

He made us in His image. That image became very broken. Jesus showed us the true image – what we were supposed to be like. When we come to Jesus for forgiveness and salvation, He remakes us (our spirits) back into that image so that we are once again in the image of God. That is the transformation process that restores His image in us.

There are a variety of things that happen in that process. Theologically speaking, when we are 'in Christ,' God doesn't just pretend that we are like Jesus, He makes us, or better, re-makes us, like Jesus by giving us the "righteousness of Christ."

Romans 3:21-24 says, *"But now God has shown us a way to be made right with Him without keeping the requirements of the law, as was promised in the writings of Moses and the prophets long ago. We are made right with God by placing our faith in Jesus Christ. And this is true for everyone who believes, no matter who we are. For everyone has sinned; we all fall short of God's glorious standard. Yet God, in His grace, freely makes us right in His sight. He did this through Christ Jesus when He freed us from the penalty for our sins."*

In plain words, God gives us a right-standing with Himself, by giving us the right-ness or the holiness of Jesus. Like someone making a deposit into your bank account, God credits our spiritual account with the same right-standing as Jesus has. In that way, we have been 'justified,' and we're 'the same as' Him.

5. Verse 24 in Romans 3 uses the term 'frees' to represent another theological term, 'redemption.' When a person redeems something, he buys it back. In Biblical days, you could become a slave if you could not pay your debts; and you could be sold by your creditor to someone else so he could recoup his loss. Your family or a friend could 'redeem' you. In other words, they would pay either the original creditor or whoever bought you as a slave, whatever amount you owed, so you could be free.

Although this is an all too mundane illustration, it would be safe to say that we redeem things that we've taken to the pawn shop. You know how it works; you take your possessions to the pawn shop. They give you money for whatever it is that you 'pawn.' If you want your stuff back, you have to pay the agreed upon price in the agreed upon time. If you don't pay that price, the shop gets to keep your things and will eventually sell them to recoup their losses. But if you redeem it; it is fully yours again and the shop has no legal claim on your goods.

The penalty for our sin was death, and we were 'enslaved' to sin. Jesus died to pay our penalty so that we could be free from our debt to sin. He 'redeemed' us so we could be free!

6. Lastly, in Romans 8:30, we see that God's intention is to 'glorify' us. I believe that this means He wants to practically restore the image that was lost to sin. Can you think of a better way for God to glorify sinful humans than to remake us back into the original image and pattern? What greater glory could there possibly be than to be made like God!?!? That's the ultimate goal of the transformation process!

Did you notice that we skipped over a line in Verse 29? It says that God chose us "...*to become like His Son, so that His Son would be the firstborn among many brothers and sisters.*" What does predestination produce? We are re-made back into the very image of God's Son ("Let US make man in OUR image...") so that Jesus would be the first of many...

The bottom line is this: God is working in every situation to rebuild us back into the image and likeness of Himself – accurate representatives of His character and His will, here on the Earth. He wants to have many sons and daughters who bear His image.

Even our name, "Christians" bears witness to God's intentions. It really means, "Little Christ's." What a huge compliment! The world should be able to look at us and say, "They're little Christ's; they remind me of Jesus."

Have you ever noticed that, in some families the kids look like little replicas of Mom or Dad? It might be the eyes or the nose; maybe it's the smile. I remember when our son, Andrew, was born, he looked amazingly like my father-in-law. My wife and I exclaimed, "It's a little Ivan Hill!" Oddly enough, as Andrew grew up, he morphed into a new and improved version of his dad. People recognize my image in my son. Happily, he's a taller and better-looking image, but he's still cast in the same mould.

I remember once, going for coffee and placing my order. The waitress then asked, "And what would your son like?" I asked how she knew he was my son. She replied, "He looks just like you." "Words to make a young man run screaming from the room!" I replied, ruefully.

Thankfully, being in the image of Father God is a much, much better thing. There is no higher calling and no greater privilege! As his dad, I'm kind of pleased that Andrew looks like me; how much more does Father God take pride and pleasure in His sons who are like Him!

If all of that is true, how is it that some 'Christians' can be such 'jerks' some of the time? If that image is so perfectly restored, why is the image still so flawed? We all know of those who profess to be followers of Jesus who are rude, selfish, hateful, manipulative, hypocritical, abusive, and destructive. Where's the image in them?

CHAPTER 4 – LET'S BEGIN AGAIN

Is any of Romans 8 true? Why is our experience so different from our theology?

Great questions! Let me give you some perspective…

The Christian life is a weird combination of what is true spiritually and what is true in the natural realm. It is also progressive. By that, I mean that, while God declares certain truths (and they are true, spiritually speaking), we still need to learn to live out that truth in the reality of our daily lives.

For example, 'salvation,' and all that is involved in it, has three distinct aspects. Let's look at it in terms of a time line – past, present and future.

In terms of 'eternity past' – before God made the universe – He planned all this, including you and me. Ephesians 1:4 says, *"Even before He made the world, God loved us and chose us in Christ to be holy and without fault in His eyes."* "Holy and without fault" sounds a lot like God, doesn't it? God chose us to be like Him.

In terms of world history, there was a day, roughly 2000 years ago, when Christ died on the cross as a sacrifice to pay the penalty for our sins. Shortly after that, He also came back to life – He was resurrected. According to Romans 1, His resurrection proves that He is God's son. Because He lives, we also will live.

Then there came a day in your personal history – or perhaps that day is still on the horizon for you – when you accepted Christ's payment as your own and changed your faith system (We all have one – the question is WHICH one?) to become a follower of Jesus Christ.

That decision was at a point in time in history. At that point, the Bible says you became 'in Christ' rather than 'in Adam' (See Romans 5:12-21). As John 3 puts it, you were 'born again' and received God's life. Your spirit, that was once dead in sin, is now alive in Christ.

2 Corinthians 5:17 says it this way… *"This means that anyone who belongs to Christ has become a new person. The old life is gone; a new life has begun!"*

Did you notice the verb tenses in that verse? If you are in Christ, you ARE (now, already) a new creature. The 'old things' passed away. That's 'past tense.' Something happened, and its effects continue – the old ceased to be and is gone; it 'died' and continues to stay dead. And the 'new things' or the 'new' has come. Again, this is 'past tense.' In other words, something new has already arrived and continues to be here. The question is, "What died and what came?"

Some theologians believe that God resurrects our old, dead, human spirit. That would certainly be in keeping with God's restorative and redemptive work. However, I believe that what died was our original spirit – what the Bible calls our "old man;" the one that was separated from the life of God. He (or she, of course) died, and a new spirit – a different one – one that is now alive in Christ and will live forever - has come to give life to the rest of our being.

Why do I say that? For one thing, the Greek tense indicates a one-time action with ongoing results. The fallen, dead human nature passed away and continues to be gone. A new nature came and continues to be here.

Additionally, Ezekiel 11:19 speaks prophetically to the Jewish people immediately, as the people of God, as well as to Christian believers. It tells us of God's plan when it says, *"And I will give them singleness of heart and put a new spirit within them. I will take away their stony, stubborn heart and give them a tender, responsive heart ..."* This verse uses a metaphor – heart of stone / heart of flesh – to indicate that God will change our hearts from being hardened toward Him, to ones that are soft and pliable and alive to Him. In any case, this verse tells us clearly that it is God's intent to put a new spirit within us. Granted, it is possible that He is just saying that we'd have a 'new attitude;' but, in light of other Scriptures, it could be taken to literally mean a new spirit.

Let's look at what the Apostle Paul said: *"My old self has been crucified with Christ. It is no longer I who live, but Christ lives in me. So, I live in this earthly body by trusting in the Son of God, who loved me and gave Himself for me"* (Galatians 2:20).

CHAPTER 4 – LET'S BEGIN AGAIN

How could we be 'crucified with Christ'? We weren't even born yet! When God says we were 'in Christ,' I believe that He means that Christ was our representative. He was our champion and represented all who would believe in Him. His death and resurrection counted for us all. In some cultures, rather than going to war with the neighbours and many people dying, each nation might select one representative to fight on behalf of the whole group. Remember the story of David and Goliath? Each man represented his nation. David conquered Goliath, and so Israel won the battle. In the same way, when Jesus, acting as our champion, died and rose again, it resulted in resurrection life for all of us who believe in Him.

There is only one outcome when a person is crucified; he dies. It sounds as if Paul is saying, "The original me has died, but a new me lives on, because Christ lives in me…"

In Romans 6:11 we read, *"So you also should consider yourselves to be dead to the power of sin and alive to God through Christ Jesus."* Why would Paul say that if it weren't true? He can't be saying, "Play mind games with yourself; tell yourself a lie; you're not really dead to sin, but, let's pretend…" No, that can't be right. What Paul is saying, is that we need to recognize this truth: our spirit is dead to sin. In other words, there is no interest in sin - no desire for sin in our new spirits. Our spirits, like God, cannot be tempted with sin. Unfortunately, our souls still are very much 'alive' to sin and have great interest in it sometimes – but that's for a later chapter!

My point here is that, when we become followers of Jesus, we are born again and the spirit within us is replaced with the true life of Christ. On the other hand, very little has changed in our human souls at this point. Until the transformation process really starts to take effect and changes our personalities, even Christians can behave in some very ungodly ways.

Remember our original diagram from Chapter 3? Although God made our human spirits to draw life and revelation and direction from Him, sin killed us; and we lost our relationship with God.

From then on, mankind was left trying to function in the natural, but struggling without the life of God. When we come to Christ and put our faith in Him, our lost relationship with the Lord is restored. Our spirit can now receive all that God intended to give to us. John 3 puts it in terms of being 'born again,' or, better, 're-born.' The diagram below depicts how we move from separation from God and without the life of God (on the left) to a close interaction with Him and having His life.

God | Human Spirit   to   God ↔ Human Spirit
                                                     Holy Spirit

When we come to Christ and place our faith in Him and make a commitment to Him, our spirit is re-born and becomes alive to God. There are many ramifications of this; too many for this chapter. Let's let one of the best-known Bible verses sum things up for us. *"For this is how God loved the world: He gave His one and only Son, so that everyone who believes in Him will not perish but have eternal life."* (John 3:16). We go from perishing to having eternal life. Such a wonderful truth!

We read what the Apostle John had to say about this: *"And anyone who believes in God's Son has eternal life. Anyone who doesn't obey the Son will never experience eternal life but remains under God's angry judgment"* (John 3:36). Elsewhere, in 1 John 5:12, he says this, *"Whoever has the Son has life; whoever does not have God's Son does not have life."* Having the life requires 'having the Son.'

That life is somehow wrapped up in relationship. John 17:3 reads, *"And this is the way to have eternal life—to know You, the only true God, and Jesus Christ, the one You sent to Earth."* What is eternal life? Knowing Father God and Jesus, His Son.

When God made Adam and Eve, they were deemed 'very good.' We might say, "Excellent!" They had the life of God flowing in them; but then sin entered the picture, and Adam and Eve 'died.' Their bodies began to decay; their souls – their personalities – experienced all kinds of negative ideas and emotions; but it was primarily their spirits that died 'on the day they ate of it.' They lost the life of God.

What happens when we are born again? Our bodies are pretty much the same; they're still getting older and heading toward the grave. Our personalities don't change all that much… Personality is the collection of all our memories, all our thoughts and belief systems, all our values, all our choices, all our habits, and everything that we know or believe to be true. Compared to the millions of 'facts' recorded in our souls, we've only made a very few changes. We've learned some truths about Christ, responded emotionally to the Spirit's working in us to bring us conviction about sin and convince us about Jesus; and we've made one decision – to come to God through Jesus.

Immediately two things happen – important things, but not everything changes… we become 'new creatures,' and our spirits become alive. Additionally, the Spirit of God comes to live in us. Wow! Talk about a mind-blowing concept!!!! It raises all kinds of questions! "How does that work?" "What does that feel like?" "So what?" It seems that the experience is unique to everyone. Some really have an immediate sense of change. Many have a huge sense of forgiveness. A few would say that, immediately, the grass was greener and the sky was bluer. Some experience a new peace… We really don't have any definitive, "This is how you know that God's Spirit has come into you…," so we must accept this wonderful truth by faith. Here are a couple of verses that will help:

When Jesus was about to be crucified, He was preparing His followers for His death and ultimate departure. To comfort them, He would send them "*…the Holy Spirit, who leads into all truth. The world cannot receive Him, because it isn't looking for Him and doesn't recognize Him. But you know Him, because He lives with you now and later **will be in you***" (John 14:17) (Emphasis mine).

John 16:5–13 is another passage that speaks to this; "*But now I am going away to the One who sent me … But in fact, it is best for you that*

I go away, because if I don't, the Advocate won't come. If I do go away, then I will send Him to you... When the Spirit of truth comes, He will guide you into all truth. He will not speak on His own but will tell you what He has heard. He will tell you about the future..."

Romans 8:9-11 gives us a wonderful summary of what happens: *"But you are not controlled by your sinful nature. You are controlled by the Spirit if you have the Spirit of God living in you. (And remember that those who do not have the Spirit of Christ living in them do not belong to Him at all.) And Christ lives within you, so even though your body will die because of sin, the Spirit gives you life because you have been made right with God. The Spirit of God, who raised Jesus from the dead, lives in you. And just as God raised Christ Jesus from the dead, He will give life to your mortal bodies by this same Spirit living within you."*

In that 'moment in time,' or 'point in history,' when we came to Christ, our spirits became alive as we entered into relationship with God; and the Holy Spirit came to live in us.

As I said, though, that's not the end of the story. It is the beginning of a life-long process – one of learning to live life as an expression of our new life and of our gratitude to God for what He has done in us. The New Testament mentions this time and time again. The Great Commission tells the church to make disciples (Followers) not just converts (profess-ors). We will spend the rest of our lives learning to live in relationship with God and how to represent Him well. In other words, we are transformed from what we were before to being like Jesus. It's a process that takes time, effort and grace.

Let me make one very clear distinction here. We do not live 'the Christian life' (whatever that is) in order to become Christians or to earn our salvation; we live as representatives of Christ because that is who we already are. Learning to do that well, though, is a life-long process.

Returning to our 'time-line,' another major change-point will come either when we die physically and our bodies go to the grave and our spirits go to be with Jesus, or, if, in the sovereignty of God, Christ returns to take us to be with Him in Heaven (John 14:1-6). It is only then, at the end of our Earthly lives, that our change-process and transformation will be complete, and we will be (exactly) like Him. 1 John 3:1-3 reads, *"See how very much our Father loves us, for He calls us His children, and that is what we are! But the people who belong to this world don't recognize that we are God's children because they don't know Him. Dear friends, we are already God's children, but He has not yet shown us what we will be like when Christ appears. But we do know that we will be like Him, for we will see Him as He really is. And all who have this eager expectation will keep themselves pure, just as He is pure."* Did you notice? We are already His children, but we still need to purify ourselves through the discipleship process.

When we come to that original crisis point, when we accept Christ, another wonderful thing happens to us. It is mentioned in the passage directly above. We become the 'children of God.' This is what is known in theology as the doctrine of 'Adoption.' We read about this in John 1:12, *"But to all who believed Him and accepted Him, He gave the right to become children of God."* God adopts us as sons and daughters. The great thing about adoption is that it is a permanent arrangement. Foster kids can be sent back to whatever agency they came from, but once you adopt, those kids are yours FOREVER!

No wonder Romans 8:15-17 explains, *"So you have not received a spirit that makes you fearful slaves. Instead, you received God's Spirit when He adopted you as His own children. Now we call Him, "Abba, Father." For His Spirit joins with our spirit to affirm that we are God's children. And since we are His children, we are His heirs. In fact, together with Christ we are heirs of God's glory. But if we are to share His glory, we must also share His suffering."* It is the Spirit of God that we have received that causes us to recognize our father-son or father-daughter relationship. "Abba" is an Aramaic term that toddlers, who are just learning to talk, use when speaking to their Earthly fathers. It is like 'Daddy' or 'Dadda' and shows the kind of intimate and innocent relationship we can have with God.

Where does that leave our friend, Joe? Well, he's placed his faith in Christ; and his spirit has been born again by faith. That brings Joe into a loving relationship with God through adoption, and gives him the assurance that he knows God in this life and will continue to live with Him in the next. In the meantime, Joe has a whole lifetime ahead of him during which he has the privilege of learning to live with Jesus, of learning to be who Joe truly is in his spirit, and of learning to do what God would have him to do. Joe's not alone in all this; God's spirit – the Holy Spirit – now lives in Joe and wants to teach Joe and guide him into the wonderful destiny and purpose that God has for him. In that sense, transformation is a co-operative effort as we humans learn to align ourselves with what the Spirit wants to do in us. God's plan so much more than just providing us with a fire escape from Hell; He intends to make us new!

As I said earlier, coming to Christ is really an issue of starting over, new beginnings, and a new direction. In some ways, that decision really does change everything.

Here is one way to 'picture' the time line we've been contemplating:

•	•	•	——	•
God chose us	Christ died & rose again	Joe accepted Christ	Joe's transformation & discipleship	Joe sees Christ - Transformation Complete
A point in time in Eternity Past	Points in time in World History	A point in time in his personal history	A process lasting the rest of Joe's earthly life	A point in time in Eternity Future

CHAPTER 4 – LET'S BEGIN AGAIN

SOMETHING TO THINK ABOUT...

1. Who is the most 'godly' person that you know? What makes you say that?

2. In what area might you have an inadequate view of God? If you don't know, you might try asking Him, "God, where don't I see You accurately?"

3. Do you understand terms such as 'born again' and 'saved' well enough to explain them to someone else? Find another believer and practise doing that together.

4. Have you ever accepted God's gift of forgiveness through faith in Jesus Christ? Why? Why not?

5. On a scale of zero to ten, with zero being totally cut off from God and ten being "as close as anyone can get," where would you place your experience? How might that change?

SOMETHING TO DO...

"The Romans Road" is a series of Bible verses that explain the plan of salvation. Look up each verse and underline it in your Bible.

Romans 3:23
Romans 6:23
Romans 5:8
Romans 10:9
Romans 10:13
Romans 5:1
Romans 8:1
Romans 8:38,39

CHAPTER 5

OF COURSE, YOU KNOW; THIS MEANS WAR!

2 CORINTHIANS 10:3-6 "We are human, but we don't wage war as humans do. We use God's mighty weapons, not worldly weapons, to knock down the strongholds of human reasoning and to destroy false arguments. We destroy every proud obstacle that keeps people from knowing God. We capture their rebellious thoughts and teach them to obey Christ…"

I learned the original quote, found in this chapter's title, on Saturday mornings, watching a kids' cartoon show called "Bugs Bunny" on TV. Often, Bugs would come up against some difficult situation and reply, "Of course, you know; this means war!" According to an internet website, "Fun Trivia," Bugs was quoting Groucho Marx, an actor in a 1933 movie called, "Duck Soup." That website also gives some insight into the original quote: "Something of the kind is supposed to have been said by one old member of the MCC (Marylebone Cricket Club) to another when they saw the bust of W. G. Grace being removed from the Long Room at Lord's Cricket Ground for safe keeping at the beginning of September, 1939." As England was being increasingly drawn into World War II and the reality of war was encroaching on her shores, the people were beginning to be aware that war was, in fact, already upon them.

Like the Englishmen of 1939, we are already at war but haven't seemed to realize it. Perhaps we can see the vestiges of this war in our lives but haven't 'connected the dots' that the trials and tests of our lives are just that – encroaching war. Whether we are aware of it or not, there is a spiritual battle going on all around us and in us.

In order to gain a better long-range perspective, let's go back to the beginning for a moment. God created the universe and all it contains. He created Adam and Eve and authorized them to 'have dominion' and to 'subdue the Earth,' as His representatives. They were to extend God's kingdom rule over the Earth. All was well. Then, into the play of World History, enters the enemy, who we know as "Satan."

According to Isaiah 14, a prophetic passage that is usually applied both to the natural King of Babylon, and also to Satan, Satan desired to usurp the throne in Heaven. There we read, in verses 12-14, *"How you are fallen from heaven, O shining star, son of the morning! You have been thrown down to the Earth, you who destroyed the nations of the world. For you said to yourself, 'I will ascend to heaven and set my throne above God's stars. I will preside on the mountain of the gods far away in the north. I will climb to the highest heavens and be like the Most High.'"*

Satan wanted to usurp the throne of God and to make himself supreme ruler over everything. Doesn't that sound familiar? How many people have said words to this effect; "I am the master of my own fate; the author of my own destiny"? Aren't they saying, "I will be my own god"?

The result was a civil war in Heaven – a war that, while a lost cause in the heavenly realms, has spilled over into the realities of our Earthly existence. Somewhere, somehow, pride entered into the heart of the Archangel, Satan; and he desired to take charge. He wanted to be 'like God.' Hey! Wait a minute! Isn't that what we're supposed to want; to be like God? What's wrong with that? The answer comes when we realize that Satan attempted to become 'like God' through self-exaltation, rebellion, and by his own merit, rather than through submission to God.

He attempted to achieve such a high and lofty goal through a political coup. He wanted to reign and be enthroned – to be the supreme ruler over Heaven and Earth. Revelation 12:4 is thought to suggest that Satan was able to muster troops that would support him in his take-over bid. In this highly allegorical and prophetic passage, we find that it speaks of a dragon that draws one third of the stars down with its tail. Many believe that this indicates that approximately one-third of the angelic realm joined in Satan's rebellion, and, as a result, were swept from Heaven with him. If Satan were actually one of three archangels, along with Michael and Gabriel, it would make sense that he would have 1/3 of the angels under his command and at his disposal. The assumption is that, because three archangels are named (Lucifer, Michael and Gabriel), there were or are only three angels that rule at such a high level, and that they all had or have an equal share of authority over the angels of lesser authority.

While very little is actually revealed to us about the details of that civil war in Heaven, Luke 10:18 is thought to explain a little about the result. The disciples had just returned from a ministry trip and joyfully reported that even the demons had been subject to their authority. Perhaps Jesus was providing a theological framework for their experience when He said, *"I saw Satan fall from heaven like lightning!"* Some believe that, at some point in history-past, Jesus witnessed Satan being thrown out of Heaven and being cast down to the Earth. Was Jesus explaining the disciples' success by saying, "Here's why they're subject to you; I saw Satan fall"?

Isn't that exactly what happens in the natural realm when a new self-proclaimed leader exalts himself, raises an army, and then launches an attack against the existing government? Civil war breaks out; the one in power manages to quell the attack, and then exiles the up-start, imprisons him, or executes him.

We assume that all of this took place in the heavenly realms either before or shortly after the earliest days of creation. While we are not told the timing of the heavenly events; we understand that, somehow and at some time, Satan appeared on this planet and continued his bid to rule by extending rebellion to humans, leading them away from loyalty and obedience to God and enslaving them to himself.

Apparently, Satan lost the war in Heaven, but has decided to continue it on Earth. Time and time again in Scripture, we find Satan (and his demonic horde) trying to gain influence and control over individuals and territories of the Earth.

Isn't that really what we know as 'temptation,' is all about? Satan tries to use even good, proper, and godly desires to lead mankind into doing things his way? "Eve, follow my suggestion; eat the fruit!" As Satan or one of his minions tempts us, and we respond in obedience, it gives him greater influence in our lives. With each little successful temptation, the devil gains authority; and this pattern continues in a downward spiral into bondage until he controls more and more of our lives.

One understanding of sin is that it is man's attempt to meet legitimate needs, using illegitimate means. For example, food is a legitimate need – one that can be legitimately satisfied by nourishing our body using healthy resources that are rightfully ours. But it can also be satisfied, either by stealing someone else's food, by consuming unhealthy 'food,' or by using food illegitimately. How many people develop severe obesity because they use food as comfort for inner pain rather than as nourishment? God wants us to meet our need for emotional healing in Him, not the refrigerator! Food, good food, healthy food can be used inappropriately.

Another example would be in our need for physical intimacy. The human sex-drive and need for intimacy was God's idea, and it was a good one – make that a great one! As originally intended, it was not shameful or 'dirty;' but it is as a person chooses illegitimate means to satisfy that legitimate need that it becomes profane. Rather than finding pleasure in the marriage bed between husband and wife, people turn to fornication and adultery or what the King James called 'licentiousness' (unrestrained, continual lust) and end up 'sleeping around' with whomever they choose.

When Satan tempted Jesus (See Matthew 4, Mark 1, and Luke 4), he used three legitimate needs as temptations for Jesus. First was the temptation in regard to food. Jesus had just finished a forty-day fast. Obviously, He would feel hunger and be in need of nutrition.

CHAPTER 5 – OF COURSE, YOU KNOW; THIS MEANS WAR!

Nothing wrong with that! The temptation came in Satan's suggestion that Jesus use His miraculous powers to turn stones into bread. "Meet Your need my way!"

That didn't work! What's next? "Jesus, You need recognition. Prove Yourself! Throw Yourself off the highest point of the temple; if You are who You say You are, God's angels will catch You." The problem was that doing so would have put God's word to the test. Not only that, but obedience Satan at any level can eventually produce bondage to him in that area. It seems subtle, but this was another attempt to get Jesus to do things Satan's way.

Lastly, came a more direct attempt. "Jesus, just bow down and worship me, and I'll give You all the kingdoms of the world!" Wasn't it always God's plan that He would rule on Earth as it is in Heaven? Has it not always been God's intention that Jesus, who is the King of Kings and Lord of Lords, be recognized as such here in our world? Wasn't it God who commissioned Adam and Eve to extend His kingdom by ruling over the Earth and subduing it? Of course, it was; but Satan would present what, on the surface, seems to be a 'better alternative.' Wouldn't Jesus get exactly what He wanted, just by worshipping Satan? Why go to all the bother of dying an agonizing death on the cross? Why not just take the easy way out and bow down? Doesn't the end justify the means?

In this last scenario, no question was raised concerning Satan's authority or ability to just hand over the kingdoms of the world to Jesus. After all, you can't give away what is not yours in the first place. Three times in the Gospel According to John, we find references to Satan as the *'ruler of this world'* (See John 12:31; John 14:30 and John 16:11). Ephesians 2:2 refers to him as *"the commander of the powers in the unseen world. He is the spirit at work in the hearts of those who refuse to obey God."* That being the case, we understand that Satan has some level of possession or ownership over the Earth. There is a saying; "Possession is nine-tenths of the law." Whether that's true or not, we have to acknowledge that Satan assumed he could hand all the kingdoms of the world over to Jesus. As the old hymn proclaims,

"This is My Father's World." Nonetheless, Satan has a great deal of influence and control in what is technically not his.

Originally, it was 1/3 of the angels that Satan led astray and into his service. Once here on Earth, Satan turned his attention to humans. That makes sense. Adam and Eve were the loyal subjects of Satan's enemy, God. Therefore, they also were Satan's enemy and needed to be conquered. Divide and conquer! Separate mankind from God and conquer them.

As Adam and Eve faltered in their loyalty to God and obeyed Satan, they not only became his slaves, they handed over their God-given authority to the one they obeyed. It reminds me of the 'domino effect.' Perhaps you've seen a video of someone with too much time on their hands who has set up hundreds and hundreds of dominoes in a strategic pattern. Tip over the first domino, so that it knocks over the second and the second impacts the third. Before you know it, an entire chain reaction has been initiated and cannot be stopped. Adam and Eve's one act of disobedience to God, as they chose to follow the serpent's suggestions, unleashed a whole host of negative consequences (Genesis 3:14-24).

In the same way, when we obey Satan, it can lead to an on-going and seemingly unstoppable chain reaction. As Adam and Eve began turning their loyalty away from God by their disobedience; they and their God-given authority increasingly came under the domination of the Enemy.

In some marriage ceremonies, the bride and groom exchange vows including something to this effect; "I give myself, all that I am, and all that I have, to you." What was once the bride's house immediately becomes 'our house.' While no formal ceremony took place, through their sin, Adam and Eve bowed to Satan's authority; and what had been entrusted to their care – the Earth – was also brought under his influence. No wonder humans are called, *"slaves to sin"* (Romans 6:6,16,17)!

We find a similar thought in Romans 12:1,2, where Paul urges the Roman believers to *"give your bodies to God because of all He has*

CHAPTER 5 – OF COURSE, YOU KNOW; THIS MEANS WAR!

done for you." If a person presents or gives his or her body to God, all that they are and have comes with it. If you own their body; you own all of them. I understand that, in some enlistment forms, the new recruit actually agrees to give his or her body to whatever military branch he or she is joining.

Apparently, the temptation to 'Eat!' was not just about a piece of fruit, or even about Adam and Eve; because the consequences were so wide-spread. Their obedience seems to have 'opened the door' for Satan to operate at greater liberty in this realm. You might call it a hostile, territorial take-over.

Little wonder that we see such carnage all around us on a regular basis! If God is good and loving and benevolent (which He definitely is), it makes sense that His enemy is also our enemy and brings just the opposite into play. Remove heat and the result is cold; remove all that is good and godly, and you reap hatred, strife, destruction, and death. What we experience now is so far removed from what it could have been; it seems impossible to even imagine a world without any evil influence and the destruction that it brings. On the positive side, we also can't imagine what life would be like if every part of it were filled with the life and glory of God's kingdom.

In light of the situation that resulted from mankind's disobedience, we need to recognize that, throughout the rest of the Biblical narrative, we find the story of God calling His people back into right relationship with Himself. World History depicts the ongoing battle between good and evil; God and the enemy. Although this battle rages on all around us and has continued for millennia, and no matter how much support Satan has been able to muster, he and all his followers are still but puny creations coming up against an omnipotent (all powerful) Creator God. Satan has surely underestimated his Foe!

So why is the battle taking so long? 2 Peter 3 is Peter's answer to this very question. In Verse 9, we read, *"The Lord isn't really being slow about His promise, as some people think. No, He is being patient for your sake. He does not want anyone to be destroyed, but wants everyone to repent."* Why does God delay in wrapping up world history and bringing an end to the battle? Because, in His patience, He waits for more people to switch their allegiance back to Him. Wooing people back into relationship with God seems to take time. God does not rob us of our free-will; He patiently works in our spirits, drawing us to Himself. Violating free-will and simply dictating a change of allegiance would be faster and much suffering could be avoided, but God has never been asking for slaves; He wants sons and daughters!

Colossians 1:13 gives us a brief glimpse of the result of all of this. *"For He rescued us from the domain of darkness, and transferred us to the kingdom of His beloved Son…"* Speaking to and of believers, Paul tells us that we were once in the 'domain of darkness,' but God rescued us and transferred (Literally, 'carried us across') into the Kingdom of His dear Son. 'Domain' and 'Kingdom' are parallel expressions. One's domain is the area in which that person has control or authority. The same could be said of a kingdom. Although we might expect that, since the first concepts (domain/kingdom) are parallel, that the next idea (darkness/dear Son) would also be a parallel, but, in reality, they are a contrast. Usually we think of the opposite of 'darkness' as 'light.' Jesus said He was the light of the world (John 8:12), and John 1 refers to Jesus as both the 'the word' and 'the light.' Satan's kingdom is a 'dark' place, but the kingdom of God's dear Son is filled with happiness and light. God was not – and is not – content to leave His people in the darkness and invites us all to come to the light.

Yes, there is a war going on all around us. It is a battle to gain and keep dominance and control; but it is also about personal recognition. Either God, the Creator of all that we see and know, will be exalted; or Satan will have his way.

The problem for many of us is that we are not aware of this battle; it is not usually at the forefront of our conscious thought but simmers away on the back burner of our minds. Occasionally, we see vestiges of the battle and may think about the evil that takes place in the world around us. This seems to be particularly true when evil is so evidently displayed in news reports about terrorism, serial murders, the sex-trade industry that victimizes innocent children, etc. In

CHAPTER 5 – OF COURSE, YOU KNOW; THIS MEANS WAR!

those moments, even the most secular and atheistic are forced to acknowledge 'evil.' Call it "Man's Inhumanity to Man," or whatever; on those occasions, when sin is blatantly displayed before our eyes, we're all forced to contemplate whatever it is that we consider 'evil.'

This raises several important questions: What is evil? Is it just some negative and nebulous force that seems to surface in the reality of human experience from time to time? Or is it more concrete and intelligent than a free-floating force? How do sin and evil, which are spiritual concepts, impact the reality of our daily and Earth-bound lives? What can be done about them? All great questions!

In the Bible, we are told that evil comes at us, not simply because of some twisted frailty or flaw in the character of other humans. There are others involved – those who are intelligent, orderly and intentional. In Ephesians 6:12, we read, *"For we are not fighting against flesh-and-blood enemies, but against evil rulers and authorities of the unseen world, against mighty powers in this dark world, and against evil spirits in the heavenly places."*

Without exception, conservative theologians understand this to be a description of the demonic forces at work around us. Satan is real, and he is our enemy. In his quest for domination and recognition, he came against God and failed miserably. Now, he has turned his attention against humanity – those who God loves dearly. The fallen angels, who were once part of the angelic host, have now become a demonic horde. In their sworn allegiance to their master, Satan, they are deployed against creation in order to bring us all under the thumb of Satan.

Although neither angels nor demons are human, but, rather, a distinct order of creation, they seem to have many of the qualities that we usually consider human. They are intelligent, have free-will, and emotion. For example, Luke 15:10 records the teaching of Jesus, *"In the same way, there is joy in the presence of God's angels when even one sinner repents."* Imagine that! Whenever one of us humans repents and comes to Christ, the angels in Heaven know about it and have some positive emotional attachment to the event!

By the way, some teach that, when a person dies, he or she goes up to Heaven and becomes an angel. I don't know where that teaching came from, but it wasn't the Bible! While we don't have the time and it isn't the purpose of this book to do a complete teaching about angels and demons, we need to recognize that both the angelic and the demonic have personalities much like our own and God's. That doesn't make angels or demons human, and it certainly doesn't make us God! By the way, have you noticed that no one seems to expect people to die and become demons – just angels. Like the movie said, "All dogs go to heaven!" but movies are hardly a reliable source for our theology!

The interaction between the physical realm and the spiritual realm is very mysterious. For example, the manifest, tangible presence of God brings physical reactions among the humans that are present. Conversely, it is no secret that demonic manifestations can produce some strange physical reactions for the person who is oppressed. Furthermore, we know from Biblical accounts that angels seem to take human form and can speak with mankind.

Hebrews 13:2 gives us a shocking insight: *"Don't forget to show hospitality to strangers, for some who have done this have entertained angels without realizing it!"* Showing hospitality seems like a perfectly normal event in human life and society. We do it all the time. Hosting complete strangers is less frequent but would hardly be considered a supernatural experience. Yet, we find that at least 'some' have done so, not to human visitors, but to angels. And they didn't even know that their guests were not just regular people!

At other times, it seems that the presence of spiritual entities was more physically obvious. When the ladies went to minister to the body of Jesus on Sunday morning, they were greeted as *"... two men suddenly appeared to them, clothed in dazzling robes"* (Luke 24:4). The messengers appeared to be men, but their shining clothes gave their true identity away. On a variety of occasions in Scripture, angels not only appeared to mankind, they brought messages and dream interpretations.

CHAPTER 5 – OF COURSE, YOU KNOW; THIS MEANS WAR!

In the same way, the demonic realm, while spiritual in nature, can have great impact on our physical world and in the lives of human beings. At one point, Jesus healed a mute boy who also had both epilepsy and a demon. Mark 9 tells us that often the demon would seize the boy and throw him into the fire. Jesus both healed the boy and cast out the demonic. This passage is way more than just a primitive interpretation that would try to blame demons for the illnesses we now understand through modern medicine. While there isn't some demon lurking behind every rock and tree, I believe that we need to be more open to the possibility of demonic interference in the physical realm. Perhaps it is more of a Western mind-set; but it seems that, in other cultures, people are more aware of that possibility. In North America, we don't 'connect the dots' as readily.

There is a fascinating story in 2 Kings 6. Elisha and his servant had been sleeping through the night while an enemy army surrounded them. The servant panicked as he emerged into the morning light to find themselves surrounded. Immediately he told his master of their dire predicament. Elisha, seemingly unshaken, replied, *"Don't be afraid!... For there are more on our side than on theirs!"* and prayed that God would open his servant's eyes so he could see 'those that were with us.' It wasn't that the servant was physically blind; he could see the enemy army quite well. It was only when God opened his spiritual eyes that the young man could see the spiritual reality – a host of angelic warriors with flaming chariots, positioned strategically and ready to defend the men of God.

Only one thing changed in that part of the story; the servant's ability to see and recognize the spiritual realities – just as significant and powerful as the natural ones that surrounded him, if not more so. It makes me wonder, "What don't I see? What might I see?"

As the saying goes, "It takes two to tango…" Yes, there is a host of angelic beings; but there is also an army of demonic forces, also ready to go into battle. As we saw in Ephesians, our battle or fight is not against 'flesh and blood' – not just the other people involved, but against an array of demonic entities. The list includes 1) rulers (principalities), 2) authorities (those with delegated authority) of the unseen world, 3) mighty powers in this dark world (those empowered since before the beginning of the world) and, 4) evil spirits in heavenly places (unclean spirits).

Theologians speculate, perhaps correctly, that these designations indicate levels of power or authority similar to the ranks of a human army; private, sergeant, lieutenant, captain, etc. Perhaps the list speaks to their types of activities or interests; maybe, it is just a variety of descriptions generally identifying all demonic spirits. No matter how you understand the verse, one thing is for sure: They're out there, and they're deployed against us!

SOMETHING TO THINK ABOUT…

1. Is there any area in your life where you are trying to meet legitimate needs in illegitimate ways?

2. Have you ever wondered if you had had an encounter with an angel? What was that like?

3. Have you ever felt like you had encountered a demon or some type of evil force? Describe that experience.

4. How aware would you say that you are concerning the struggle between good and evil?

5. Have you ever asked God to open your eyes so you could see the supernatural realm? Why or why not?

SOMETHING TO DO…

If you are able to do so, look up pictures of both demons and angels from different cultures (Asian, African, South American, European) and from various time periods. (You might want to ask God to protect you before doing that! We don't want to expose ourselves needlessly.) Compare those pictures with how Hollywood portrays both entities. Do you notice anything in particular? Why do you suppose that the pictures of demons are so similar?

CHAPTER 6

PLUNGING HEADLONG INTO BATTLE!

Romans 12:2 "Don't copy the behavior and customs of this world, but let God transform you into a new person by changing the way you think. Then you will learn to know God's will for you, which is good and pleasing and perfect."

Ok! Time for some balance, here. After reading the last chapter, you might be inclined to think that I'm suggesting that you look for demons behind every rock and tree. I knew one lady who, if anyone sneezed, wanted to cast a 'cold demon' out of them (True story!). Taken to an extreme, this line of thinking could end up in schizophrenic paranoia: "The bad guys are in my head, and they're out to get me! AAAAAHHHH!"

Let's not get carried away. Perhaps, though, it is time for a bit of a paradigm shift. A 'paradigm' is a framework of thinking that we assume to be true and automatically and unconsciously apply to every situation. For example, if, at some level, you believe, "I'm a bad person," it would impact every area of your life.

The Western or North American mind-set has often become very secularized or naturalistic. Since demons cannot be proven as scientific fact, or so it is presumed, our naturalistic minds tend to overlook such a possibility. If someone gets sick or has some sort of 'accident,' the LAST thing that most North Americans, including many Christians, consider would be demonic attack.

It is not that way in Africa or the Far East. Many in those cultures and of that experience would, because of their paradigm, automatically assume that the situation does involve the demonic. If that proves not to be the case, then they would look to a more naturalistic cause.

In 2007, I had the privilege of traveling with a friend for 7 ½ weeks through Uganda, Kenya, and South Sudan. In Juba, the capital of South Sudan, we were working with two young evangelists, Robert and Justin. While we were with them, they were asked to go and minister to a young man who had been in what I suspected was catatonic depression (But I'm no psychiatrist!). He had just laid on his bed, staring blankly into space, hardly moving a muscle for over eight years. The fact that he had not had a bath in over a year was painfully obvious. (You can imagine the stench!). During that time, his mother found it necessary to spoon-feed him.

When we arrived for a 'ministry session,' Robert and Justin and their students automatically assumed that some demon or another had taken control of the young man and proceeded to very loudly command the spirit to leave. The yelling and shouting went on and on for well over an hour, without result. The boy hardly breathed and didn't even blink. By this time, I was thoroughly embarrassed and had a headache from all the racket. I was wondering if he'd had cerebral malaria or some other debilitating disease and had been reduced to a vegetative state. I was thinking that all of this praying and yelling was just a waste of time.

Suddenly, Robert declared, "Warfare songs! We need warfare songs!" and began singing the old hymn, 'There's Power in the Blood' in Swahili, I think. Maybe it was the Bari dialect. With that, the young man, his face contorted in agony, brought his hands up to his temples and started shrieking in pain. My paradigm shifted quickly, to say the least! Once the demon exposed its presence, it was not long before it was cast out. The young man gave a violent gasp as if wind was being forced from his lungs; then, he laid back down in peace.

Within the hour, he had been bathed, was freshly clothed, and in his right mind. The filthy rags he'd worn and the bed sheets and mattress were burned. He was sitting upright and asked for a drink as he said

CHAPTER 6 - PLUNGING HEADLONG INTO BATTLE

he was thirsty. Immediately, he downed six large glasses of juice, one right after the other. He'd been so thirsty but had been unable to even ask for a drink. Suddenly, everything seemed to be functioning normally; he interacted with his family, who came with tears of joy streaming down their cheeks, to greet their son. It reminded me of the widow of Nain who received her son back from the dead when Jesus brought him back to life.

Why do I tell this story? To help us be aware that spiritual warfare is real. There are demons on assignment against us. Thankfully, that's not the whole story! God has released His angels to act on our behalf and has given us His Holy Spirit to guide and empower us. Logically, if Satan took only one-third of the angels with him, it means that we have twice as many angels ministering on our behalf!

While the battle rages on all AROUND us, it is also WITHIN us. While most theologians believe that the demons cannot read our minds, they, nevertheless, have great influence, introducing their suggestions into both our conscious and un-conscious minds.

Before we came to Christ, we were under the domain of darkness and were slaves of sin and Satan. Somehow that sounds so vilified, as if we are all depraved, wild-eyed and out of control. Thankfully, it isn't always that obvious.

When we become Christians, there is an instantaneous event, as God places a new, or born-again human spirit within us. This spirit is distinct from the indwelling presence of the Holy Spirit, who also lives in us. This renewed spirit is as pure and as holy as Jesus is; and, like Adam and Eve before the fall, is untainted by sin. That makes us Satan's enemy and a threat to his kingdom. Apparently, Satan does not like it when he loses control. After all, his agenda is world domination. Because we move from being his slaves to being his enemies and a friend and child of God, we can rightfully expect that the attacks from Satan will escalate as he comes against us with temptation or with some scheme to harm us.

What makes us so susceptible to attack is that, while our spirit has been renewed, our soul has not. Our mind is full of inaccurate belief systems; our emotions continue to have wounds and the damage that life has done to us; and our wills follow along in line and in response to what is in our mind and emotions. Even the habits that were formed in us before we came to Christ continue to exert their influence in our lives. All of these serve as opportunities for the enemy. If we think of our souls as a recording device, our thoughts, attitudes, words, and actions are all the data that has been recorded there as we lived out our lives. In fact, experience has even shown that memories and emotions have been recorded in the souls of babies while still in the womb; and these are carried with them throughout life. It may even be that there is such a thing as cell memory or memories recorded in our DNA, that can be mysteriously passed down from generation to generation. That's an amazing concept!

Obviously, not everything recorded in our memory-bank is evil. Many of our thoughts, attitudes, words, or actions may be good and godly and in line with the character and will of God. Unfortunately, all that is in our soul is not that way, and may not be true or accurate. We may believe those concepts and act accordingly, but that doesn't make them true.

For example, for centuries, people believed in a 'flat' Earth. The prevailing thought was that, if you sailed too far from home, you might come to the edge of the world and fall off. That would explain why some ships never came back again. Apparently, there is still a "Flat Earth Society" functioning today. Its members have a sincere faith, but not an accurate one. Believing in a flat Earth is hardly a 'sin;' but it is not in agreement with God's scientific truth, so it needs correction.

For years and years, 'civilized' people believed that slavery was a good and beneficial practice. It was an accepted and acceptable social construct. Questioning that idea was almost considered blasphemous. It was only as Biblical insight and attitudes prevailed

CHAPTER 6 – PLUNGING HEADLONG INTO BATTLE

against the culture of the day that slavery was abolished in Britain and in the south of the USA.

Most of us have learned how to get our own way by using ungodly tactics. It may involve using anger to force people to do our bidding or to punish them for some perceived failure or shortcoming. How many of us have used a 'little white lie' to escape the consequences of the truth? How many angry spouses have communicated, "You'd better not do that again!" with a cold shoulder at bedtime? We've all learned coping skills that are ungodly to some degree or another and will use them, particularly when our stress-level is high. We use them because they work or because we hope they'll work. That doesn't make the natural way a godly one!

If we could picture a believer in a diagram, we'd see that their soul or personality, comprised of mind (intellect), emotions and will, is loaded with belief systems, thoughts, memories, actions, reactions, plans, emotions, and ways of behaviour. Essentially, our natural personality is just the cumulative outworking of all of these things, interacting in our souls.

It might look something like this, with the checkmarks representing the good, godly, and true things, and the x's representing the ungodly or untrue aspects of our personality. One problem with a diagram such as this is that, in reality, there are no blank spaces in our souls; they are completely full, and there is no neutral territory. Granted, somethings are amoral; they have no moral attributes to them. For example, it is morally neutral to prefer the colour green over the colour purple. It's neither right nor wrong. Although purple is also a part of Jesus' colour palette, preferring green is not sinful.

When it comes to moral issues, it might be better to picture a person's soul as a war-map. Every square millimetre is under someone's control and is either dedicated to Jesus Christ, or it is subject to the thinking and ways of the enemy. Think of it this way; in terms of morality, everything on the map is either like Jesus or it is not. Every place that is like Jesus is a checkmark; every bit of space that is not like Him is an 'x.' As we grow to be more like Jesus, we increase the number of checks and reduce those x's. Sounds a lot like discipleship, doesn't it?

Circle #1 – Natural Man   Circle #2 – Some Growth   Circle #3 – More Growth

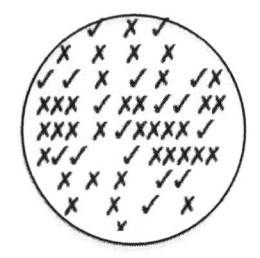

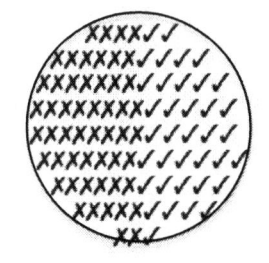

When we come to Christ, we have learned a few truths about Jesus; we may have struggled with some emotions (conviction, sorrow, etc.) and made one choice – to respond to the gospel and surrender to Jesus – so we have a very few nice, new checkmarks in our souls. There were already check-marks from before we came to Christ as well. Other than that, we're filled with all kinds of knowledge, emotions, and decisions that may not be in line with the character and will of God or with truth. In the diagram, Circle #1 shows the good, the bad and the ugly all swirling around in one big mixture of thoughts, feelings, and choices. It is not possible to somehow sift them into two divisions with all the checkmarks over here and all the x's on this side (As in Circles #2 and #3).

This is not to be confused with the Confucian understanding of yin and yang, depicted by those circles with two equal swirling halves, one representing the "good" part of us, and one representing the "bad" side. This is not an equal fight; let's not forget that the supernatural Spirit of God is also involved.

The Bible speaks of believers who are 'carnal' (See Romans 7:14; 8:6,7; 1 Corinthians 3:1,3,4, etc.). Our English term 'carnal' reminds us of the Spanish word carné which means 'meat' or 'flesh.' Chilé con

CHAPTER 6 - PLUNGING HEADLONG INTO BATTLE

carné literally is "chilés (and beans) with meat." Biblically speaking, someone who is carnal, is a believer who continues to live a life that looks pretty much like the rest of the world or very similar to what you'd expect if the person were not a believer. The 'carnal' (fleshly) side of our soul is comprised of all the beliefs, attitudes, words, and actions that are not in line with the character and will of God. In other words, the person lives naturally, as if they have not been impacted by God's revelation or the work of Holy Spirit in their lives. The outworking of this is that they really don't look or behave much more like Jesus than they did before they became Christians. You must know that there's something wrong with that! Obviously, Satan and his horde are quite happy with the carnal side of a believer and are only too happy to promote and reinforce that side of things.

Romans 12:2 puts it this way: *"Don't copy the behavior and customs of this world, but let God transform you into a new person by changing the way you think. Then you will learn to know God's will for you, which is good and pleasing and perfect."* In a sense, our personality has been formed and conformed as we grew up in this world. After conversion, it needs to be re-formed, not by the natural processes of the world but by the transforming application of God's Word by the Spirit of God. It will take the renewing of our mind (personality) if we are to experience God's will, and, by our experience, find that it is good and acceptable and perfect. We are either being conformed (to the world) or being transformed (to the image of Christ). At times, it seems that people 'coast' spiritually in a season where they are neither growing spiritually nor regressing backwards to the attitudes and behaviours of the flesh. That's a dangerous situation. It is almost impossible to coast uphill or up-stream. Usually, coasting will take us in the opposite direction!

This process is likened to a war or a battle or to a wrestling match in 2 Corinthians 10:3-5. *"We are human, but we don't wage war as humans do. We use God's mighty weapons, not worldly weapons, to knock down the strongholds of human reasoning and to destroy false arguments. We destroy every proud obstacle that keeps people from knowing God. We capture their rebellious thoughts and teach them to obey Christ."*

Did you notice that this battle is primarily in our mind, meaning our personality? We destroy speculations, which are 'logical' arguments or conclusions – the things that we've figured out naturally – and every high-sounding idea that is contrary to our knowledge of God. Additionally, we are to take EVERY THOUGHT captive and make it obedient to Christ. It is those remaining speculations and un-captivated thoughts that cause believers to act in ungodly ways.

Essentially, this verse teaches us to go through our data bank and inspect every piece of data – all the information that is stored there – to see if it is in line with the character and will of God. When we find something that is not obedient to Christ, we need to do away with it altogether and replace it with truth that is under the lordship of Jesus.

This is the basic process of repentance. 'Repent' literally means to 'think again,' or to change our mind on a topic. If we were to truly change our thinking or belief system, it would change our behaviour. It seems that often people say that they believe one thing but act in a way that is not in line with their belief. In actuality, we always act in line with what we believe the most deeply. The bottom line is this; if you want to know what you really think, look at how you act! Ouch!

For example, probably all Christians would say that they believe in prayer; that prayer 'works.' The sad reality is that many Christians do not pray on a regular basis. Why is that? Maybe they've prayed and prayed for something but didn't get the answer they wanted. Perhaps they have believed the lie of the enemy that they aren't good enough to expect God to answer their prayer (As if God's grace is a merited thing!). What they've held to, theologically, hasn't worked itself out in the reality of their experience, so they've stopped praying. Whatever the reason, if they don't pray, we can be pretty sure that they don't really believe in prayer.

CHAPTER 6 – PLUNGING HEADLONG INTO BATTLE

For many of us, we know far more truth than what we put into practice. Knowing is not the issue; it is what we really believe or commit to that is behind what is causing the trouble. Sometimes this struggle is pretty obvious: we know very well that what we are doing or are about to do is wrong, but we can't seem to help ourselves. We find ourselves in such a position, partly because we have not had our minds renewed according to Romans 12:2 – the carnal thoughts and emotions are still there.

Part of the struggle may be because the enemy of our souls, Satan, has one of his agents at work tempting us and sneaking his suggestions into our thinking. We are told that Jesus was tempted in every way that we are tempted (Hebrews 4:15) and understands what we go through. Most of us react something like this, "Come on: Jesus can't have dealt with what I'm facing. If you only knew…" But that is what the Bible says. Thankfully, we know that He never gave in to such temptations and is without sin. We also read about Jesus being tempted by Satan in three of the four Gospels (Matthew, Mark, and Luke). If Jesus could be tempted by Satan himself or by lesser demons, wouldn't it be pretty naïve for us to think that we aren't susceptible to the same tactics? Anyone who is honest, including the most spiritual Christian you know, has to admit that they deal with temptation on a regular basis.

Sadly, just being tempted seems to be enough for us to experience shame and condemnation. We don't have to fall into sin; apparently just momentarily contemplating it is something that is hard to admit. It may be fear of rejection or of being condemned. "I mean, what would people think if they knew what I was thinking about?"

God never brings that kind of condemnation; that's the work of the enemy. God does bring conviction, however. Conviction is the work of the Holy Spirit in our lives to help us change our behaviour from what is ungodly to what is Christ-like. Condemnation is the work of Satan to make us ashamed of who or what we are. People can change their behaviour; but they can't change who they are. For example,

Satan actively tempts us to do a certain ungodly behaviour by putting the suggestion into our mind; sometimes it echoes around in there, repeating the idea over and over until we give in. If we could record the conversation, it might look like this: "Go ahead do it; you'll like it; no one will know. Go on; do it; *do it;* ***do it...***" But as soon as we obey, we hear, "Now look at what you've done! And you call yourself a Christian? Shame on you! You're in trouble now!"

What does Satan use to do this to us? First, there is all the ungodly material recorded in our mind, emotions, and will. Secondly, there are the external suggestions that are too available in our society. You'd practically need to be both blind and deaf in order to avoid the temptation triggers that we encounter on a daily basis! But there is a third element, and that is the area of what the Bible refers to as 'strongholds.'

Ephesians 4:17-32 is an extended passage that also speaks of the transforming process that Romans 12 addresses. Verses 22–24 say this: *"...throw off your old sinful nature and your former way of life, which is corrupted by lust and deception. Instead, let the Spirit renew your thoughts and attitudes. Put on your new nature, created to be like God—truly righteous and holy."* Summary version: "Stop doing things carnally (according to our natural desires); learn to think and live like God (spiritually)." This is a choice each of us must make. The clothes you're wearing didn't just leap out of your closet this morning and land on your body; you chose what to put on and what to take off. In the same way, we can choose our thinking patterns and behaviours – if we decide to do so.

That same passage goes on to list a variety of activities that should be laid aside and some that need to be put on. In the midst of this list we find this: *"And don't sin by letting anger control you. Don't let the sun go down while you are still angry, for anger gives a foothold to the devil"* (Ephesians 4:26,27).

CHAPTER 6 – PLUNGING HEADLONG INTO BATTLE

That word, foothold, is the Greek word, topon. and means *'a place'*[1] for Satan to find a toehold or a base of operations. In the NASB, it is translated, "opportunity." 2 Corinthians 10:5 calls these 'strongholds' or 'fortresses.'

In my younger days, I loved rock climbing. It was such an adventure to see if I could conquer the side of the cliff and make my way from the bottom to the top. Every once in a while, I'd seem to get 'stuck.' I'd get so far up the face of the rock; and, suddenly, the 'path' just seemed to disappear. Down lower, I'd been able to find a ledge on which to stand or a crack that was big enough to get my fingers into – places that would give me 'purchase.' But then, it would seem that there was no place to put my other hand or foot; and nothing was in reach. All opportunity seemed to disappear as all I could see or feel was a smooth vertical surface of rock – no cracks, no ledges – so I'd have to back down and find another route.

These verses tell us to be like that smooth, flat rock surface and to not give the devil any opportunity to lay hold of our lives or any place to stand.

When we accept Christ as our Saviour, we give our lives to Him, but that doesn't automatically remove Satan's influence or control over some areas of our lives. That general decision needs to be worked out in the specifics of what we believe, how we deal with our emotions, what we say, and what we do. The passage in Ephesians 4 lists a number of ways in which we give Satan that room to operate. Some people, read, *"... Don't let the sun go down while you are still angry, for anger gives a foothold to the devil,"* and assume that the only way we give Satan an opportunity is to prolong anger over a drawn-out period of time. Obviously, we can give Satan a chance to work in our lives in many more ways than just our anger issues. On the other hand, this verse may be providing some insight into the ways in which Satan gains such control over us.

One possible translation for the term, 'opportunity,' is the idea of a 'stronghold.' We might think of it as a "fort" or "fortress" or perhaps an "enclave." Perhaps the idea of a terrorist 'sleeper cell' works well. Such is the language of war. In order to protect its borders, a nation may build strongholds or forts as a defence against intruders. When an enemy army invades a nation, it will seek to establish its own strongholds. In this case, a stronghold is a place in a country that has been invaded by enemy forces and has fallen to them. That small area, now under the enemy's command, then becomes a base of operations from which the enemy can infiltrate near-by areas and also take control there.

For example, (a ridiculous one!), we Canadians might decide to invade the USA. Either we'd row across Lake Ontario to up-state New York or take the Ambassador Bridge from Windsor to Detroit and move onto 'foreign soil.' Once there, we'd look for a place to conquer. It might just be one room in a hotel or a building; but, from there, we'd continue to spread our influence, taking over, first the whole building, then the neighbourhood, and, eventually, the whole city. Have we conquered the USA? Not yet, but it would be a start. But, if we can bring Detroit under our control, perhaps we could eventually take all of Michigan. From there, our conquest could spread into the Mississippi Valley and go on to take the whole continental United States (Would they be provinces by then? – My apologies to our American friends!).

In the same way, all Satan needs in our lives is one or two toeholds or fortresses (2 Cor. 10:4,5) from which he can spread his influence. Remember, he is all about domination; one little area of your life isn't enough; he wants it all.

Have you ever thought about spider plants or strawberries? You start with just one plant, but eventually, as the original plant gains health and strength, it will send out these long tendrils; stems with baby plants on the end of them. Once those baby plants find soil, they

CHAPTER 6 – PLUNGING HEADLONG INTO BATTLE

develop roots and bury into the earth. The process is repeated and repeated until the one mother plant has taken control of the whole garden! Satan works in the same way; as the saying goes, "Give him an inch, and he'll take a whole mile." Give Satan one small area of your life, and he'll spread his control over other areas that you had no intention of giving to him. Few, if any, set out to become raging alcoholics. No one plans to become a sexual pervert; but one thing can lead to another, and it's all down-hill from there.

Such fortresses can be established in our personalities in a variety of ways. As Ephesians 4 may indicate, allowing one area of sin to be prolonged in our lives is a way that Satan gains opportunity. Hebrews 12:15 tells us that a poisonous root of bitterness will spring up and 'corrupt' many. Bitterness settles in when we are slow to grant forgiveness or harbour and rehearse the details of an offence. Bitterness will spread its influence and defile many people. Have you ever met a bitter person? Not a pleasant encounter! Perhaps, a woman has been betrayed by her husband; he's left her for another woman. In her pain, she may decide that, "All men are pigs! Trust none of them!" Her relationship with all the men in her life has just become tainted or defiled as the pain of one encounter now colours all the others.

Fortresses are built by prolonging sin; they are also established when a person repeats the same sin over and over again. I remember having this visually portrayed in church when I was maybe 10 or 12 years of age. They asked for a volunteer, and my friend went forward. The teacher tied a piece of sewing thread around his arms, pinning them to his side. She asked if he could break free; and, of course, he was able to do so. Then the teacher looped the thread around him 3 times. Again, he was able to easily break free. Six loops were more difficult. You guessed it; eventually my friend was no longer able to free himself. What was once easily conquered by my friend had now conquered him! It is the same way with sin. Do it often enough; and, eventually, you can't stop; Satan has taken control of that area of your life.

A third way that a stronghold may be established is by force. This is not necessarily a sin done by the person, but may be something done to them. A very traumatic event, although only a one-time situation, may be an opportunity for the enemy to create a stronghold for himself. Someone only needs to be raped one time for a stronghold of defilement and lust to be created in his or her life. Bitterness and hatred against the offender may settle in. The victim may take on a 'victim mentality,' which will influence how they see themselves and by which they start to interpret all of life. Additionally, it might be the trigger for the person to label themselves as 'damaged goods' and assume that, "No one will ever want me." The greater the offence; the greater and longer-lasting its effects. One event may create a number of strongholds.

The offence doesn't have to be sinful or intentional. I know of a man in the town where I grew up who was backing a panel van into his driveway and did not see his elderly father standing in the way. Sadly, the gentleman was run over and died. Imagine the internal struggle for the son and the condemning self-talk that took place in the poor guy's life! I wonder if he was ever able to forgive himself.

Perhaps you noticed that this chapter is entitled, "Plunging Headlong into the Battle." There's a reason for that title. Most of this battle for control seems to take place in our 'heads.' External temptation comes at us through our senses, but the battle is fought primarily in our minds. i.e. One innocent glance in the wrong direction can trigger an inner battle with lust, can't it? Demonic suggestion comes as mental talk – that nagging voice that we hear internally.

The sin in our natural lives also impacts the health of our spirits. We know that the Holy Spirit can be made to experience sorrow (Ephesians 4:30) as well as be stifled (1 Thessalonians 5:19) by the sin in our lives. In the same way, I believe our human spirits, while made new and sinless, can be ignored, grieved, and weakened, according to 2 Corinthians 5:17. Much like our physical body, it can suffer from malnutrition. Like our muscles that atrophy because of lack of use, our spirits can be weakened when not fed or exercised regularly. Psalm 34:18 speaks of spirits that are 'crushed.'

We know that we empower Satan in our lives in three ways: 1) By agreeing with what he thinks, 2) by saying what he says, and by 3) doing what he does or what he tells us to do. If the enemy tells us, "You're stupid," we are tempted to believe him and think or say, "I'm so stupid…" It doesn't matter whether that voice was internal suggestion or if he got another human to deliver his message for him; (How many frustrated fathers have said, "How can you be so stupid?") if we believe his pronouncement, we're hooked.

Where does all this leave us? Are we just stuck and imprisoned by what the enemy has done to us? Or is there hope for us? The answer is, "Absolutely!" Although there is neither time nor space for a full treatment on spiritual warfare in this book, we do have some specific strategies to employ in order to free us from that captivity.

If we empower Satan by agreeing with him, saying what he says, or doing what he wants us to do; we can also disempower him by moving in the opposite direction. Along this line, James 4:7 gives us a powerful weapon. There, James provides a two-step strategy: First, we are told to *"… humble yourselves before God."* and then we are to *"Resist the devil."* That means that first, we, as an act of our will, humble or submit ourselves and place ourselves under God's direction. The Greek word for submit, hupotasso, literally means, "to set an array under." [2]

This word reminds me of working with a tool that house painters use. It is called a 'colour deck.' It is a stack of strips of paper on which all the available paint colours are displayed. Basically, the painter spreads it out before his client and says, "Here; you choose whatever colour you'd like." Then the client gets to choose. When we set an array – a complete list of all the options – before the Lord, we're basically saying, "Father, I want what You want; and I gladly let you choose what I should do."

Imagine praying that in a moment of temptation! "Father, is this what you want me to do? I gladly give up what I want, whatever I feel like doing right now, for whatever it is that You want." That's submission!

The second step, once you've completed the first, is to do exactly the opposite with Satan. Rather than submit, you resist him. To resist (Greek: anthistemi), is 'to set over against.'[3] Titus 2:12 says, *"And we are instructed to turn from godless living and sinful pleasures. We should live in this evil world with wisdom, righteousness, and devotion to God..."* The NIV puts it this way, *"Saying, 'No!' to ungodliness..."*

'Opposite' and 'oppose' are closely related words. When you oppose someone, you go in the opposite direction or do the opposite of what they're doing. This is painfully obvious in an old-fashioned tug of war. Perhaps you'd participated in one of these at school, at a church picnic, or at a workplace social. A group of people on one end of a rope pull back in their direction while a number of folks on the other end pull in their direction. Eventually, someone tires or loses their foothold; and one side prevails against the other.

The same thing can happen spiritually. When we submit to God and let Him choose the path we'll take, we can confidently expect that God will empower us to walk in obedience to His will. We cannot expect God to anoint us to do Satan's will. Once we're rightfully submitted to the Lord, then we are ready to oppose or stand against Satan, and just say, "No!" until we gain the victory. Is it really as easy as that? I can tell you from personal experience, that it is! I suggest you try this for yourself; you'll be amazed! I was.

That is the kind of power available to us, if we'd just do those two steps: Submit to God; resist the devil. I love the response that we can expect from Satan... Take those two steps and you can fully anticipate that, *"...he (Satan) will FLEE from you."* When I picture someone 'fleeing,' I envision him running away in terror, perhaps screaming in panic, shrieking at the top of his lungs, and waving his hands about hysterically. Did you realize that you have the power to make Satan and every one of his demons do that? What an awesome concept!

One time, I was doing ministry with a young man who had demonic issues; and, oddly enough, he could hear their conversation 'in his head.' As we approached the time for deliverance, the fellow started chuckling, so I asked him what was happening. He said something to this effect; "I can hear them talking. They're saying, 'It's no use; we can't stay. Let's just get out of here!'" With that, they all took off, exiting hastily out of his mouth. Rushing out on someone's breath is not the only way that demons leave the physical body, but it is one way. When we resist, they flee!

Where does such authority come from? Great question! Ephesians, Chapters 1 and 2 paint an amazing picture for us. There, Paul depicts the spiritual reality that we so often fail to grasp from our Earth-bound vantage point. In Chapter 1, Paul portrays the resurrected Jesus, seated on a throne at the right hand of God, the Father. Culturally, this shows us that Jesus is sitting as second in command. In our culture, we sometimes speak as our most valuable assistant or support as our "right-hand man." We go on to read that, not only is Jesus at God's right hand, He is seated, "*... far above any ruler or authority or power or leader or anything else—not only in this world but also in the world to come*" (Vs. 21).

In this picture, the great difference between the power and authority of Jesus, compared to all other authorities, including the demonic, is demonstrated in terms of distance. Jesus is FAR ABOVE them, so He is far more powerful!

Chapter 2 adds another focus in the picture. There, God has done a variety of things for believers. Verse 6 says that God has "*... raised us from the dead along with Christ and seated us with Him in the heavenly* *realms because we are united with Christ Jesus."* If Jesus is far above the demonic powers, and we're seated with Him, it makes sense that we, also, are far above the demons. Just as that distance indicates the superiority of Jesus' authority, our authority is at least almost as strong, for we are with Him! That's why I never want to back down from an encounter with the demonic or shy away when we know for sure that they're involved in a situation. I have authority, and I know it! Do demons ever hate that!

Not every encounter is such an, 'in-your-face' experience. Most of the time, it seems to be just internal suggestions that should be denied. This brings us back, pretty much to where we started, in 2 Corinthians 10:4,5,6. How do we tear down these strongholds? Like the corny, old joke, "How does one man eat an elephant? ... One bite at a time."

In the same way, we tear down strongholds one thought at a time. Some of our thoughts are morally neutral. For example, "I'm hungry!" is not a moral issue; it is just a fact. When it comes to moral issues though, we should inspect our thoughts to see with whom they line up. Are they in agreement with Jesus, or do they agree with Satan? Bring everything into captivity – to obedience to Jesus. This takes practice and patience.

Sometimes, taking thoughts captive to Jesus also takes intervention as a person receives ministry from a pastor or Christian friend who will help them identify the thoughts and ideas involved in that area of the person's life. That's one thing about deception; it's deceiving. If we could clearly identify the deceptions in our lives, we would not be tricked by them; and we'd be able to deal with them. It is only when the deception is revealed as such that we recognize it for what it really is. When a demonic entity is clearly active in the person's life, as was the case of the young man in South Sudan, it may take a ministry session to set the person free.

Winning the battle and gaining our freedom isn't just about tearing down the areas already under Satan's influence or recovering the

CHAPTER 6 - PLUNGING HEADLONG INTO BATTLE

ground he's previously taken in our lives. Victory involves a proactive choice to walk in righteousness. Doing so will protect us from future attack, so that Satan won't be able to capture new ground in our lives.

In Ephesians 6, Paul told the Ephesians to *"Put on all of God's armour so that you will be able to stand firm against all strategies of the devil"* (Vs.11). He was using a metaphor, drawing a comparison between the pieces of armour that the Roman soldiers wore and the various godly characteristics and life-choices that protect us from attack. He lists the following: a belt (truth), body armour (Chest-plate – God's righteousness), shoes (the Gospel of peace), a shield (faith), a helmet (salvation), and a sword (of the Spirit – God's Word). With these things, we will be able to stand firmly against the attacks of the enemy.

Some Christians take this passage very literally and have a morning ritual of 'praying on' their armour, and so they pray through the list before the Lord every day, saying, "Today, I choose to put on the belt of truth…," or "I choose to walk in righteousness today…" Doing so functions as a reminder to the person that those attributes are what they choose to walk in for the day. On another level, we do not know who all hears our prayers; both angels and demons may eaves-drop on our prayers. Such a declaration may serve as an encouragement to those who are sent to minister to us as well as to push back against the enemy. One way or the other, if I've pre-determined to walk in these godly ways, I'll be stronger when the attack of the enemy does come. I'll already have a mind-set that is opposed to what the enemy wants to bring into my life. Choosing to live righteously will help to protect us from attack and help us gain freedom and victory!

For our part in the battle to get free and stay free, we have effective strategies and strong armour; but that is not the whole story. Additionally, the Holy Spirit is in us, the angels fight for us, and God is working in us and through us to bring us to victory; but that's for another chapter.

SOMETHING TO THINK ABOUT…

1. Think about the most dysfunctional person you've ever met. How do you think they got that way?

2. Have you ever met a person who was clearly demonized? What did that look like?

3. In your own life, identify 2 specific areas that are not like the Lord Jesus. What do you want to do about them?

4. Do you remember a time when you practised the James 4:7 principle, "Submit and resist!"? How did that work?

5. Think about Psalm 139:23,24 in the context of this chapter. "Search me, O God, point out anything that offends You, and lead me along the path of everlasting life." What do you think that the Psalmist was asking?

SOMETHING TO DO…

Practise letting God choose your options for you. When I used to teach 'prophetic activation,' I'd tell the students, "When you go to the cafeteria, ask God where you should sit. Wait for Him to speak or to get you to notice a particular seat. Go; sit there and see what happens." Sometimes the outcome won't even matter to you or to God, but practising hearing from Him and being led by His Spirit is a good discipline. Sometimes something supernatural might happen!

CHAPTER 7

IN THE M*A*S*H UNIT

Isaiah 61:1-3 "The Spirit of the Sovereign Lord is upon me, for the Lord has anointed me to bring good news to the poor. He has sent me to comfort the brokenhearted and to proclaim that captives will be released and prisoners will be freed. He has sent me to tell those who mourn that the time of the Lord's favor has come, and with it, the day of God's anger against their enemies. To all who mourn in Israel, He will give a crown of beauty for ashes, a joyous blessing instead of mourning, festive praise instead of despair."

In every war, there are casualties or, at least, wounded soldiers. In the spiritual sense, all of us are already wounded, perhaps even before we enter the battle. We've all come that way. As our lives have unfolded, we've also gotten hurt.

Sometimes, the wounds are on the outside; we can see the physical scars that some traumatic event has left recorded on our bodies. While some of these, like a small scratch on the back of you hand, may be relatively minor or hardly even noticeable, others command our attention. Obvious wounds, such as the scars left on the face of a burn victim or a missing arm, the result of a tragic car accident, demand our attention.

Inner wounds are often much more difficult to recognize. Usually, people like to keep their inner wounds hidden away so they don't have to deal with them and so that others don't know the reality of their inner lives. Occasionally, a wounded person really wants to be identified as a victim in order to gain sympathy or to avoid responsibility, or because his or her inner pain is just too much to keep bottled up inside. In this case, they're very open about sharing their 'stuff!'

Most of us would rather keep our private issues to ourselves. In some ways, it is much easier to just ignore the pains and wounds of the past and just limp along through life as best we can. No one really wants to rip the scab off his elbow to see if the road-rash has healed up!

There is a famous saying, "Time heals all wounds!" NO; it does not! If that were true, all of us would automatically out-grow our emotional wounded-ness. The reality is this; it just doesn't work that way. I know this because all you need to do is ask an adult about the most painful memory from their childhood. As the story begins to unfold, those pesky buried emotions come seeping up to the top, and the emotional pain bubbles out. Actually, the expression of emotions may be very helpful as tears may begin to fall or other physical reactions to suppressed emotions begin to release the buried pain. Such release is healing. Not only that, these newly released emotions help us to identify their root causes and open the door for healing.

These negative emotions, whether from our personal, ancient past, or as fresh as yesterday's encounter, stay with us until we are healed. Because we are so inter-connected, what's going on in our memories has strong implications for our emotions; and what's going on in the immaterial man begins to manifest itself physically in our material body. These days, it is a well-recognized fact that emotions impact our physical health, either positively or negatively. No wonder Proverbs 17:22 says that, *"A cheerful heart is good medicine, but a broken spirit saps a person's strength."* Without doubt, our emotions impact our physical wellbeing. They can also impact our human spirits.

I believe that our newly-born human spirit, given to us when we accept Christ, is holy and righteous, just as Jesus is. As time unfolds, it can be impacted, both positively and negatively, by what is going on in our souls. Similarly, those who are physically ill will experience negative changes to both their personality and their human spirit.

CHAPTER 7 – IN THE M*A*S*H UNIT

The same is true for the Holy Spirit, who lives in believers (Romans 8; Galatians 2, etc.) and can be grieved (Ephesians 4:30). Imagine that! The Holy Spirit of God is saddened and experiences negative emotions in response to our human behavior! I don't believe that the Holy Spirit is so much angered by our sin as He is sorrowful for the pain and destruction our sin will bring into our lives. In the same way, we and others can damage our human spirits. Thankfully, God can heal us on all three dimensions; body, soul, and spirit!

Sometimes, I try to picture or imagine what my spirit looks like or what is it doing. I know that many Christians shy away from visualization because of so many New Age associations with the practice. On the other hand, God was the creator of our imaginations; and when they are surrendered and available to Him, He can sanctify them for His purposes and use them to communicate His truth to us. Furthermore, God says that His children will see visions and dream dreams.

I think of these experiences in much the same way as I interpret the parables. Jesus told stories, using natural, Earthly things and events to illustrate spiritual truth. Does every aspect of the 'picture' of a parable apply to our lives? Of course, not! Earthly illustrations are just that; illustrations that convey a general impression or a central truth that God wishes to convey to us.

For example, a number of sane, credible Christians would claim to have seen a vision of Jesus. Because these pictures are not all exactly the same, does it mean that there is no validity to the vision or dream? If the Jesus in my vision has longer hair than the Jesus in your dream, does that mean that both experiences were pure hoaxes? If the teeth I 'saw' when Jesus smiled at me in my vision, aren't the same teeth that you saw when you had a vision, does this mean we should dismiss the whole thing as just the after-effects of last evening's overly-spicy pizza? Or could it be valid for us to just recognize that Jesus isn't angry with us, or that He's pleased with our progress?

When we study Scripture, there are three or four steps to interpreting and applying its message accurately. First, we read the passage and understand what it actually SAYS. Then we look for the MEANING; what the author was trying to convey and what the original recipients would have understood. Thirdly, we look for PRINCIPLES to be applied to our daily lives. Lastly, we look for APPLICATIONS, ways to put those principles into practice. We could treat any godly dreams and visions in pretty much the same way. What principles do we need to apply in order to encourage and build up our spirits and our souls and in order to free them from Satan's influence?

Am I suggesting that God is little more than the product of whatever our imagination might suggest? Absolutely not! God is much more than just whatever I can comprehend Him to be. But just because we can't understand Him fully or completely accurately doesn't mean that we shouldn't at least try to see Him for all that He is!

Whether we get a vision of them or not, our human spirits can become withdrawn, disappointed, or discouraged, depending on what is happening in the other areas of our lives. Conversely, when we're doing well, it encourages our spirits. At the same time, what is going on in our human spirits also impacts what's happening in the soul and in the body. The more our souls are wounded, the greater the negative influence on our spirit and on our physical beings. The opposite is also true; when your spirit is strong in God, it impacts our soul and body in wonderful, positive ways!

At salvation, we switch our allegiances back to God and become the enemy of Satan's kingdom. Therefore, it makes perfect sense that he moves from 'control' to 'attack' mode. Not only that, we can anticipate that his work in our lives might increase. His tactics might change, but his motive does not; he still wants to bring each of us under his control. Naturally, it would be easiest for him to continue his assaults against our freedom by building on those strongholds in our lives that he had previously. Perhaps it might be helpful to think of each of our wounds as a place where Satan still exerts a level of control. In the Kingdom of Heaven, there is no sickness and no wounds because Jesus is reigning there. All tears will be washed away and *"sorrow and mourning will disappear"* (Isaiah 35:10). If we

CHAPTER 7 - IN THE M*A*S*H UNIT

have wounded-ness, it is in an area where the Kingdom of God has not yet been applied.

Such freedom from the wounds of our experience has forever been on the heart of God. Just listen to the words of Isaiah 61:3; *"To all who mourn in Israel, He will give a crown of beauty for ashes, a joyous blessing instead of mourning, festive praise instead of despair. In their righteousness, they will be like great oaks that the Lord has planted for His own glory."* These words reflect the heart and intent of the Lord. He takes us from being broken, mourning, heavy-spirited individuals and transforms us so that we experience joy and are clothed with praise. In the end, we are established or planted by the Lord. The result is that God would be glorified.

As usual, a desire or intention without a plan is just a dream. God had more than a dream; He also had a plan. That plan is explained for us in Isaiah 53.

"Who has believed our message? To whom has the Lord revealed His powerful arm? My servant grew up in the Lord's presence like a tender green shoot, like a root in dry ground. There was nothing beautiful or majestic about His appearance, nothing to attract us to Him.

He was despised and rejected — a man of sorrows, acquainted with deepest grief. We turned our backs on Him and looked the other way. He was despised, and we did not care.

Yet it was our weaknesses He carried; it was our sorrows that weighed Him down. And we thought His troubles were a punishment from God, a punishment for His own sins! But He was pierced for our rebellion, crushed for our sins. He was beaten so we could be whole. He was whipped so we could be healed.

All of us, like sheep, have strayed away. We have left God's paths to follow our own. Yet the Lord laid on Him the sins of us all.

He was oppressed and treated harshly, yet He never said a word. He was led like a lamb to the slaughter. And as a sheep is silent before the shearers, He did not open His mouth.

129

Unjustly condemned, He was led away. No one cared that He died without descendants, that His life was cut short in midstream. But He was struck down for the rebellion of My people. He had done no wrong and had never deceived anyone. But He was buried like a criminal; He was put in a rich man's grave.

But it was the Lord's good plan to crush Him and cause Him grief. Yet when His life is made an offering for sin, He will have many descendants. He will enjoy a long life and the Lord's good plan will prosper in His hands. When He sees all that is accomplished by His anguish, He will be satisfied.

And because of His experience, My righteous servant will make it possible for many to be counted righteous, for He will bear all their sins. I will give Him the honors of a victorious soldier, because He exposed Himself to death..."

If we unpack this prophetic passage about Jesus a little further, we notice that there are a number of unpleasant experiences or emotions that He experienced at the cross. These include, being tender, so easily 'bruised,' not being particularly attractive, having people turn away (ignoring?) from Him, being despised, and not being recognized or appreciated (not esteemed). While He carried our sorrows and griefs, He was wrongly accused, as people believed that God was punishing Him for His own sins. He was crushed, pierced, chastened, and scourged.

We also know that, at the cross, Jesus felt exposed, hanging stretched out and naked for all to see. He was mocked as both the soldiers and the crowd made fun of Him. Not only that, He suffered all kinds of physical pain; whipped with a cat-of-nine-tails, slapped, crowned with thorns, nailed to the cross, endured thirst and suffocation, not to mention the other accumulated physical agonies of crucifixion. Additionally, Jesus knew the emotional pain of pleading with the Father to remove the cup of suffering before His arrest, and then having to deal with the disappointment of "unanswered prayer." The feeling of being forsaken or abandoned and separated from

CHAPTER 7 - IN THE M*A*S*H UNIT

His Father was especially painful. Thankfully, Jesus also knew the sacrifice of bowing to God's will.

Perhaps we can sum all this up this way: At the cross, Jesus experienced all the negative emotions that we face. All of them, except the guilt and shame caused by His own sin – He never sinned so was not personally guilty until He took our guilt and shame on Himself. He can identify with us in those experiences. Not only does He understand our negative emotions, He also died to provide healing and freedom. Looking back at Isaiah 53, we see that *"He was pierced for OUR transgressions"* (the sins that took us where we weren't supposed to 'go'); *"He was crushed as payment for our iniquities"* (the ways in which we are not godly), and *"He was chastened for our well-being."* Additionally, it was because Jesus suffered the scourging that we can be HEALED.

All of this was part of the eternal plan of God and a divine transaction, as Jesus died to pay the penalty for our sin, giving His life for ours. He was our guilt offering. Did you notice the very last line? Jesus would justify (make the same – make righteous) the many (all the believers) by bearing our iniquities.

In evangelical circles, we are pretty familiar with the idea of taking our sin to the cross. In other words, we come, with all our sinfulness and history, to the cross and ask Jesus to forgive us for our sins. We seem to have no trouble believing that He is willing to do that for us. What we are less familiar with, is the concept that we can take, not just the sins that we have done and their consequences, but the sins that others have done to us and the wounds they've inflicted on us, to the cross. There, we may ask 'Doctor Jesus' to heal us.

Do you get it? Jesus has already provided the way and the means for us to be healed; body, soul, and spirit. He's done it all! Our part is only to accept what He offers to us: divine healing! How do we do that?

Much like at a hospital operating theatre, or, in warfare, at a MASH (Mobile Army Surgical Hospital), there are routines and procedures that are designed to bring healing. It is the same in the spiritual or emotional realm. If we follow the right procedures, we can be healed. One proviso: just like physical surgery, there is more than just one routine. Surgery and inner healing are not exact sciences. You can't approach every patient the way you did the last one. There is no cookie-cutter protocol. As the saying goes, "One ear to Heaven; one ear to Earth!" In other words, you have to listen to both the person who comes to receive ministry as well as to the Lord. In almost every session, we eventually have to ask, "Ok, Lord, what do we do with this?" or "Lord, what's the truth here?" The process of inner healing isn't simply working through the same check-list for each 'patient,' and it isn't always just taking their version of the story at face value. Often, God will provide additional insight and strategy, particularly when we attend to Him as we move along in the process.

Thankfully, though, there does seem to be a typical pattern; one that generally can be used with success – under the direction of Holy Spirit, that is. I am sure that there may be other approaches that also bring healing, but I've seen this one work well.

Just a note or two of caution: It is usually not a great idea to self-diagnose. Taking your own appendix out is always risky business. The Bible quotes the mockers, "Physician, heal thyself," but that is still not a good idea! In this area of ministry, you never know what is going to come up until you're well into the 'thick of things.' It is both safer and more effective to work with someone who knows what they're doing in this field. You might trust a dear friend explicitly, but if they're a plumber and not a surgeon, you probably don't want them picking up a scalpel!

No matter what the situation you think you might want to deal with, it might not be what the Father wants to begin working on. So, you start by asking the Lord what He wants to work on that day. Oddly enough, His priorities might not line up with our own.

Having established the event or wound that the Lord intends to heal, it seems necessary to begin with our own 'stuff.' Generally speaking, this includes the need to affirm our commitment to Jesus Christ as Lord. A person who is not willing or able to give the control over their life to the Lord may not be in a position to ask for healing. After all, Jesus Christ did not die to make our flesh more comfortable or to pamper it! The process of gaining our freedom is like so many of the other paradoxes in the Bible; getting there seems to require that we move in exactly the opposite direction – the way to be first in the kingdom is to place yourself last. Go down to come up. The first shall be last, and the last shall be first. When it comes to obtaining true freedom, it begins with total surrender and giving the control of your life to the Father. Even if the person's commitment to the Lordship of Christ may be in question, we can't ignore the graciousness of God as the basis for anything we might ask or expect from the Father.

Next, we need to move on to deal with anything that we might need to confess or for which we need to repent. "Where have I been 'wrong' in the story?" That might mean anything that we did to precipitate the problem. The hurtful memory about a huge fight with his father might have been avoided if the teen had just come home on time. It could be that we've harboured bitterness against our offender. Perhaps we believe a lie about what happened (We assume that, "She did it on purpose!"). Maybe we've thought or proclaimed judgments about our offender (What a jerk!), or cursed them in angry reaction ("Go to _____!"). Have we issued pronouncements against them ("You'll never amount to anything!")? Did we gossip about the person? You get the idea; the list goes on and on. I suppose that some of those actions and reactions are clearly 'sins,' but some are not so obvious. The bottom line is, "Is this what Jesus would have thought, felt, said, or done?" If not, then it is something to be confessed!

If we ask Him, God will show us everything that we need to confess. According to His word in 1 John 1:9, *"... if we confess our sins to Him, He is faithful and just to forgive us our sins and to cleanse us from all wickedness."* We can count on God's willingness to forgive us and to cleanse us from the guilt of that sin.

Having been forgiven ourselves, it is now our turn to do the forgiving. God takes our need to forgive others very seriously. In the "Sermon on the Mount," Jesus taught that, if we want to be forgiven, we also need to forgive. What we call "The Lord's Prayer," includes, "... *forgive us our sins, as we have forgiven those who sin against us.*" Jesus goes on to add, *"If you forgive those who sin against you, your heavenly Father will forgive you. But if you refuse to forgive others, your Father will not forgive your sins."* Another one of Jesus' hard sayings!

While we might prefer that Jesus hadn't said that, we have to acknowledge that He did. What might help is that we do not forgive others for their sake alone, but for our own also! It is probably true that the other person is not sorry for what they've done and hasn't apologized for it; they might not even be aware that they did something wrong. Regardless of where they are in all this, you need to forgive for the sake of your own freedom and healing. Forgiveness is part of the process by which you take your own life back. If you don't forgive, the other person still has a hold on your life. If you don't forgive, you are allowing the other person to control your emotions, even in the present. You're just not 'free' from your offender or from the past.

Think of someone who seriously offended you, years ago. Does the very mention of his or her name bring emotions of anger or resentment to your soul? If so, you're not free from their influence today, and the event of ancient history still owns you. There is only one way to get free; forgive.

It seems that some people believe that they just 'CAN'T' forgive. I suspect that this is for one of two reasons. First, there may be an actual demonic stronghold in that area, due to the open door in the victim's life. Second, there may be a false belief system, that the person is incapable of forgiveness. The truth may be that it would be painful for the person to grant forgiveness. The reality is that God has given us free will – the ability to choose for ourselves, regardless of how painful the consequences may be. Even when someone is holding a loaded pistol to your head, you still have a choice. You can

CHAPTER 7 - IN THE M*A*S*H UNIT

comply with the gunman's demands, or you could refuse and let him shoot you. Either way, you have a choice.

I remember debating with a student about the quality, or lack thereof, of their work. They claimed that it was their very best work and that they couldn't possibly do the assignment any better than they had already done it. The student changed their tune quite quickly, when I offered, "If I give you $50, could you do it better?" "Can't" changed to "Could" almost immediately! If you want healing, you have to forgive.

Someone might protest, "But they don't deserve to be forgiven!" or, "But they haven't asked for it," or, "But they're not sorry for what they did!" Sadly, that may be true, but remember, forgiveness is the price you pay for YOUR freedom.

One additional point here; do not confuse forgiveness with lack of discipline. Matthew 18 makes it clear that we have a responsibility to confront someone who has offended us; especially another believer. Forgiveness does not negate the responsibility to follow through on what we are told to do if a person refuses to repent, particularly after confrontation. Remember the whole point of a confrontation is to secure reconciliation through repentance and forgiveness. If the offender refuses to repent, the victim should still forgive them, but also hold the person accountable by treating them as an unbeliever and a tax collector. In other words, treat them as if they are not part of the church.

That would be a sad situation; but forgiveness, repentance and reconciliation are great causes for celebration! Reuniting with a brother or sister, particularly one who is 'in Christ,' is a joyous occasion. It also is opportunity for deep healing in the lives of all who are involved. Additionally, it is the doorway to great freedom.

Speaking of being free or not free, we often find that people are connected to others in either a positive or a negative way. The stronger the relationship, the greater is the potential to form either positive or negative emotional ties to the other person. On the positive side, when two or more people engage in godly, kingdom activities, it creates a godly relationship and healthy, positive emotions. The Bible speaks of the healthy and godly relationship between Jonathan and David. It says that, *"There was an immediate bond between them, for Jonathan loved David"* (1 Samuel 18:1). In spite of how some people might try to interpret this verse, it depicts a pure and free relationship. Along the same lines, Judges 20:11 speaks of the Israeli army, saying that, *"So all the Israelites were completely united, and they gathered together to attack the town."* The KJV says that they were, *"knit together as one man."*

If people participate in evil together, it produces a negative association. Some people call these 'ungodly soul ties' or 'relationship bondages.' Whatever the label may be, the effect is the same; you own a little piece of the other person, and they own a piece of you. For example, if two people commit a robbery, they are forever associated. Should your partner in crime come 'clean' and confess or get caught, he will incriminate you as well. You both will have to take that enslaving secret to the grave; if one goes down, you both do!

This even works if a person sins against you and you do nothing except hold anger and bitterness against them; the bondage is still there, and the sting is still present. Again, mention their name, and see what emotions come bubbling up.

How do we get free? By forgiveness and inner healing.

Once forgiveness has been granted, it is possible to 'cut or sever the ungodly soul-ties' between the two people or to break the ungodly relationship. Often, though, the offended person needs to receive inner healing before this can happen.

I have found that one of the most effective ways for a person to receive inner healing is via the process known as visualization. Many secular psychiatrists don't seem to be in favour of exploring old emotional wounds in this way; but, with the help of Holy Spirit, it can prove to be very effective. Again, we need to trust that Father God can sanctify and anoint our human imagination for His purposes and that He is also at work in the process. In Acts 2:17, Peter quoted from

CHAPTER 7 - IN THE M*A*S*H UNIT

the book of Joel when he said, *"Your sons and daughters will prophesy. Your young men will see visions, and your old men will dream dreams."* If the Lord can give us visions, He can also speak to us through what we might call sanctified or surrendered imagination.

Essentially, the person sees himself or herself standing before the cross with whatever experience or negative emotion that needs to be dealt with. Perhaps you've read a Christian classic novel, "Pilgrim's Progress," written by John Bunyan, centuries ago. In this allegory, the main character, "Christian," finally comes to the cross and kneels there, demonstrating that he recognized his own need of a saviour and for the forgiveness of sins. When Christian kneels there, the backpack that he's been carrying around throughout all his life, suddenly falls off his back. It is filled with rocks, which represent the weight of his sin and guilt. It falls from his back and rolls down the hill and out of sight and is gone. Christian does not bear that burden any longer.

When we come to the cross with our sin or the sins that others have done to us and all the negative emotions that those things produce in us, we can picture or imagine them in some way. It seems that everyone has their own unique way of describing or picturing their particular situation and emotions. Once, when I was receiving some ministry, I was dealing with what I had automatically described as "a whole boat-load of pain." Actually, it was about a situation that had caused me much grief eight years prior to this ministry time; but, this night, someone was talking about that event, and it began to bring some pretty strong emotions to the surface. I found myself in tears, releasing long-buried pain.

Just as with our sin, we need to bring these events and emotions to Jesus at the cross and ask Him to deal with them. We might ask, "Jesus, will You take my shame for me?" or "Jesus, what do You want me to do with my fear?" or something along those lines. In this case, I asked Jesus if He would take and deal with my boat-load of pain. What I 'saw' in my mind, was Jesus, taking my boat, lighting it on fire, and then blowing into its sails, sending it across the water and out of sight beyond the horizon. After it was out of sight, there was a puff of smoke; and the boat was gone. So was all my pain.

Nothing had changed; all the circumstances were exactly as they had been. History was still history, and I still remembered all the sad details; but, miraculously, all the negative emotions were gone. I don't really know how this process works; but, amazingly, Jesus had dealt with my pain and grief – just because I asked Him to. I was free, and the sting was gone!

I've seen the Lord extend the same grace and love to well over one hundred of His children. Often people tell me that they don't see visions or that they don't hear the voice of God; but, time and time again, the Holy Spirit comes through, honours their mustard seed of faith, and heals their wounds in a compassionate and personal way. Such negative emotions have been pictured as hand-cuffs, mud, a ball and chain, a heavy, water-soaked hooded robe, rocks on their chest, etc., etc. The person asks Jesus what He wants to do with these things or what He wants the person to do with them. Sometimes, Jesus asks them to bury their item at the foot of the cross; sometimes He nails it there for them. On another occasion, Jesus just let His blood drip down onto the thing they'd brought; and it melted. The details of the story or the nature of the wounds don't seem to matter; what is important is bringing them to Jesus to deal with. He has always been faithful to meet us at our point of need. No wonder we call Him, "Wonderful Counsellor!" One can hardly describe the elation and joy experienced by someone who has just been healed emotionally. They are free, and they know it. It is always an occasion for great rejoicing at the kindness of our God!

It seems important that the person decide to actually leave that burden at the cross and not take it home with them. Some people seem to want to pick it up again and keep the burden and the pain. Perhaps they haven't forgiven themselves. So often, we only think of forgiving the person who offended us but forget to forgive ourselves. It seems as if the enemy uses either real or imaginary guilt and condemnation to convince a victim that they somehow deserve what happened. They might believe, "This was my fault; I shouldn't have gone there in the first place." I know a young lady who had

CHAPTER 7 - IN THE M*A*S*H UNIT

been date-raped. When she confided in her parents, her father's first words were, "Well, you must have seduced him or he wouldn't have done that," which was not true. Although it is not the only reason that people take back their wounds and negative emotions rather than leaving them at the cross, one issue is that they believe that they deserved what happened to them and have not forgiven themselves for whatever part they played in their story. Other people seem to lack faith and so don't believe that God could or would heal them. Others don't feel worthy or that they don't deserve to be healed and, therefore, reject the healing that God offers them. Finally, others have a religious spirit and performance orientation. They know that they have not earned God's healing favour. Whatever the situation, restoration and freedom was available, but they subconsciously dismiss it.

I've seen this in the natural realm as well. One late night, the Lord completely physically healed a friend in a miraculous, reconstructive way. A number of us saw it; there was no doubt that they'd been healed. The next morning, everything was back to 'normal' – just as it had been before the healing took place. As I asked the Lord why my friend had 'lost' the healing, He said it was because the impediment was actually a part of my friend's identity – how they saw themself. Take away the disability and you take away their life-style. In that case, being healed would mean taking greater responsibility for the person's own life – something they were afraid to do.

If we refuse to give our issues to Jesus, we get to keep living with them. We can stay in our bondage, if we'd like to. But what a shame! Whether it is our wounded-ness or our sin, if we don't bring it to Jesus, we have to live with it. Can you imagine such a thing? The military ambulance speeds up to the MASH hospital and unloads a severely wounded soldier, but what if no one takes him into the surgery? What if he refuses to go in? "No way! They'll cut me open, and it will hurt. I could die in there; I refuse to go in there!" Chances are he'd bleed to death lying there outside the very tent where his life could have been saved. It would be equally sad for Christians to continue dealing with their wounds, unattended and unhealed, simply because no one brings them to the cross or because they don't believe that it will help.

John 8 talks about the healing and freedom that Christ wants us to experience. There, we read, *"... And you will know the truth, and the truth will set you free"* (Vs. 32). *"...I tell you the truth, everyone who sins is a slave of sin. A slave is not a permanent member of the family, but a son is part of the family forever. So, if the Son sets you free, you are truly free"* (Vs. 34-36). Apparently, God wants Jesus to set us free, but even He can't help us if we don't go to Him for help, forgiveness and healing.

> **SOMETHING TO THINK ABOUT…**
>
> 1. What are the memories and emotions in your life that Jesus might want to heal?
> 2. Is there anyone you need to forgive? Someone else? Yourself? God?
> 3. Is there anyone, who, if you hear their name or see their picture, it causes a negative emotional response in your soul?
> 4. Is there some kind of event that typically triggers your negative emotions?
> 5. Ask God if there is something in your life that He'd like to work on.
>
> **SOMETHING TO DO…**
>
> Although we have not talked about our need to be forgiven by those we've offended, you might ask God to bring to mind someone who needs to forgive you for what you've done to them. You may want to go to that person and ask for their forgiveness. Before you do so, you need to be prepared to accept, with God's help, whatever their reactions might be (even legal ones!). Consider your wording ahead of time. What would you like to hear, "Sorry," or, "God has shown me that it was wrong for me to _____. I have asked Him to forgive me, and now I am asking for your forgiveness"? Only go to the person if and when the Spirit of God directs you to do so.

CHAPTER 8

IDENTITY ISSUES – YOURS, MINE AND OURS
(Who? Me? A Warrior?)

2 Corinthians 5: 16,17 "So we have stopped evaluating others from a human point of view. At one time, we thought of Christ merely from a human point of view. How differently we know Him now! This means that anyone who belongs to Christ has become a new person. The old life is gone; a new life has begun!"

In Chapter 6, we were looking at strongholds, and only briefly mentioned the whole issue of identity, which is a major stronghold for all of us. Our identity is not just who or what we perceive ourselves to be, but also how we present ourselves to the rest of the world.

Soldiers in the army wear what they call, "Dog Tags." These small metal plates hang from a chain that is worn around the neck of each soldier. On the plates, you find three pieces of information; the soldier's name, his rank, and his serial number. The gruesome reality is that this would be an accurate way to identify the body, should the soldier be lost in battle. I believe that they also serve a secondary purpose. It gives the soldier a sense of identity. We know that, when a soldier is taken captive, he or she is only supposed to reveal those three pieces of information: their name – which identifies them individually, their rank – which indicates their level of authority, and their serial number – which identifies them corporately. Nametags also remind the soldier of who he is and what or whom he represents. No wonder so much time and energy is spent drilling into the recruits a sense of identity and pride! Just look at the army, navy, air force, or marines; they're very proud of who they are and are expected to perform accordingly.

Spiritually speaking, it is no wonder that the enemy does not want us to know who we are, what our level of authority is, or our place in the army of Heaven. He does everything he can to keep us from walking in our true spiritual identity and to tear it down so that we do not know where we belong or what we are authorized to do.

In the natural realm, 'identity' can come from a variety of places. Some of us get our identity from our jobs or careers. Frequently, when we meet someone for the first time, we might ask, "So what do you do?" meaning, "I can identify who you are by what you do." We also tend to evaluate or rank people based on this one clue regarding who they are. It would be an interesting experiment to be in a situation where you can meet lots of new people and tell some that you work in a coffee shop but tell others that you're a university professor – just to measure their reactions and evaluate how they respond to you.

Our identity is important to us; it is also significant to Satan. He knows an truism found in Proverbs 23:7, *"For as he* (a man) *thinks in his heart, so he is"* (NASB). In that context, the author is writing to warn his son that outward appearances are not necessarily accurate. In other words, what a person really thinks inwardly – their true thoughts and intentions – are what is real, and what will eventually find outward expression. Unless someone is very transparent, we rarely really know what is going on in the other person's head or heart! Eventually, though, their true thoughts and intentions will be exposed in the reality of life.

The same principle applies to the area of our identity. It is unusual to really know what the other person actually believes about himself or herself. Knowing that identity is a key issue, Satan will do all that he can to influence what we believe about ourselves. If he can convince a person that he or she has no value, that belief will eventually work its way into how that person lives.

CHAPTER 8 - IDENTITY ISSUES - YOURS, MINE AND OURS

Satan has done this since time immemorial, and it is one of his prime manoeuvres. Remember how the serpent deceived Eve with three attacks against her self-image? Just eat the fruit; and 1. Your eyes will be opened (You're spiritually blind now.), 2. You will become like God (You're not like God now. Even though you were created 'very good,' and in His image and likeness, you need to become like Him through your own efforts and by following my lead.), and 3. You'll know the difference between good and evil. (You lack the experiential knowledge of evil; just assume that it's a bad thing that you do). In one short discussion, Eve went from feeling completely acceptable and unashamed to believing that she was spiritually blind, ungodly, and ignorant. How did that happen? Satanic suggestions re-formed her self-concept and identity.

Throughout all of our lives, and even before birth, Satan, the enemy of our souls, is at work, attacking our identity. If he can convince us that we are somehow defective or, at least, insufficient; he can limit our potential and diminish our destiny.

There seem to be three factors in regard to the destiny that believers have in Christ. These are 1) our identity (especially who we are in Christ), 2) our personality and natural abilities, and 3) our spiritual gifts. If I know who I am in Christ, understand myself, know my strengths, and can identify my gifts; I have some pretty strong clues regarding the destiny God has for me. Many Christians love the verse, Jeremiah 29:11; *"'For I know the plans I have for you,' says the Lord. 'They are plans for good and not for disaster, to give you a future and a hope.'"* Deep down, we want to believe that God has good plans for us; but, as ALL of us struggle with self-image issues and self-esteem questions, it makes it difficult for us to believe God for a positive future. Not knowing the destiny to which God is calling us makes it even more difficult! Satan knows that too; and, if he can keep us from knowing who we are in Christ, it will prevent us from fulfilling our destiny and limit the threat that we pose to the Kingdom of Darkness.

There is an Inuit community in Northern Quebec called, 'Quaqtaq,' more or less pronounced, "Kwawk-tawk." One of the churches there,

Quaqtaq Christian Fellowship, has an inner healing service called, 'Aaqitauvik Healing Centre.' 'Aaqitauvik' is pronounced, 'Ow-key-tau-vik,' and is an Inuktitut word meaning, "I can fix it." In that context, "I can fix it," is a wonderful concept and an important ministry in the community. Unfortunately, Satan has used an, 'I can fix it' belief system to pre-occupy people and to distract them from what will truly heal their identity issues; a relationship with God in Christ. Instead, Satan will pre-occupy us with a variety of ways with which we might be able to 'fix' whatever is supposedly wrong with us.

While there is no denying that there is some true evidence against us – others are taller, better looking, smarter, richer, whatever…, and that our behaviour is less than exemplary on occasion, we need to recognize that Satan multiplies the negative evidence against us and draws us to an exaggerated conclusion. For example, I know of one student who, if she ONLY got 95% on a test, would literally slap herself up the side of the head and cry out in sincere anguish, "Why am I so stupid!?!?" That response may feel correct but certainly is not an accurate reflection of her intellectual abilities! You must know that Satan was having a proverbial heyday in that poor girl's heart and life.

I've been amazed at some of the, "I am _____" statements that I've heard over the years. I'll ask a recipient to describe himself in one word and usually get a negative response. One time, a person shocked me by claiming to be "stupid." This person had a 4.0 Grade Point Average in more than one graduate degree. I was wishing I had their brains and thought, "You're not stupid; you're crazy!" Seriously, though, most of the outside world would be shocked to learn what is going on inside a person. Beautiful women feel ugly; great musicians say that they don't play well; and, sometimes, those students who MUST get 100%, do so to prove to themselves and to the world that they aren't stupid.

It seems that Satan tells us all that, whatever we are, it isn't enough. Women with straight hair want curly hair. Some who have curly

CHAPTER 8 - IDENTITY ISSUES - YOURS, MINE AND OURS

hair spend hours straightening what they have. The following will sound totally ridiculous, but it is true. At one time, I was working with two young men who didn't know each other but had the same first name. I was helping them with their inner healing needs. I happened to ask the same question to both of them; "What don't you like about yourself?" Among a variety of other things, the first young man said, "I hate my body; I have no chest hair. Everyone knows that real men have lots of chest hair; I guess I'm not a real man." Later that same day, the second one included this statement in his litany of supposed faults, as he answered the same question; "I hate my chest hair; it grows everywhere, and I have to shave all the time; I'm a disgusting, hairy ape." True story! Good grief! So few people are genuinely happy with who or what they are! We all do the comparison checklist to see if we measure up physically, intellectually, in the areas of giftedness or social status, or about our skills and abilities, etc.; and we can usually find someone who seems 'better' than we are. Chalk one up for the Enemy!

These negative feelings become our silent or spoken judgments or curses against ourselves. All of us learn that, in some way, we aren't good enough and give the power of our agreement to the voice of the enemy. Because we don't like feeling that way, we find ways to shore up our damaged egos.

If, for some reason, a young man can't compete in sports, he may find another way to 'establish' his worth. It might be that he throws himself into his studies and finds both affirmation and satisfaction by scoring "A's" on his assignments or exams. He medicates the pain in his soul by doing well academically. He says to himself and to the rest of the world, "I'm not a loser after all!" This isn't a sin; it is a coping mechanism. The problem is that this kind of medication may be just enough to dull his pain, so that he doesn't find true healing and identity in Christ.

As I mentioned, everyone deals with this kind of thing. Some of us have felt the sting of being that last to be chosen when divinely appointed captains take turns choosing or calling out their teams! The academically challenged but physically gifted 'jock' finds recognition in being the captain of the team or by lifting more weights than anyone else. Some people become appearance focused and NEED to have just the 'right' clothes, latest fashion, and most stylish hair-do. I know of one young lady who absolutely cannot leave the house in the morning until she is 'perfect' in this area – every hair in place, make-up expertly applied, trendy clothes fitted perfectly and arranged 'just so,' etc. It takes her almost two hours every morning just to get ready to leave the house. That's bondage!

But what happens when the most handsome young man in high-school – the heart-throb of all the girls – the King of the Prom – goes off to university and recognizes that there are probably one hundred other guys who are more handsome, better built, taller, or more gifted than he? The king of the castle has been dethroned! What happens to his self-esteem then? If a person's identity is all wrapped up in their career title, what happens when they retire or, worse yet, get fired? They may not know who they are any more.

Depending on how damaged a person's self-esteem or identity is, they will typically take one of two or more options. If there is the slightest glimmer of a hope that, with enough effort and luck, they can become a 'winner,' they may throw themselves headlong into the effort to overcome their deficiencies. To this end, they will form an "IF ONLY LIST;" a list of attributes that, should it be achieved, would make them a worth-while person and a 'winner.' Depending on who they are, their list might read something like this:

"If only I were taller; if only I were shorter; if only I were smarter; if only I were blonde; if only I were married; if only I were single again; if only I had a better job; if only I were thinner; if only I could gain weight; if only I could win the lottery; if only I'd had different parents; if only I had his spiritual gift; if only that hadn't happened to me; et cetera, et cetera, et cetera." You fill in the blank!

In the end, this kind of thinking results in transformation by performance and human effort, rather than through identity in

CHAPTER 8 – IDENTITY ISSUES – YOURS, MINE AND OURS

Christ. It may provide some relief of the inner pain, but it doesn't cure the wounds; and it doesn't last!

The big problem with "If Only Lists" is this; they don't work any better than Eve's plan – just eat the fruit! This reality came as an epiphany one time when I was on a ministry trip with the organization I was working for. We were doing a conference, teaching on a variety of inner healing topics. A young man asked for a private session, and I was asked to meet with him.

At first glance, this guy had many attributes typically found on many an 'if only' list and then some. He was blond, tall, handsome, built, 25 years of age, made good money, had his own company, owned his house, a pick-up truck and a sports car, and was engaged to a beautiful young lady, played in the band at church, etc. His list of positive attributes just went on and on. He had his act all together; he was living the dream! Surely, he was a 'winner!' What most guys wouldn't have given to be him!

Then came a hard dose of reality! Why had he come? He was messed up worse than I had ever been and was coming to me for help. Yikes! It was then and there that it hit me square up the side of the head, and the proverbial light-bulb went on as it does in the cartoons. Everything that we think might make us a winner; all that we dream about becoming and long to be, is nothing more than a chasing after the wind – a useless and unproductive pursuit. Our 'if only's' will never 'fix' us! How depressing! That hard dose of reality was a real revelation. But what a valuable lesson!

On the other extreme, we find those even less fortunate individuals who, for their own reasons, believe that there is absolutely no hope for them. Why fight it? They're just too damaged to ever claw their way out of the hole in which they live to ever have a happy, productive, or fulfilling life. So why not just lay down a wait to die? They no longer dream any 'if only' dreams; all vision is lost. Taken to an extreme, they conclude, "There is no hope; I'm just too _____ to live; I might as well just put myself out of my misery and end it all now."

How sad is that, especially when we recognize that much of what goes on in our heads is actually a lie of the enemy? They don't know that God is happy to take us, *"...out of the pit of despair, out of the mud and the mire. He set my feet on solid ground and steadied me as I walked along"* (Psalm 40:2).

In the first case, where the person still has some hope for a brighter future, Satan has derailed the person, occupying them with chasing 'if only,' rather than pursuing the destiny God has for them. This leaves them feeling dissatisfied until whatever their fantasy is comes true. In the second instance, the person does not have enough faith to believe that anything good would be their final result, so they don't even try. Rather than pursuing destiny, they settle for the status quo and just hope to survive. Either way, Satan wins!

In both situations, people live out what they really believe. Most, if not all, of our social interactions are impacted by our self-image issues. When I started at Bible College, I was very shy. My shame-based identity pretty much controlled how I related to people. My general rule of thumb was, "If I know you and you speak nicely to me, I will speak back to you; but if I don't know you, I will not start a conversation."

On the evening of the first day at college, I saw a young lady at an Orientation Week activity. Obviously, I was not in her league! The very next day, I went to the post-office a few blocks down the street. As I was going in, that same girl was leaving. I saw her and recognized her; but, because of my shyness, I just put my head down and kept on walking. Over time, we did become friends; but I still was not in her league; and we never dated or anything like that.

She graduated a year ahead of me; and, after a post-graduation party, we were about to say our farewells. Suddenly, she confronted me with a conversation that went something like this; "Before we say, 'Good-bye,' there's something I need to confront you about. I know you don't remember this, but on our second day here, we ran into each other in

CHAPTER 8 - IDENTITY ISSUES - YOURS, MINE AND OURS

the post office; and you were so stuck up that you wouldn't even say, 'Hello,' to me!" I was dumb-founded! The fact was that I did remember it clearly, and I quickly explained the reality of my situation. She was floored and went on to say that she'd felt such rejection and had held that judgement against me for almost three years.

What was going on there? My self-esteem issues ("I'm not good enough to speak with her!") were interpreted by her as, "Apparently, I'm not even good enough for him to talk to me!" Her inner voice that said, "I'm not good enough," was triggered by how she interpreted what she experienced. In actuality, we'd triggered each other's self-esteem issues unintentionally, and didn't even know it!

I tell you that story to say this: Our self-esteem issues, springing from Satan's deception, will colour how we interpret life and how we live our lives, even if our conclusions are not based on reality. Was it true that I wasn't 'good enough'? No; but it was what I BELIEVED; and because I believed it, I lived it out. Remember, *"As a man thinks in his heart..."* (Proverbs 23:7).

Until we deal with our identity issues with the Lord's help, we're left to our own devices – those 'I can fix this' plans to become something or someone of value. But what happens between the reality of "now" and the dream of "eventually"? We find the need to protect ourselves. Being as damaged, insufficient, wrong, ugly, stupid, fat, etc., as we apparently are, we don't want anyone else to know our sad reality. We are convinced that, "If they really knew who I am, they wouldn't like me any more than I do." We try to keep our 'reality' hidden by hiding behind 'masks.' There is only one purpose for a mask and that's to hide our true identity. People can 'see' us, but not the real us. Often people have more than one mask and exchange them according to the situation at hand.

I believe that this is what psychiatrists would call 'adaptive personality.' That's how we present ourselves depending on the circumstance in which we find ourselves. For eight years, I taught in private elementary school. In the classroom, I was responsible to maintain a certain level of order, and found that, if I relaxed or did anything out of the usual routine, it seemed as if chaos broke out very quickly. I took on a very different, highly disciplinarian role that really did not reflect who I was. Nobody wants to be a crabby teacher; and I certainly didn't, but it worked!

In the opposite direction, when we are so sure that whatever we are is not good enough, we put on a 'mask' - a public presentation that we hope will be more pleasing to the crowd. For example, when a young couple are dating, both of them will put their 'best foot forward;' and they put forth the extra effort to impress the other. Although some guys are perfectly comfortable in a stretched out, smelly t-shirt and baggy track-pants, they usually don't show up for a hot first date looking like that.

Sometimes, it isn't until after the ceremony that their true persona rises to the surface. The guy that was always so polite and considerate while they were dating, suddenly is a less attentive and somewhat demanding husband. The girl-friend who would wait on the young man hand and foot becomes the wife who snaps back with, "You've got legs; get it yourself!"

I remember one young lady who was always smiling. That sounds great, but there was a sad reality behind it. She'd been taught that, "No one wants to marry a sad girl, so always keep smiling." No one knew the burden of sadness that she actually carried.

What creates further issues is that, when two people fall in love; they actually fall in love with the other person's mask, rather than who the person really is. Everyone believes in the fantasy of 'wedded bliss,' and expects that their marriage will always be a little slice of Heaven on Earth. Nobody can wear their masks 24/7; and sooner or later, off they come! The honeymoon ends quickly when that happens! Suddenly, each person realizes who or what they've just committed the rest of their life to, and aren't so impressed. Sometimes, a couple

CHAPTER 8 – IDENTITY ISSUES – YOURS, MINE AND OURS

can spend the rest of their lives trying to get their partner to put the mask back on and keep it on! Hence the nagging, criticism, etc. "You're not the man/woman I married! Where'd he/she go? I want him/her back!"

Where does that leave us all? Wounded... ashamed... in hiding... and either hopeful or hopeless. We cling to our looks, athletic prowess, intellect, bank account, career, spouse, or children to give us meaning and a level of acceptability. Thankfully, it doesn't have to be that way.

One of the great themes of Scriptures is that God is in the restoration or transformation business. He restores our relationship with Himself in Christ Jesus. When we are born-again, He gives us new life and, in our position in Christ, restores our righteousness (right standing with God) to a level equal to the righteousness of Jesus. His goal is to restore His image in us. In doing so, God is also willing to restore our value and worth.

You see, it doesn't really matter what others think of you, or even what you believe about yourself; what matters most is what God has to say about who you are and what your worth is. Those of us who had the privilege of growing up in church already know the correct "Sunday School" answers; we know the theological words and church lingo. We can even use big words such as, 'justified,' 'redeemed,' 'reconciled,' or 'propitiation' with some level of intellectual accuracy.

Unfortunately, Sunday School answers and theological constructs do more for the brain than for the heart. The best-known verse in the Bible, John 3:16, says, *"For this is how God loved the world: He gave His one and only Son, so that everyone who believes in Him will not perish but have eternal life."* Many of us have quoted it from memory for years. We know its truth intellectually and theologically, but many of us miss it in our heart-level experience. We do not know what it is to FEEL loved by God. Love is meant to be experienced; not just read about or discussed!

Without that experiential knowledge of God's love for 'me as an individual,' we read John 3:16 more like this; "God so loved the world, except for me, that…" or perhaps like this; "God so loved the world (and by default, me) that…" If we allow our feelings (I'm useless, damaged, unlovable goods) to dominate our experience, we tend to believe that God couldn't possibly love someone as mediocre or damaged as we are, so that verse really can't be true of us personally.

Time for a testimony! By the way, some Bible teachers say that you can't let a person's testimony shape your theology; testimony and experience are not as reliable as God's word. That's true; experience can be misinterpreted; we never catch all the facts of an experience, and we should not build our theology based on experience. On the other hand, theology that does not 'work' in the reality of our lives is useless, at best; and may very well be inaccurate, at worst. Theology and experience should work hand in hand to give us a more complete understanding of life. Experience should help us interpret our theology, and theology should help us interpret our experience. I will say this, though, in the end, it is God's Word that has final authority.

So, here's my story. I was raised in a great Christian home with loving parents, enjoying our Canadian slice of the 'American dream' and going to an evangelical, conservative church. I knew that people were saved by faith in what Jesus had done at Calvary; that salvation was a gift, received by faith, and not the result of works (Ephesians 2:8,9). Somewhere in the midst of all of that, I 'learned' that my relationship with God was supposedly based on my performance. I was pretty sure that I had not read enough, given enough, prayed enough, or witnessed enough; and that I had sinned more than enough… My experience had taught me that *I* was not enough.

Eventually, I began attending another church, one that was even more legalistic. It was both handy and comforting to have a long list of 'shoulds' and 'shouldn'ts,' so that I could measure my 'right standing' with God. As year turned into year, I became further engrossed in the legalism and the letter of the Law. To be honest, I

CHAPTER 8 - IDENTITY ISSUES - YOURS, MINE AND OURS

had turned into a pretty controlling Pharisee (a teacher of the Law in the Bible). Looking back, I believe that I was really hoping that, in my self-righteousness, I could get God to notice me, and perhaps even win His favour. How many times did I ask, "God, do You even know that I'm down here?"

I even went into ministry, although my own preference would have been teaching High School Math. I worked hard, eventually holding positions in the pastorate, Christian Education, and Missions. Some unfortunate work experiences taught me this; I was expendable; and, no matter how much I did, it wasn't enough.

By the Spring of 1997, I found myself exhausted and frustrated; nevertheless, I pressed on. Eventually, I ended up in the hospital emergency ward. The first doctor said I was having a heart attack; the second said it was angina. The heart specialist said, "I'm not sure what's happening; we'll keep you in until you settle down. Then you can go home; but don't do anything more than a slow walk or lift anything more than five pounds; because, if you do, your heart will explode, and you'll be dead by the time you hit the floor." I had totally "burned out." When a car runs out of gas, it just stops working. I had run out of gas; in fact, there weren't even fumes left in the tank. I was 'gone' physically, emotionally, and spiritually. I didn't know who I was or who God was. I resigned from my position at the church, and went home to tell my wife, "If God does not touch my life, I will be dead in two weeks." I was not suicidal; but there were no resources left to sustain life.

The decision was made to visit my brother, Doug, and his wife, Lois. Several years before this, they had joined a 'charismatic' church. I wasn't exactly sure what that meant, but I was pretty convinced it wasn't good! In my hour of need, I knew I had to go there for prayer. A friend of Doug's came over and prayed for me. That prayer session lasted about four hours – and it changed my life forever!

Doug's friend, Mike, put his hand on my chest and prayed for my heart to be healed. As he did so, two things happened. First, his hand got so hot that I expected to find a hand-shaped sunburn on my chest. After prayer, I looked in the bathroom mirror, just to check it out. The other manifestation came as what I can only describe as "waves and waves of electric love, flowing down over me from head to toe." In the process, it seemed to 'fix everything.' I had been given my life back. A few days later, Doug and I jogged 8 kilometers in 42 minutes. Less than a week before, I'd been afraid to go to the airport, thinking that I'd have to carry my 'certainly more than five pound' suitcase, and wondering if I'd even make it to the plane. Complete physical healing had taken place!

Back then, I knew nothing of inner healing; I hadn't even heard of it. But God was not finished with just physical healing. Without any warning, Mike prayed and asked God to show me what my 'spiritual identity' was. I had never heard the term before and had no 'theological box' for such an idea. I had a spiritual identity?????

As you can well imagine, my self-esteem and identity had taken quite a beating; but now Mike was praying about my spiritual identity! "What did he just say?" Nothing in that request 'computed,' to say the least. Mike had no sooner made his request, when I heard a voice in my head say, "A Warrior!" You must know that there was no way that I'd have come up with that answer on my own! Believe me, my church had not taught me to hear voices or see things. In fact, we believed that such fanciful events were more likely to be demonically inspired than from God. Nevertheless, that's what I 'heard.' In my head, I was arguing somewhat with God, thinking, "A warrior!?!? You've got to be kidding me! I could be a mud-puddle; I'll just lay here and let people walk on me; that's all I have the energy for." Again, the voice came, "No! A warrior!" For some reason, I stopped debating the point and said, "All right then; I'll be a warrior."

With that, I 'saw' a vision of a beautiful silver sword with a gold hilt, hanging in mid-air in front of me. I'd never had a vision before; but, in the vision, I reached out and took hold of the sword with my right hand. The arm that I saw – my arm – was strong and muscular

CHAPTER 8 – IDENTITY ISSUES – YOURS, MINE AND OURS

and looked more like Arnold Schwarzenegger's than my own! I remember wondering if that could possibly be MY arm.

What had happened? In response to Mike's short prayer and by God's grace, I had received a personal revelation. The Bible calls this a rhema word – a personalized word from God. The Bible is the written Word of God and is God's Word to all people for all time. Personal prophetic revelation is a word that applies to an individual or a group in an immediate situation for a specific time or season. I learned my 'spiritual identity' through a rhema word and a vision. I really can't explain it, but that picture or metaphor of a warrior has really become my spiritual identity. Interestingly enough, the person in the Bible that I have always identified with most is Joshua, the warrior-leader who led the people of God into the Promised Land.

Immediately, I remembered how Jesus had read from a well-known passage in Isaiah 61. *"The Spirit of the sovereign Lord is upon Me because, He has anointed Me to..."* Of all the things found on that list, one leaped off the page and into my heart; it just applied to me and resonated in my spirit: *"to set the captives free,"* – another military picture.

One thing that was so amazing was the timing of such a powerful revelation. When I was completely broken, when I had come to the end of myself, when I had absolutely nothing to offer God or anything that would commend me to Him, and when I finally dropped my control issues and let God do whatever He wanted to do, that's when He loved me the most! Correction: That's when I felt His love the most, and I learned the meaning of 'grace!' The days that led up to that experience had been horrible, to say the least; but the ecstasy was worth every bit of the agony that preceded it! I never want to go back to where I was before; but I am so thankful that God allowed me to go through those experiences so I could come through the brokenness to the place of healing.

The events of that evening changed the course of my life and my ministry. Over the years, I've had the privilege of leading several people into a similar encounter. Each session follows the same pattern:

Often, it is necessary to start by breaking the power of our agreement with what the enemy has taught us. It might sound something like this: "Father, I confess believing what the enemy says – that I am _____. I break the power of my agreement with him and ask for You to forgive me and cleanse me from such unrighteousness."

We continue by confessing the lies of the enemy, asking for cleansing and forgiveness, forgiving those who taught us the lies, and asking God to speak words of revelation or to bring a picture of who the recipient is in God's eyes. "Father, when you look at me, who do You see? When You think about me, what do You feel? Speak to me with a word or a verse; show me a picture…" Almost every time, God has been so faithful to provide the person receiving ministry with some revelation of their identity. A Bible character might suddenly come to mind or a verse, or just some thought. Some people receive a vision – a mental picture, like a dream, but they're awake. Jesus is always in the picture and always has some specific word to speak to the recipient of the ministry. In each experience, the person tells us that they would never have said that or thought that about themselves – it just seemed too good to be true. Often they leave with a whole new perspective on life.

Let me back up a bit. Life teaches us about who we are or what our natural life is like. Given enough time to think about it, we can even come up for some metaphor that 'pictures' our lives, even as believers. One person said that every day, demons that looked like trolls were beating them with clubs and chains, trying to take them down into Hell. The natural pictures are always pretty ugly; some are even gross! But God's pictures are always wonderful. I wish I could share them with you, but I need to respect the privacy of my friends. Let me tell you my natural picture.

If I were to paint you a picture of how I lived my life in the 'natural realm,' it would be like this: I am a clown, riding an 8' tall unicycle on an old Vaudeville theatre stage. I'm juggling about 18 balls in the air, trying to impress the crowd with my skill and unfailing ability.

CHAPTER 8 – IDENTITY ISSUES – YOURS, MINE AND OURS

To make matters worse, there is some guy trying to throw more balls to me to juggle with all the rest; but I'm already going as fast as I can. In my picture, I know this; I can't keep up this pace forever. When I can't, I'll drop all the balls, fall off my unicycle, and come crashing down. When that happens, the whole audience will 'boo' and throw rotten fruit and vegetables at me; and one of those old-fashioned shepherd's crooks will come out from behind the curtain, wrap itself around my neck, drag me from the stage, and toss me into the back alley behind the theatre like last week's garbage. The next act will appear, and life will go on without me.

How do you live, if that's your life? I can tell you from my experience, you're nervous, angry, and resentful. You know that, regardless of how well you're performing, someone wants more from you. You know that you can't keep it up forever, and, when you can't, you're done. Keeping the crowd impressed is all that matters. And if you think that anyone out there actually cares about you, you're wrong! That's quite a depressing picture!

And what a contrast to what God says! If you're a warrior, what are you like? Strong, confident, trained, capable. If you mess up, you take your licks and get up, dust yourself off, and keep going. Most importantly, there is only one person you have to impress and that's the "Captain of our souls," Jesus (and He already loves us!). What a freeing concept!

I no longer care to impress the crowd and care little for what the audience thinks of me. I only have to please One Person and answer only to Him. "I hear; and I obey and let the chips fall where they may!" If my life pleases God, the details will work themselves out. The only reason I need to care what the crowd thinks, is that I represent the Lord God, my King, my Captain. If Jesus is happy with my stewardship, I'm happy too. Life is SO much better this way! I am free!

Does one short ministry experience really change your whole life? Can it really be that easy? The answer to those questions is, simply,

"Yes and No!" "Yes," because believing what God says about you, no matter how ridiculously wonderful it is, really does change your perspective. It helps to heal up those emotional 'hot buttons' stemming from our emotional and spiritual wounded-ness.

On the other hand, the answer is, "No," because it is a daily, if not moment-by-moment, choice to live in light of God's revelation or to go back to what life has taught you. Who do I choose to be today? A clown or a warrior? The choice is mine to make; but, if I don't make that choice, the 'default setting' is to 'clown.' It takes conscious effort to choose "Warrior" and to walk like one in the reality of life.

At ten o-clock one morning, while I was at work, the second in command in the organization called to say that she and the director wanted to meet with me at one o'clock that afternoon. As it happened, I'd had a previous similar experience when #2 called at 10:00 a.m., to say that he and #1 wanted to meet with me at 1:00 p.m. That day, I was unemployed by 1:30. This time, all of the clown in me came rushing to the surface. As I hung up the phone, the only thoughts in my head were, "What have I done now? How much trouble am I in? Am I getting fired today?" By lunchtime, I was so 'tied up in knots' I couldn't eat anything.

The truth of the situation was that my immediate supervisor had resigned, and they wanted to offer me the position on a temporary basis, until another member of the leadership team could take over. I was saddened to learn that a good friend was leaving the organization, but I was more relieved that I still had a job! Why was I all 'tied up in knots?" Because I was living as a clown and hadn't chosen to be a warrior that day! I wonder what the morning would have gone like, if I had approached the situation as a warrior.

Over the years, God has both patiently and graciously added to the picture of me as a warrior. Each time, He has affirmed His original word. I know who I am and what my life is to be about. I'm called to set the captives free and to do so by teaching, inner healing, and

CHAPTER 8 – IDENTITY ISSUES – YOURS, MINE AND OURS

evangelism. And when I walk in my identity, I also step into my destiny. And that is transforming my life!

Our personal identity is one of the largest strongholds Satan can have in our lives. As 2 Corinthians 10 says, we have the spiritual weapons and strategies to tear down, destroy, and demolish Satan's strongholds. Good-bye, Mr. Clown! God's revelation tore down that picture and gave me a new one. Interestingly, the warrior is more joyfully obedient to Jesus Christ than the clown ever was!

The good news is that I'm nobody special; no super-saint; no one unusually spiritual or Christ-like. I am just another one of God's children. What My Father has done for me, He'll gladly do for you as well!

SOMETHING TO THINK ABOUT…

1. What has life taught you about who you are? How did it do that?

2. If you were asked to paint or imagine a picture that represented your natural life, what would that picture be?

3. When you think about what life has taught you about yourself, how would you describe yourself in one or two words?

4. What do you think Jesus thinks of you? (No 'Sunday School' answers!)

5. Have you asked the Father who you are in His eyes? Why? Why not? What has He spoken to you or shown you?

SOMETHING TO DO…

Paint/draw/scribble (whatever you can do) 2 pictures of yourself – guess which ones!

CHAPTER 9

FOLLOW THE LEADER; IT'S NOT JUST A KIDS' GAME!
(Learning to follow orders)

Matthew 4:19 "Jesus said, 'Come, follow Me…'"

Thinking back several thousand years to when I was a child, I can remember a number of fun, free-time activities. Capture The Flag, Simon Says, Cowboys and Indians (That was long before we'd even heard of something called, "Political Correctness"), and Follow The Leader, along with a variety of board games and sports like swimming, biking, and skiing, happily filled our days.

When I think of how we are supposed to live our lives as Christians, two of those games stand out as examples of learned obedience. In 'Simon Says,' one kid, "Simon," was the leader; and the rest stood in a line, awaiting his instructions. Basically, the game was just a test to see who was the most attentive and obedient. If Simon began his orders with "Simon says…" you were supposed to obey. If you didn't hear, "Simon says…" then you were to remain as you were. "Simon says, 'Stand on one foot.'" "Simon says, 'Touch your nose,' etc., etc." Eventually the orders would come more quickly, and even the most attentive would get fooled into illegitimate obedience.

The other game was 'Follow the Leader.' This was less of a contest and more of a practice. Basically, we were being taught obedience, although it just seemed like a game. At all times, you had to keep your eyes on the leader and just do whatever they did, say what they said, and go wherever they went. And you had to do it in the same way that the leader did it. I believe that teachers thought up this game just to reinforce the whole idea of obedience into their students. Perhaps it was some parent; who knows?

In a culture that frequently displays the message, "Nobody is going to tell me what to do," we find that the Christian life, or, at least, how the Christian life is supposed to be lived, is exactly counter-cultural to what we see in much of society. Biblical concepts such as surrender to the will of God, obedience to authorities, and the Ten Commandments seem to be offensive to many secularized people who might consider these concepts as antiquated relics that are no longer applicable today. Nevertheless, without God to determine truth and morality, there is no standard for right and wrong except the prevailing public opinion of the day.

The "Nobody tells me what to do," message is a direct descendent of atheism and springs from the philosophical stance known as relativism that says, "What's true for you might not be true for me, and what's true for me might not be true for the next person."

The logical conclusion, if you follow that line of thinking through to its ultimate end is, "Everything can be considered true and everyone's opinion is valid." If everything is true, then nothing can be false. The result is that everyone is 'right,' whatever they do is 'ok,' and whatever they believe is 'true.'

Without God and His revelation, individuals, and even our legal and court systems, have no foundation for morality, except man's opinion. Granted, some laws of the land do uphold Biblical values. For example, we have laws against murder, whether or not the lawmakers recognize that such a principle is Biblical in its origin. If we fail to recognize God and His ethical code, what other foundation do we have, except what seems good to those in power or the opinion of those with the loudest voice in society?

CHAPTER 9 - FOLLOW THE LEADER...

If one follows relativism through to its logical conclusion, it becomes impossible to be wrong – unless you point out that someone else is wrong; that would definitely be wrong. "Who are you to say that I'm wrong or that what I do is wrong?!?!?" Tolerance has become the mantra of the day and everything is tolerable, except intolerance, of course. Proverbs 30:12 reports accurately, *"They are pure in their own eyes, but they are filthy and unwashed."* Sound familiar?

Recently I was confronted by someone who was offended by the stance our church took about a social issue. I was told that it was inappropriate for the church to 'judge' or to tell others how to live. According to this person, people should be free to do whatever they want to do – as long as it doesn't hurt anyone. My response was this; "You just quoted a moral absolute at me. You're imposing your standard of righteousness – 'as long as it doesn't hurt anyone' – on me. That's the very thing you won't allow the church to do. Why is your opinion more valid than ours?" (Hopefully, it didn't sound as harsh then as it reads now!) They seemed shocked that I didn't just cave in to their standard of morality. Hopefully, I gave the person something to think about in that brief exchange. What I noticed was how readily they'd accepted the social convention of our culture and hadn't thought it through to its ultimate end.

Decades ago, people were expected to do the 'right thing.' That became, "If it FEELS RIGHT, do it." Now, we hear, "If it FEELS GOOD, do it." And our culture is now officially adrift on the amoral sea! Even in church we might find those with "felt-led disease." These are the people who claim to have heard from God on a particular matter or course of action. "I felt led to..." is their frequent rationalization. Refusing to be accountable to anyone else, they take the stance, "I've heard from God, so you have nothing to say about the matter." They seem to have forgotten that God might speak to others who also listen to His voice.

Those who prescribe to the "anything goes" life-style often regard the Church as harsh, judgemental, and condemning. Unfortunately, that has, too often, been the case, particularly when religious legalism is loudly portrayed as the heart of the Father. Some people might say we are not gracious, especially if they expect that 'being gracious' means happily accepting any and all behaviour.

Titus 2:11,12 gives us a more accurate picture of grace. *"For the grace of God has been revealed, bringing salvation to all people. And we are instructed to turn from godless living and sinful pleasures. We should live in this evil world with wisdom, righteousness, and devotion to God…"*

Self-discipline does not come naturally, but it seems inconsistent for a 'believer' to want the benefits of salvation but to kick against the idea of self-denial. Grace, when fully applied, teaches us to live lives that turn from or deny (Say, "No!" to…) ungodliness and to 'sinful pleasures' and to live lives that are sensible, righteous, and godly. Remember, God's grace wants to rescue us from the destruction that ungodliness and sin produce. Legalism may be somewhat graceless, but false grace is lawless. Only true grace loves the person enough to lead them into a righteous lifestyle.

Standing in stark and almost absurd contrast to the prevailing culture, we find Christ's challenging message, *"If any of you wants to be My follower, you must give up your own way, take up your cross, and follow Me."* Three of the four Gospels (Matthew 16:24; Mark 8:34; and Luke 9:23) quote these famous words of Jesus. To 'give up our own way' or 'deny oneself' is simply to say, "No!" to your selfish desires. Remember the concept of the flesh and the spirit? Our flesh – our natural personality's way of doing things, has a will. It WANTS to do things in the old, familiar, tried-but-not-so-true way and in the ways of the world. It FEELS like doing things, and that can make us self-centered. While not everything our 'natural man' feels or wants to do is evil, some of its ways are.

Dr. Larry Crab was a leading Christian psychologist in the late 20th century. Although we wouldn't want to put words in his mouth, you could try to summarize his teaching this way: "Sin is man's way of trying to meet legitimate needs in illegitimate ways."[1] I might feel a legitimate need for job security. I could try to work hard and make myself invaluable to the company, or I could steal other people's ideas and take the credit. One way would be legitimate; the other would be sinful.

If I sense a legitimate need to defend myself from someone who is verbally attacking me, I might feel like punching my offender in the mouth; it might feel good to do so. My fists are clenched; my muscles are tightening up, getting ready to spring into action; but I don't do it, because it would not be good to do. A fistfight might break out; I might get arrested for assault, etc.; so, I say, "No!" to what I feel like doing... Anyone who has tried dieting knows all about the power of saying, "No," to one's desires. I might feel like gobbling down a large slab of Black Forest Cake – with a healthy dollop of ice cream, or going for that third helping of mashed potatoes and gravy; but self-discipline says, "No!"

No matter what temptation we face, we either say, "Yes," to our flesh and the clues of the enemy OR we say, "Yes," to the Spirit of God. There is no way around it: we can only say, "Yes," to one of the two at a time.

I remember hearing a very corny, old joke several years ago, but I don't know its origin. A pastor was addressing the congregation about the need to overcome temptation and asked if there was anyone there who never struggled with it. Eventually, a sad, defeated-looking man shyly put up his hand. The pastor was amazed and asked him to come forward to tell the others how he did it. His answer brought much chagrin to the pastor when the man replied, "As soon as a temptation comes along, I just give in right away; there is no struggle at all!" That may be slightly amusing (maybe not!); but, behind that answer is a sad reality; that man lives much of his life in defeat and in bondage.

Those of us who have really struggled with temptation know that, "Just say, 'No!'" is more easily said than done. Many of us seem powerless to overcome the lure of the needle, the computer, or the refrigerator! Just because something is 'hard,' doesn't excuse us from the responsibility to follow through obediently. Where can we find such strength?

Some folks are intellectually focused. If it is logical and makes sense, that's the way to go! End of story. Other people may have a very strong will – once their mind is made up and a decision is made, they'll doggedly follow through until success has been achieved. Neither emotions nor logic will sway these folks from their decision. These are the kind of people who say, "Don't confuse me with the facts; my mind is made up!" Thirdly, a person may be more emotionally driven and live according to how they feel in the moment. Should a temptation present itself, their feelings take over, bringing both their minds and body into obedience to their emotions.

Is that it? Are there any other options available to us? Are we just left on our own to muddle through as best we can, sometimes failing and sometimes managing to stave off the attacks and temptations of the enemy?

Thankfully, such is not the case, because God is the consummate administrator. He never, ever assigns His children a responsibility without giving both the authority and power to complete the assignment. In other words, He provides us with what's necessary to deny our flesh and to live an obedient life.

Where does that power come from? From Jesus, through His Holy Spirit! 2 Peter 1:3 tells us, *"By His divine power, God has given us everything we need for living a godly life. We have received all of this by coming to know Him, the One who called us to Himself by means of His marvelous glory and excellence."* Such an amazing thought! God's power has ALREADY given us EVERYTHING pertaining to the Christian life. We already have it all; we just need to learn to use what we have. Apparently, all of that came to us as we learned the truth of the gospel message and responded to it as God called us to faith.

Just listen to the encouraging truth found in 1 Corinthians 10:13: *"The temptations in your life are no different from what others experience.*

CHAPTER 9 – FOLLOW THE LEADER...

And God is faithful. He will not allow the temptation to be more than you can stand. When you are tempted, He will show you a way out so that you can endure."

As Jesus was preparing the disciples for His death, resurrection, and return to the Father in Heaven, He told them that He would not abandon them as orphans; but, when He left us, He would send us His Holy Spirit. That Spirit of Jesus would not just be WITH the disciples; He would also be IN them (See John 14,15,16). If you are a believer in Jesus, the Holy Spirit is IN YOU! What a wonderful concept! You can't get any closer than that! No wonder Jesus said, *"My sheep listen to My voice; ... and they follow Me"* (John 10:27). So why do many believers consider it a strange thing to 'hear' the voice of God as an inner voice? Isn't that where Holy Spirit lives – inside of us?

Paul told the Corinthian believers, *"Don't you realize that your body is the temple of the Holy Spirit, who lives in you and was given to you by God? You do not belong to yourself, for God bought you with a high price. So, you must honor God with your body."* (1 Corinthians 6:19,20).

Since the Day of Pentecost (Acts 1,2), God no longer dwells in a house made with human hands, but INSIDE believers – all believers. As Paul put it in Romans 8:9, *"But you are not controlled by your sinful nature. You are controlled by the Spirit if you have the Spirit of God living in you. (And remember that those who do not have the Spirit of Christ living in them do not belong to Him at all.)."* The bottom line is simply this, if you do not have the Holy Spirit, you do not belong to Christ. All true believers have Holy Spirit living inside of them. You are His temple – His permanent dwelling place!

It would seem logical to anticipate that, when Holy Spirit 'moves in,' it would automatically bring about a number of obvious changes. For many, there may be a heightened awareness of sin and a greater sensitivity to conviction. Surprisingly, though, if people aren't taught to attend to or pay attention to Holy Spirit, they may continue to go through life with little or no awareness of His presence and activity in their lives. This is such a shame as it tends to deprive them of the necessary guidance they so desperately need.

It would be like a soldier who is lost in the jungle, separated from his company, and not sure where to go or what to do next. The soldier has obviously been through basic training, and like the Boy-Scouts, has been taught to "Be prepared!" but, in that situation, what he really needs most is direction! What better way to get direction than to pull out your compass and allow it to provide perspective? It would be sad, even ludicrous, for the soldier to not know or to forget that he was carrying a compass in his pack and to continue just wandering through the jungle, hoping to find something that would help him get his bearings.

God has already given believers a 'compass:' something, actually, SomeONE, to help us get our bearings and chart our course in life. That compass is the Holy Spirit, who lives in us. The problem is that we may not be very aware that we have been given such a gift or that we have not learned how to 'use' our compass. 'Use' is actually a terrible word; 'cooperate with' or 'follow the direction of' would be much better expressions. The Holy Spirit is not something that we use for our own purposes; He is not some tool in our hands. He is, however, available to be our Helper and our Guide in life. His part is to lead us, and our part is to attend to what He is saying and to 'Follow the Leader' in obedience. This means that we must walk in humility and in surrender to His will, so that we can let Him lead, rather than expecting Him to do whatever we might demand.

Some Christians have had their faith either weakened or lost when God failed to do what they thought He should do. It is our flesh, pride or self-centredness that expects God to serve our purposes or to provide whatever we think we might want. God is not some Cosmic Butler, duty-bound to fetch us whatever we ask, expect, or demand. Talk about nerve! We can't imagine some private in the army barking orders at a general. Oddly though, we seem to have little trouble giving God our orders (in 'prayer,' of course). That would be like us deciding which way is north and expecting our compasses to come into line with us rather than us letting the compass determine our direction.

CHAPTER 9 – FOLLOW THE LEADER…

Perhaps you've seen an old war movie when the troops are stealthily moving through enemy territory. They might be in a forest or a jungle. As they go along, the Captain gives orders. He might hold up his fist, indicating that the rest of the troop should stop immediately. Amazingly enough, one simple hand-gesture has the power to make a whole bunch of grown men 'freeze!' Why doesn't some private just keep moving forward? Why doesn't he protest, saying, "I don't want to stop right now; I'm standing in a puddle, so I'm going to keep marching ahead"? A soldier would never think of telling the Captain, "Who do you think you are? You can't tell me what to do!" Why not? Because a good soldier knows that his life and the lives of everyone in the company depend on his instant obedience.

Sadly, many of us journey through our Christian lives like that, only obeying when we're in a crisis or if we know that there will be terrible consequences if we disobey. But what about when everything is going well – when life is good? Are we as diligent in following Heaven's orders at that point? Perhaps not so much.

As was mentioned earlier, it seems that some believers are not be very aware of the Holy Spirit's presence in their lives. He's there already and active, but they might not realize it. For some folks, it might take quite a bit of time before they recognize His work or presence in them. Perhaps they don't recognize that it is His voice bringing some intuitive warning to mind. Maybe they've had an experience that, when they met someone for the first time, their immediate and inexplicable reaction was, "Don't trust that man!" Where did that come from, if not Holy Spirit? It amazes me that the same Christians who must admit that they have no trouble hearing the voice of the enemy when he brings tempting thoughts to mind, might also deny their ability to hear God.

Some believers seem to have a kind of 'crisis' experience sometime after their salvation when, suddenly, it seems as if the Holy Spirit powerfully comes upon them in a more tangible way. They might refer to this experience as being 'baptized in the Holy Spirit.' There are a number of passages that talk about a baptism in the Holy Spirit, but perhaps not in the way some people use the term. Listen to the following passages:

Mark 1:8 *"I (John) baptize you with water, but He (Jesus) will baptize you with the Holy Spirit!"* Here, John the Baptist was prophesying that Jesus would baptize His followers with the Holy Spirit.

Acts 1:5 *"John baptized with water, but in just a few days you will be baptized with the Holy Spirit."* In this passage, Jesus was referring to John the Baptist's prophetic word and telling the disciples that the prophecy was about to be fulfilled. In Verse 4, Jesus was reminding them of John's words, and Verse 6, applies that prophecy to what would happen on the Day of Pentecost. Jesus was telling 'the boys' to wait for the Holy Spirit to come on them.

Acts 11:16 *"Then I thought of the Lord's words when He said, 'John baptized with water, but you will be baptized with the Holy Spirit.'"* Here, Peter was reporting about what had already taken place on the Day of Pentecost when the Spirit visibly descended on them as tongues of fire and like a dove. He was saying that John the Baptist's prophecy had been fulfilled with that event.

That was fine for the early believers, but what about us today? Are all of us baptized in the Holy Spirit, or are some reduced to second-class late-comers?

The early verses of Acts 19 might shed some light in answer to our question. Paul was dealing with some recent converts, who, by their own admission had not received the Holy Spirit. In fact, they didn't know anything about Him; they hadn't even heard of Him. While some would use this text as proof that some believers suffer a lag-time between when they believed in Christ and when they received Holy Spirit, a closer look at the passage shows us that these 'believers' had only been instructed in the way of John the Baptist; they had repented and turned to God and been baptized with John's baptism – a baptism of repentance.

At that time, baptism was a common ritual, and not just a Christian event. When a person switched religious belief systems or perhaps adopted another god in their poly-theistic world view, they would be 'baptized.' Baptism is a type of very short, silent play or mime. It uses the imagery of a burial and resurrection to depict the change that had already taken place in the person's life. As the person is tipped back down under the water, it demonstrates 'death' – death to their old world-view or philosophy, their religious belief system, and subsequent way of living. When the person is raised back up out of the water, it depicts that they have been raised from the dead to embrace and walk in a 'new life' – one dedicated and devoted to a new belief system and life-style.

By the way, the Greek word for 'baptism,' "baptizo" literally means to 'plunge into water.' That's why our church uses the immersion method, rather than dipping or sprinkling, and puts the whole person under water to more accurately depict their death to their old system of belief and then being raised to walk by a new faith.

If you were to baptize a pail, the pail would be in the water and the water would be in the pail. Similarly, baptism depicts that the believer is already in Christ and that Christ is already in the believer. Remember, baptism is a picture to demonstrate what has already taken place. We don't get saved when we're baptized. I'm not saying that; nor am I equating water baptism with a baptism in the Holy Spirit. While I don't believe that baptism saves people, it does bring the general blessing that any act of obedience merits.

In the Acts 19 passage, it becomes clear that the 'believers' had been baptized either to show their new-found faith or to demonstrate their repentance from their former, sinful manner of life to embrace a more godly life-style. Paul then explained the rest of the Gospel – that Jesus was the Christ. As John's converts embraced faith in Jesus and were again baptized to demonstrate their new-found faith in Christ, they received the Holy Spirit.

Having said that, experience shows us that, from time to time, sincere Christian believers seem unaware of the Spirit's presence in their lives. Perhaps, like I had been, they just hadn't been educated about His real-life activities. Then, suddenly, and for a wide variety of reasons, they have some sort of crisis experience (a good one!) when it seems as if a dam breaks and there is a flood of the Holy Spirit into their awareness. Some testify that it felt like water or oil being poured down over their heads. In my own experience, I would say that I felt wave upon wave of what I can only describe as liquid, electric love. Others might comment about feeling as if energy came bubbling up from deep within, usually down in the 'pit of their stomach.' The physical manifestation seems to be much less significant than the fact that they became aware of His presence in them. Some would call this a "baptism in the Holy Spirit." What you call it is not as nearly as important as that we experience the manifestation of Holy Spirit in our lives.

All of this reminds us of Jesus' words found in John 7:38,39. *"Anyone who believes in Me may come and drink! For the Scriptures declare, 'Rivers of living water will flow from his heart.' (When He said 'living water,' He was speaking of the Spirit, who would be given to everyone believing in Him. But the Spirit had not yet been given, because Jesus had not yet entered into His glory.)"* It is God's intention that His children get so full of Holy Spirit that He (The Spirit) automatically overflows out of their spirits and into their day-to-day experience.

Another expression that we often hear in Christian circles is that we should be 'filled with' or 'full' of the Holy Spirit. In fact, we are COMMANDED to be filled. Ephesians 5:18 says, *"Don't be drunk with wine, because that will ruin your life. Instead, be filled with the Holy Spirit..."* We are told to be filled. Because this verb – be filled – is in the present tense, it means that we should continuously be filled. All the time, be filled! Any "baptism in Holy Spirit" is a one-time event, but being filled is to be the regular, on-going experience for each believer.

The big question then becomes, "How, can we be filled?" First, we need to recognize that, if God commanded us to be filled, then it is His will that we are. Second, this is a "passive voice" verb. That means that the filling is something done 'to' or 'for' us. We don't fill ourselves; we let it happen. God does the work; and we receive its effects. Years ago, a pastor from Uganda was asked, "Why did

CHAPTER 9 - FOLLOW THE LEADER...

God visit Uganda and bring such a mighty revival?" His answer was telling, "Because He was invited!" Why will the Father come to fill us with His Spirit? Here are two answers: because we invite Him to do so and yield ourselves to be filled, and simply because He wants to fill us with His Spirit.

Another important question is, "How full is full?" In some sense, it would require a completely sinless life for us to be completely filled with Holy Spirit. That suggests that we can only be filled when we are perfect. This is not the case. Perhaps a simple, natural illustration will help. If you took a glass jar or perhaps one of those old "Mason Jars" used for canning fruits or vegetables, and put a number of stones in the jar, it might look 'full' of stones; but you could more completely 'fill' the jar with water, simply by pouring the water into the jar and letting it fill up all the 'empty' places between the stones. In one sense, the jar is full of both stones and water, but you could still say that you had filled the jar with water. Obviously, the fewer the stones, the more water the jar could hold.

If we were to draw a spiritual application from that natural illustration, we might realize that our lives can 'hold' more Holy Spirit when more and more of our lives are yielded to Him and as the sin is removed from the various parts of our lives. Through confession and repentance of sin, we remove the 'stones' and make more room for the Holy Spirit. The more full we are of the Holy Spirit, the more easily He can guide and empower us, and the more obvious His presence in our lives becomes.

Being filled is not just a matter of sitting around waiting for God to do something. "Waiting on God" is not that passive. If we are to experience the power of God's Spirit, it will require that we cooperate with Him. Such a concept is not unusual in Scripture. God does His part, and we must do ours if we are to experience the desired result. Of course, there are times when God just seems to sovereignly move, even without the 'help' of his people. Most of the time, though, He seems to wait for us or on us to do our part in the program. This goes right back to Creation and God's purpose for mankind – to be His image and likeness – His representatives on Earth, and to reign here on His behalf. God reigned through Adam and Eve who had been instructed to "Go and reign." In order for us to fulfill His purposes for us, it will take the fullness of the presence and power of God's Spirit in our lives.

Later, when the Lord was preparing the Israelites to enter the Promised Land – the land that He had sworn to give to the Jewish ancestors – He gave the following instruction, recorded in Deuteronomy 9: 23: *"And at Kadesh-barnea the Lord sent you out with this command: 'Go up and take over the land I have given you.' But you rebelled against the command of the Lord your God and refused to put your trust in Him or obey Him."* God had brought the Israelites out of Egypt, led them through the desert, provided all their needs, and brought them up to the border of their land; but they still refused to obey. God had done His part; they failed to do their part. He told them, "YOU go and posses what I have already given you." Unfortunately, at that point they were unwilling to do what they were told. Interestingly, God points out in this passage that their failure to obey was rooted in their failure to believe. This lack of follow-though on the part of His people is described as 'rebellion.' For the Israelites to possess what God had promised required that God would do His part AND that they would do theirs.

I believe that there is a parallel here between that scenario and how God extends His offer of salvation to all people. He has already done all that is necessary as Christ died on the cross to pay for our sin and was raised for our righteousness. God makes the offer – a complete gift – something that we do not need to pay for. Sadly, though, some people decide not to accept such a wonderful gift. Why? Because of their rebellion and unbelief. Could it be that so many Christians are regularly 'not filled' with Holy Spirit, because of their unbelief?

In the same way, we must choose to live by faith and in obedience if we are to experience the freedom from temptation and the transformation that God has already provided for us. How do we do that? By following the leading of God's Spirit. Perhaps this is a poor illustration, but it might help. Think of the Holy Spirit as a friend with whom you spend your life. Remember that Jesus called the disciples His friends in John 15:15. In the same way, we can be the friends of the Holy Spirit. Such a friendship is NOT a peer to peer relationship, however. It is a Creator to creation relationship and a Master to servant or Commander to Private way of relating. Yes, God does invite us to be His friends, but we must never lose perspective in regard to who is the Teacher and who is the disciple. My point is that, if we are to walk with the Holy Spirit as both Friend and Lord, we must do so as obedient follower. In the game, the kids took turns being "Simon." In our spiritual life, there can only be one "Simon," and it's not you or me! It is God's Holy Spirit!

There was an old saying, "If God seems distant, guess who moved!" So true! If God is not our closest Friend, it is because we are not following closely enough! Friendship with God and learning to walk WITH Him means allowing Him to set the course and do the leading. That's His part; our part is to follow the leader.

As we learn to walk with the Holy Spirit and are led at His direction, we move into a whole new level of life-transformation and experience. Under His leading, we can find the power and wisdom to overcome temptation, are kept in safety from encroaching dangers, and can be led in wonderful adventures in the Kingdom of God. On the other hand, God will never lead us, empower us, or anoint us to do something that He is not already doing or that would weaken our fellowship with Him. Besides, why would we do anything that would distance ourselves from the Holy Spirit?

1 Thessalonians 5:19 tells us, *"Do not stifle the Holy Spirit."* The NASB used the term 'quench.' When you 'quench' something you put it out. For example, you quench a fire by dousing it with water. You quench your thirst, by taking a drink and removing that desire. We 'quench' Holy Spirit by failing to listen to His voice or by disobeying His instructions.

I remember when I was in teacher training, we were told, "If no one is listening, quit talking." That really worked. While I was teaching a lesson, if the students all started talking amongst themselves, I would just stop talking. Eventually they'd realize that I was not saying anything and become quiet themselves. In some ways, they had quenched my voice. In the same way, we quench or put out the Spirit's work in our lives when we do not attend or listen to Him. Sometimes we just keep talking and talking ourselves so that He never gets a word in edge-wise.

That might lead to what the Bible refers to as 'grieving' Holy Spirit. (Ephesians 4:30 NASB). A person is grieved when they do not like what is happening. How many parents have been grieved by the behaviour of a teenager who is going astray? They see their darling son or daughter making unwise decisions and sowing a harvest that they will not want to reap. In the same way, the Holy Spirit is grieved when we fail to obey Him or when we do something that will eventually hurt us or other people. While some people read this verse as if it says, "The Holy Spirit is grieved; and when He is grieved, He is angry!" I think that the passage really means that He mourns over the damage we do to ourselves and to others. I believe that He is sad. And if Holy Spirit is sad, so is our human spirit, particularly if we are close to Him!

I so appreciate the words of Galatians 5 because it tells us how to walk in victory over temptation and sin – no matter what that temptation might be.

"So Christ has truly set us free. Now make sure that you stay free, and don't get tied up again in slavery..." (Vs. 1).

So, I say, let the Holy Spirit guide your lives. Then you won't be doing what your sinful nature craves. The sinful nature wants to do evil, which is just the opposite of what the Spirit wants. And the Spirit gives us desires that are the opposite of what the sinful nature desires. These two forces are constantly fighting each other, so you are not free to carry out your good intentions. But when you are directed by the Spirit, you are not under obligation to the law of Moses... (Vs. 16-18).

When you follow the desires of your sinful nature, the results are very clear: sexual immorality, impurity, lustful pleasures, idolatry, sorcery, hostility, quarreling, jealousy, outbursts of anger, selfish ambition,

CHAPTER 9 – FOLLOW THE LEADER...

dissension, division, envy, drunkenness, wild parties, and other sins like these. Let me tell you again, as I have before, that anyone living that sort of life will not inherit the Kingdom of God (Vs. 19-21).

But the Holy Spirit produces this kind of fruit in our lives: love, joy, peace, patience, kindness, goodness, faithfulness, gentleness, and self-control. There is no law against these things! Those who belong to Christ Jesus have nailed the passions and desires of their sinful nature to His cross and crucified them there (Vs. 22-24).

Since we are living by the Spirit, let us follow the Spirit's leading in every part of our lives (Vs. 25).

This important passage teaches us a variety of 'secrets' about life in the Spirit. First, we need to notice the purposes of God. Christ wants us to be FREE! In the context of these verses, we're talking about freedom from the religious performance orientation of the Old Testament. It also means that we can be free to follow Holy Spirit's leading rather than adhering to a bunch of rules and regulations. Nothing is more freeing or more transforming than being led by the Spirit.

Second, we learn the secret to over-coming temptation. From the human perspective, we might think of living a 'holy' life, as NOT doing this and NOT doing that. In other words, it is a sin-focused or temptation-focused life. For someone on a diet, staring at the Black Forest cake doesn't help! Obviously, there are times when we need to "Just say, 'No!'" but the secret to overcoming temptation is to focus our attention on the Holy Spirit and to follow His leading. If our gaze is constantly on God and our relationship with Him, the things of this world and the temptations we face lose their power.

Why is that? Because, like someone using a microscope, you can only focus on one thing at a time. How many of us, as budding junior high students, fiddled in frustration with the classroom microscopes? What you saw depended on how you adjusted the microscope. Turning the knob on the side of the scope adjusted the depth of field. Sometimes you could see something clearly; adjust the knob and something else would come into focus, and what you were looking at changed. Sometimes – too often – everything was just blurry!

Life is like that; if we move away from the Holy Spirit, our focus changes toward the sins and temptations of the world. Move closer to God's Spirit by immediate obedience, and a new focus captures our attention. How do we avoid temptation? Simply by focusing on the Holy Spirit and walking in obedience to Him (See Galatians 5:16).

Really? Can it be that simple? Absolutely! Wouldn't that be boring? Always denying yourself and never getting to do what you felt like doing? Ask any Spirit-filled, Spirit-led believer and they'll tell you just the opposite! It is the most satisfying, exciting way to live!

The third thing we need to learn is simply this: We can identify how we're living or the source of our behaviour, simply by looking at the fruit that is exhibited in the reality of our lives. We can identify the tree by the fruit it produces. If you see an apple on a tree, you know it's an apple tree; it isn't an orange tree. Our flesh produces a variety of 'fruit,' and our spirit produces different kinds. So, we read, "The works of the flesh are…" This is followed by a whole list of what the flesh produces; things like envy, burning anger, divisions, etc., etc. Whenever you see these things, you know that the flesh is behind them.

A few years ago, I was teaching this passage at a men's retreat for our church and had been contrasting the fruit of the Spirit to the works for the flesh. Talking about the works of the flesh and sniffing loudly a couple of times, I said, "Smells like flesh to me!" It was hilarious! Anytime some guy did something that was on the first list, another would sniff loudly and proclaim, "Smells like flesh to me!" That went on for the rest of the retreat; in fact, you'd still hear it on occasion years later. My point is this; we need to be aware of how we're operating; in the flesh or in the spirit!

Alternatively, we also have a list of the wonderful characteristics that the spirit produces in us: love, joy, peace, patience, kindness, goodness, faithfulness, gentleness, self-control. Whenever we see one or more of these qualities in our lives, we can assume that it is because we are being led and empowered by Holy Spirit. In broad daylight, the flame of a single candle might not seem like much; but, in the deepest darkness of a cave, it is the source of great perspective and comfort. In the same way, all of these positive attributes shine brightest when produced during a time when darkness is all around.

I believe that the actual proof of the Spirit's presence and work in our lives is found in these attributes, called the 'fruit of the Spirit' in this passage. In some circles, the gift of tongues (the ability to speak in naturally unlearned human or angelic languages) is interpreted as the 'proof' or 'the sign' of having the Holy Spirit. Unfortunately, we have all known of someone who exhibits the gifts of the Spirit but not the fruit of the Spirit. In other words, they have gifts and abilities but not the maturity of character to sustain their work. They remind us of the people to whom Paul referred in 1 Corinthians 13. They do all kinds of 'ministry' but do not have love (the first in the list of the fruit of the Spirit). The more a person demonstrates the fruit of the Spirit, the greater their ministry can be.

Fourthly, we need to learn the truth behind how Paul summed up this discussion: *"If we live by the Spirit, let us also walk by the Spirit."* (V.25 NASB). If we have been made alive through the Spirit of God (If we have accepted Christ and been born-again) then we ought to 'walk' by the Spirit. In other words, it is our responsibility to listen for His direction and to be obedient to how He is leading us.

What should we do when we see the fruit or works of the flesh in our lives? That's where our free-will comes into play. I've learned a variety of things over the years, and one of those lessons is simply this: When I see myself producing the fruit of the flesh, it's a reality check. For example, if I'm in a snit about something – all worked up and 'pitching a fit' as they say in the southern U.S., I realize that, "I'm operating in the flesh right now." At that point, I have the opportunity to repent – to change my thinking and my behaviour – and to say a quick prayer. Usually, my prayer goes something like this:

"Father, I confess that I'm operating in the flesh right now. That's not what either of us wants. As an act of my will I choose to move into operating in the Spirit. Please bring my emotions and my behaviour into line with the Spirit. Help me to walk in the Spirit." With that, something amazing seems to automatically take place. All my angst dissipates, and I seem to have a whole new attitude about my situation. Is it really that simple? Does it really work? Sure does! That's being transformed in the reality of our every-day lives!

> **SOMETHING TO THINK ABOUT...**
>
> 1. On a human level, what should we do when we make someone else sad? How might you apply that to your relationship with Holy Spirit?
>
> 2. Have you experienced a season when the "Holy Spirit's fire" seems to have been quenched or put out in your life? What might you need to do about that?
>
> 3. Review your life recently. What do you find; the work of the flesh or the fruit of the Spirit? What might you need to change?
>
> 4. Are you better known for your gifts or for the fruit of the Spirit in your life?
>
> 5. Are you good at playing "Follow the Leader" with Holy Spirit?
>
> **SOMETHING TO DO...**
>
> Ask Father God to fill you with His Holy Spirit. You might confess any sin that comes to mind and then pray something like this: "Father God, I want everything You have for me, as long as it is really You. According to Your Word, I ask You to fill me afresh with Your Spirit; I trust You and yield to You now. Thank You for Your gift of the Holy Spirit." Wait and see what happens.

CHAPTER 10

NO MAN IS AN ISLAND
(A band of brothers...)

1 Corinthians 12:27 "All of you together are Christ's body, and each of you is a part of it."

John Donne was a famous poet and a cleric in the Church of England who lived in the late 1500's and early 1600's. He has become well-known for his poems and what we might call 'deep thoughts.' Probably the most famous of these is his 'Meditation 13' in "Devotions upon Emergent Occasions." Perhaps that could be translated, "Thoughts on Current Events." Nonetheless, two phrases, "No man is an island," and "...for whom the bell tolls..." are the best known. Here is the writing in its complete and more modern form:

'No Man is an Island'

> "No man is an island entire of itself; every man is a piece of the continent, a part of the main; if a clod be washed away by the sea, Europe is the less, as well as if a promontory were, as well as any manner of thy friends or of thine own were; any man's death diminishes me, because I am involved in mankind. And therefore, never send to know for whom the bell tolls; it tolls for thee."[1]

That sounds more than just a bit depressing, but it holds an important truth. We need each other. This is never more apparent than in the Christian church. Spiritually speaking, it is true that no man is an island.

Yes, each of us will stand alone before the judgment seat of Christ; and, one by one, we will give an account for what we have done during our earthly life-time. We primarily find this teaching in two New Testament passages. Romans 14:10 says, *"So why do you condemn another believer? Why do you look down on another believer? Remember, we will all stand before the judgment seat of God;"* and 2 Corinthians 5:10 reads, *"For we must all stand before Christ to be judged. We will each receive whatever we deserve for the good or evil we have done in this earthly body."*

In these passages, Paul is teaching that we, individually, will answer to God for how we have lived our lives. As the wonderful, old hymn rightly proclaims, "Jesus paid it all; all to Him I owe…"[2] He has fully paid the debt of our sin, and we will never be expected to re-pay that penalty. At the same time, Paul reminds the early Believers, as well as us, that we should not busy ourselves with worrying about how others are doing in their service but look to ourselves.

Nevertheless, we are, at the same time, very inter-connected. As Donne said, "No man is an island." Not only do we individually need the others in our local congregations, but the others also need us. In long passages in the books of Romans and 1 Corinthians, Paul used an extended metaphor to illustrate the inter-connectedness of God's children. That word picture is presented as a human body. Each of us is like a particular part of the body, and the body needs every part in order to be healthy and whole. Granted, we cut our hair and clip our toenails, tossing away the trimmings without thought; but both hair and toenails have a specific function in the body.

In the same way, each believer plays a unique and important role in the life and health of the church. Should some part be removed, whether through some accident or intentionally by surgery, the whole body both suffers and is diminished. A person missing his or her right arm does not have the same capacity as someone who has both arms. Someone might be able to live after his or her stomach has been removed – but life is just not the same. The entire system is weakened, and adjustments in life-style will be required just to maintain a somewhat diminished life.

CHAPTER 10 - NO MAN IS AN ISLAND

In 1 Corinthians 12, Paul was addressing one or two particular problems that he identified in the early church. It is no secret that we're all different; we come with different strengths, personalities, gifts (Holy Spirit generated abilities), talents, and callings. Each of us sees the world differently because of who we are and what we've experienced. We're a pretty random bunch, to say the least. At the same time, God expects us to be unified – to enjoy unity or oneness – without uniformity. He made us different; He expects us to see things differently; and He has given us unique abilities. God does not make 'cookie-cutter' Christians, with everyone looking and behaving exactly the same. This situation provides an opportunity for two problems to arise. In our human frailty, we drift in our thinking toward the snare of comparison, especially on the natural level; and it is this that gives rise to two extremes.

The first could be recognized as pride. While this form of pride may parade itself with the appearance or an air of superiority, any haughty attitude is actually rooted in insecurity. We've all know those individuals who seem to be naturally 'blessed.' They enjoy great looks, heightened intellect, amazing ability, awesome spiritual gifts, and incredible influence. They're the 'winners,' or the 'movers and shakers' in the church and in the world. Like mythological Midas, everything they touch turns to gold. They've been born with the proverbial 'silver spoon' in their mouth. Voted most likely to succeed in High School, they go on to enjoy great success and to command respect and influence. They've never known either the physical pain of a cavity or the public embarrassment of a zit, and every hair automatically falls into place.

In the church, they publicly exhibit amazing spiritual gifts and talents. They sing exquisitely. They can preach up a storm as well as prophesy publically and have no trouble bringing a word in the spiritual gift of tongues. Seemingly without effort, they rise to positions of influence and office. They are the 'winners!'

From the lofty and exalted place attributed to them on the corporate ladder, they may be tempted to look down on the mere mortals who also populate their local assembly. If they do succumb to such pride, Paul typifies their reaction in the erroneous words, *"I don't need you..."* (1 Corinthians 12:21).

In stark and somewhat painful contrast, most of us identify with the 'others' who seem to be 'less blessed.' We don't quite measure up on one or more levels. We may not have been born into the same economic stratus. Some of us had to take the bus to school rather than drive the new sports car we didn't receive for our sixteenth birthday. We may not be actually ugly, but we're not cut from the same bolt of cloth as our 'superiors,' to say the least. Rather than capturing attention as the quarterback, we serve in obscurity as the water-boy. In band, we get stuck with the clarinet, rather than the trumpet.

In church, our gifts may be among the less exciting. Nobody prays for the gift of helps. Probably even fewer look forward to the gift of giving. We may only long for the recognition and admiration that the silver-tongued orators and ruby-throated song-birds command. The gift of administration, while absolutely necessary to turn great vision from mere fantasy into reality, doesn't seem to be as highly esteemed as it might be. Unlike their counter-parts with the 'greater gifts,' these folks shy away from "I don't need you," only to profess the other extreme, "You don't need me!"

Such thinking – in either direction – is un-biblical to say the least. Paul makes this clear in 1 Corinthians 12:12-26.

"The human body has many parts, but the many parts make up one whole body. So it is with the body of Christ. Some of us are Jews, some are Gentiles, some are slaves, and some are free. But we have all been baptized into one body by one Spirit, and we all share the same Spirit.

Yes, the body has many different parts, not just one part. If the foot says, 'I am not a part of the body because I am not a hand,' that does not make it any less a part of the body. And if the ear says, 'I am not part of the body because I am not an eye,' would that make it any less a part of the body? If the whole body were an eye, how would you hear? Or if your whole body were an ear, how would you smell anything? But our bodies have many parts, and God has put each part just where He wants it. How strange a body would be if it had only one part! Yes, there are many parts, but only one body. The eye can never say to the hand, 'I don't need you.' The head can't say to the feet, 'I don't need you.' In fact, some parts of the body that seem weakest and least important are actually the most necessary. And the parts we regard as less honorable are those we clothe with the greatest care. So we carefully protect those parts that should not be seen, while the more honorable parts do not require this special care. So God has put the body together such that extra honor and care are given to those parts that have less dignity. This makes for harmony among the members, so that all the members care for each other. If one part suffers, all the parts suffer with it, and if one part is honored, all the parts are glad."

As we can clearly see, each believer plays a significant role in the life of the church. This makes it all the sadder when some believers opt out of the body and quit attending church or fellowshipping with other believers altogether. Others seem to feel at liberty to just pack up and move to another church, should they be offended by someone or something where they have been attending.

Granted, it is important to find a local assembly that nourishes you spiritually and socially, where you are in theological agreement with the rest of the body, and where there is a place of service for you. Should it be that a person finds himself in a position where that is not the case, it would probably be best to relocate to a church that is better suited for him.

Unfortunately, though, people tend to take their hurt feelings and personal preferences more seriously than their need to give and receive ministry. Someone or something makes them angry, so they pack up the family and run off to find a different venue. (Sounds a lot like our current cultural situation regarding divorce!) They go 'church-hopping' and look over the selection, picking and choosing as if they were filling their plates at a smorgasbord. In our small city, there are over 68 different churches of the evangelical ilk to choose from. So, if I'm 'disenchanted' with where I am now, I still have lots of options.

The sad reality is that people come and people go. Granted, some may actually be led by the Spirit to relocate; but probably the majority of transfers are the result of consumer orientation or a fleshly, knee-jerk response to some unpleasing situation. We've heard the horror-stories of churches that split over such critical issues as aluminum offering plates verses wooden ones! Shame on us!

When people leave, it creates a spiritual vacuum because the body has just been diminished. Those who are left behind are now deprived of the gifts and contributions of the newly departed. If a person's recent exodus from one local assembly 'makes no difference' (We don't need you!) that should tell us something: The person wasn't using his or her gifts for the benefit of the body! We're ALL supposed to make a difference. If we aren't, something is wrong.

One of the battles that the North American church continually faces is what we call "consumer mentality." In other words, people attend church for what it can do for them. They come to get. When they don't get whatever it is that they want or expect, they go shopping for another church and take their participation and money elsewhere. While consumerism is a spirit of the age, particularly in the West, I believe that it is also a by-product of faulty evangelism. People are encouraged to come to Jesus for what He will do for them, for how it will help their lives be better, and for a fire-escape from Hell. But how often do we hear an evangelist exhort his or her audience to come to Christ simply because He is God; and, as such, He is worthy of our undying love and allegiance? People conveniently forget the fact that their sin is an affront to a holy and righteous God who, not only pronounced them guilty, but is willing to pay the penalty for their sin. We hear too little of that kind of commitment to the cause of Christ or to the Kingdom of Heaven.

CHAPTER 10 - NO MAN IS AN ISLAND

It always amazes me when I hear of the brave men and women who volunteered to go off to fight in some war. Why would they do that? Why place themselves in mortal danger for the sake of some strangers living half a world away? What was there in their character that would motivate such a self-less move? We might call it 'altruism' – doing something just because it is the right thing to do. It might be a sense of compassion for those suffering at the hands of evil and greedy aggressors. Maybe it was more of a 'do unto others before they do unto you,' kind of thing. We don't really know what it was, but I'm pretty sure it wasn't a consumer mentality, or a "What can I get out of this?" line of thinking.

In some circles, people are urged to "give their lives to Jesus" or to make Him "Lord of their lives." Paul certainly would agree; listen to his words in Romans 12:1,2: *"And so, dear brothers and sisters, I plead with you to give your bodies to God because of all He has done for you. Let them be a living and holy sacrifice—the kind He will find acceptable. This is truly the way to worship Him. Don't copy the behavior and customs of this world, but let God transform you into a new person by changing the way you think. Then you will learn to know God's will for you, which is good and pleasing and perfect."*

Because God has been and continues to be so gracious towards us, there is only one 'acceptable' response; and that is to give ourselves – our very bodies and everything associated with them to Him. Total surrender is what God's grace calls for. If I were to give you something – anything – a new car, a dog, a sandwich, whatever; once I gave it to you and you accepted it, that thing would be completely yours. I would have no more legal claim on it; I had surrendered ownership to you. As the owner, you could do whatever you wanted to the thing I gave you; and, in reality, I'd have nothing to say about how you treated it.

But, when it comes to surrendering our lives or giving our bodies and everything else to God, we believe that we, somehow, still maintain some right by which we are entitled to tell the New Owner what

He should to with it. I remember hearing the man who was once my boss, Steve Chua, say, "Christ did not die to pamper your flesh; He came to kill it!" Ouch! He was speaking of the ungodly parts of our personality, not our physical bodies, of course. Sadly, we have some misconception that our lives should be a bowl of cherries if we follow Christ and live for Him. So many of what we call testimonies center around the same theme, "I came to Jesus, and now everything is wonderful."

If we were to actually adopt a completely different stance, "Take me as I am, Jesus; I'm yours. Do with me, with my time, my talent, my resources, my future, whatever You want…," how different our inner and corporate lives would be! What if the churches were filled with people determined to contribute, to sacrifice from their time, talent, and resources for the sake of the Kingdom and the Bride of Christ, the Church? What if every believer pulled his weight by whole-heartedly throwing himself into just one area of ministry? What could be accomplished for the Kingdom?

At our church, we're aiming to see every believer involved in one weekly worship service, one fellowship group where he or she could be spiritually fed and cared for communally, and one area of service where they are blessing others by what they do for Christ. Would that be too much to ask? The individual and corporate spiritual growth and that of our community impact would be staggering!

No wonder no man is an island. If each of us were an island, living out our faith in isolation, whom would we serve? Perhaps one of the greatest tests of our devotion to Christ is not so much what we do for Him, but what we do for others. The whole story of the sheep and the goats (See Matthew 25 31-46), indicates that what we do to our fellow men, we do to Christ.

Going back to the whole area of spiritual gifts for a minute, let's reconsider why God gives them to us and why we have them. There is really only one reason – to build up the body of Christ. They're not here for us. We don't have them to get "warm fuzzies" or experience supernatural entertainments, but to cause the body of Christ to grow. Ephesians 4 explains how God has given gifted individuals to the church so they could train ALL believers to do the work of the ministry. Listen to what Verses 15 and 16 have to say: *"Instead, we will speak the truth in love, growing in every way more and more like Christ, who is the head of His body, the church. He makes the whole body fit together perfectly. As each part does its own special work, it helps the other parts grow, so that the whole body is healthy and growing and full of love."*

Individual and corporate maturity requires the proper working together of EACH PART. Without that, very few of us actually come to the place of maturity. So, let me ask you, "How spiritually mature or healthy can you be if 75 or 80% of your local church body is doing little or nothing?"

Let's just consider our spiritual gifts for a moment. In the New Testament, spiritual gifts are actually called 'graces' – abilities that are supernaturally given to us in order to do a spiritual work. For example, a person may be a very good teacher; teaching just comes naturally to him or her. Professionally, they've taught Grade 2 for years. They have the ability to teach. But when the Holy Spirit produces a supernatural, unlearned ability to teach spiritual truths, we've moved from the natural ability to teach to the supernatural gift of teaching.

In Scripture, there are at least 4 passages that enumerate the various gifts of the Spirit. These are Romans 12, 1 Corinthians 12–14, Ephesians 4, and 1 Peter 4. None of these are complete lists; the lists they provide vary in number and nomenclature. We are not even told if, added all together, they would create an exhaustive list of the gifts of the Spirit. Here is what has been listed: prophecy, serving, teaching, encouraging, giving, leading, showing kindness, … ability to give wise advice, messages of special knowledge, great faith, gifts of healing, power to perform miracles (events outside the realm of natural laws), ability to prophesy, ability to discern spirits, ability to speak in unknown languages (tongues), ability to interpret (tongues), apostles, prophets, teachers, miracles, gifts of healings, helping, leadership, speaking in unknown languages (unlearned human languages and/or the language of Heaven and the angels), interpretation… apostles (those called to plant churches and continue to have authority in the churches), prophets, evangelists, pastors and teachers… speaking and helping.

We occasionally hear people speak of the gift of discernment – the ability to distinguish what is right and true from that which is false and evil. Hebrews 5:14 says, *"Solid food is for those who are mature, who through training have the skill to recognize the difference between right and wrong."* This verse suggests to us that some things, like the use of spiritual gifts, can take training and practice. We know that in the Old Testament there were "Schools of the Prophets," where people could get training and opportunities to practise hearing God for themselves and others, so that they could deliver the words and message of God to the people. It took practice!

In the same way, we need to practise and exercise our spiritual gifts if they are to be used easily and effectively. I remember starting out and taking very tenuous baby-steps, when exercising my gift of prophecy. Boy, was I nervous! As time went on, I began to be more confident, not in myself, but in God's ability to speak to me – often through mental pictures – about what He wanted to communicate to an individual or group of people. While doing so can still be a bit stressful, it is fun! And powerful! I especially love it when people respond, "How did you know?" My only answer, "God told me," tends to freak them out!

All of these gifts have been given by God for one or two specific purposes. Listen to the revelation in 1 Corinthians 12:4-7 *"There are different kinds of spiritual gifts, but the same Spirit is the source of them all. There are different kinds of service, but we serve the same Lord. God works in different ways, but it is the same God who does the work in all of us. A spiritual gift is given to each of us **so we can help each other.**"* (Emphasis mine.) Other translations express it this

CHAPTER 10 - NO MAN IS AN ISLAND

way: *"for the common good."* In other words, gifts are to generally strengthen the whole church, although individuals may be blessed in the process. The word 'gift' in Verse 7 is 'manifestation' and is like a 'revelation.' It is what happens when something that was unseen or unrecognized suddenly becomes visible and known. We can 'see' or experience the Holy Spirit at work as the gifts He produces in our lives are operative in the church. The purpose for such a manifestation is for the building up of the church spiritually. 1 Corinthians 14:12 instructs, *"Since you are so eager to have the special abilities the Spirit gives, seek those that will strengthen the whole church."* Herein is our motivation; to build up the church and make it spiritually stronger and more mature.

Verse 3 of the same chapter speaks of the gift of prophecy and identifies the three by-products of New Testament prophecy: "strengthening," (building up, edification), "encouragement", (exhortation, calling people forward to godly action and life-style), and "comfort," (consolation when needed). If a supposedly prophetic word does not accomplish or work toward at least one of these three, it probably is not an authentic word. i.e. If a 'word' only leaves the audience feeling rejected and condemned, it is likely not a true 'word' or it was delivered in a wrong way.

The one exception to this 'common good' rule is a comment made about the use of the gift of tongues. In 1 Corinthians 14:4, Paul said, *"A person who speaks in tongues is strengthened personally, but one who speaks a word of prophecy strengthens the entire church."* When I attended a seminary where they taught that the supernatural gifts were no longer operative in the church today, I was informed that it was a bad thing to edify yourself – that prophesying (to them, that meant preaching the Bible.) for the church would build up the church – and that was a good thing. But if you spoke in a tongue (unknown language) you were edifying yourself. That was interpreted as 'blowing your own horn,' or 'puffing yourself up,' or 'putting on a show to make yourself look important by impressing everyone with your gift.' Indeed, God does not give us gifts so we can put on a show or to pander to our flesh.

The problem with such an interpretation is that both situations – building up the church and building up yourself use the exact same word. In the first line, edification is seen as a good thing, but a few words later, in the second line, it is deemed to be an evil thing. I believe that both references refer to good things; I certainly need all the edification I can get! I would say though, that one's personal edification should take a back seat to the edification of the group and should not inhibit the growth of the larger congregation. To prevent that type of situation, Paul gave some pretty specific rules for how the church should operate in a public meeting. As 1 Corinthians 14:40 says, *"But be sure that everything is done properly and in order."*

I believe that there are two major factors that will help an individual or a local church to grow spiritually and to ensure that things unfold in a beneficial way; coaching and accountability.

We're pretty used to the idea of having a coach, particularly on the sports field or in the arena. In such settings, it is not at all unusual to find one or more sportsmen or players wilfully submitting to and following the instructions of the coach. Coaches are usually older athletes with more experience and greater expertise. That pretty much goes without saying; nobody asks someone with lesser ability to tell or show them how to play a game. Coaches are, more or less, experts in their field. It might be boxing, hockey, track and field, or any number of athletic competitions. Not only are coaches experts in their sport, they coach the sport in which they're experts. When was the last time you saw an expert hockey player coaching volleyball? It just doesn't happen.

When it comes to athletics, there is no shame and very little hesitation to realize that, "I could get better at this, if I had someone to show me how to improve my game."

CHAPTER 10 - NO MAN IS AN ISLAND

One other thing about coaches; they expect to be obeyed! Rightly so! And the person in training also expects to obey, even when it hurts, even when they feel like they can't do another lap or one more rep. But the coach is encouraging them to keep going, and so they do.

A current cultural phenomenon is the idea of a Life Coach. Entire organizations have been established to standardize and legitimize the whole concept and practice of life-coaching. When it comes to selecting and engaging a life coach, you're looking for someone with more life-experience and greater insight and wisdom than what you have. No one hires a recognizable fool to coach them through life! While life-coaching is considerably less directive than coaching hockey, the goal is pretty much the same; to help the recipient become more skilled at, and more successful in, life. People engage life-coaches, not to be told what to do, but so the coach can help them think through for themselves what the best way forward might be. People pay big bucks for this kind of help.

Oddly though, we seem to shy away from getting the same kind of help when it comes to spiritual matters. Many have adopted an, "I can do this on my own," mentality. Others seem to content themselves with the line from the old chorus, "It's just Jesus and me!" The reality is that we need help – all of us do – if we are going to grow and mature in the Christian life. We may need someone other than the Holy Spirit to help us find our way and to internalize Biblical principles to the point that they become part of who we are. In the Church, we call this kind of life-coaching, mentoring, although that term is used elsewhere, too. We might even recognize it as discipleship.

Perhaps no one has stepped forward to make themselves available to coach because of the time, energy, and personal commitment it might take. Maybe no one has ever suggested that we get someone to walk with us in our spiritual journey. It might be that we just don't want anyone to know about all our spiritual 'junk,' or the reality of our personal lives. So, we struggle along, doing our best to see what works and what doesn't. It's almost like expecting a newborn baby to have sprung from the womb, already self-sufficient and capable of looking after itself. If that scenario were played out in the natural realm, most infants would not live long enough to see their first birthday.

We have to wonder how many baby Christians didn't last in their commitment to Christ because no one walked with them in the early days of their faith. I've met people who sadly said, "I tried that Christianity thing, but it didn't work for me." I am pretty sure that it wasn't so much that Christianity didn't work, but that no one coached them to the place where they realized that it does. So sad!

Over the last number of years, it has been my joy to be somewhat associated with a great church in Mbarara, Uganda. King of Kings Church has had phenomenal growth right since its inception. By 2016, they'd started over 120 daughter churches all through western Uganda and into South Sudan, the Congo, Rwanda, and Burundi. King of Kings is my church home away from home.

One Sunday morning while we were there, an invitation was given to anyone who wanted to receive Christ as their Lord and Saviour. (This was before the message, even though we all know that preaching MUST come before the invitation!) In any case, five people came forward and prayed to received Christ – out loud and in front of everyone. That was wonderful but not what amazed me. One by one, they were asked their name and where they came from. If one of the converts said that he was from the town of Masaka, the pastor would call out, "Who from our King of Kings family is from Masaka?" Immediately, someone would shout out, wave, and come down to the front. They'd run over, give the new believer a big hug and take them back to sit with them. I thought that this was a pretty neat reception and a great way to welcome someone into the Family of God. Then the pastor explained to me that the K of K's member had just taken on the responsibility to mentor the new believer in order to see them grounded in Christ and to disciple them into a solid understanding

CHAPTER 10 - NO MAN IS AN ISLAND

and practice of the faith. What a great idea! Immediately, each new Christian had a coach to show them how to live as a believer.

Such a relationship requires transparency and a willingness to learn. That implies another whole concept of... Wait! Wait! Are you ready for it? That other word – the one that's not so popular? Accountability! "Gasp!"

As was mentioned earlier, some people resist accountability; they want to do their own thing and balk at the idea of accountability. The Bible describes a culture where such an attitude prevailed by saying, "... *all the people did whatever seemed right in their own eyes*" (Judges 17:6 & 21:25). The start of both of those verses says that in those days, there was no king in Israel. Where there is no authority, people are not just free to do what is right in their own eyes, they're DOOMED to do so. In every way, we need God-ordained authorities in our lives to help us live lives that are worthy of our calling to faith and Christ-likeness.

But those who resist and resent authority wilfully choose to do whatever they might want. "Accountability" is regarded as rights-depriving oppression. While there is no doubt that many in authority have used their power to abuse those under them, both authority and accountability can be helpful and productive tools when used properly.

Before we leave the topic of spiritual mentors, let me encourage you; find one! Become one! Allow a more mature believer to school you into maturity. At the same time, begin to pour your life into a younger Christian. Allow someone to walk with you and be prepared to walk with another. In the Bible, Barnabas encouraged Paul; and Paul helped to train Timothy. Find someone you can respect and look up to spiritually; ask them to help shape your life. Then pass that blessing on as you come along side someone younger in the faith. Doing so will bring you some of the most rewarding experiences of your life!

Just as with a sports coach who might say, "Don't lower your left shoulder when you swing the bat," or "Keep pointing your toes," or "Pass the puck to…," we need spiritual mentors who will show us, not just tell us, what to do and how to do it. We also need to be held accountable and to follow-through obediently.

Sadly, finding a good spiritual mentor is not always easy; and, unfortunately, many churches are gun-shy when it comes to accountability. They tolerate this 'Do whatever is right in your own eyes,' thing and do not hold their people accountable for how they live. You might well imagine the backlash if a church board dared to confront sin in the lives of their members and adherents! "How dare you try to tell me what I can and cannot do! That's not very tolerant; that's not loving; that's not gracious!"

Speaking of 'grace,' there seems to be a lack of balance when it comes to a Biblical understanding of what grace really is. At its very core, God's grace can be easily understood in these terms: "God's grace gives us the good things we haven't earned and don't deserve." In contrast, God's mercy is understood when God does not give us the bad things we do deserve." His mercy covers a multitude of our sins. It is available because one of the reasons Jesus died was to pay the penalty for sin – He took all the bad things we deserve for us. God's grace, like His mercy, comes from God's heart of unfailing love. Because He loves us, He shows us favour and gives us good gifts.

A poor understanding of grace has partly been the by-product of the, 'Everyone should get to do what's right in his own eyes,' philosophy; and partly it is due to soft-sell evangelism that proclaims, "Come to Jesus for what He will do for you," rather than, "Come and acknowledge a Holy God and allow Him to save you from your sin." "Come and get," has replaced, "Come and give," (your life to Jesus). But any 'gospel' that does not include repentance for sin and a desire to life a godly life in thankfulness for God's forgiveness and grace, is flawed at best! It pretends to cancel out our need for both grace and mercy.

CHAPTER 10 – NO MAN IS AN ISLAND

Even in the church, we may fall prey to false ideas about grace. We hear that God's grace only says, *"Neither do I condemn you,"* a partial quote of what Jesus said to a woman who'd been caught in the very act of adultery. In reality, He also said, *"Go and sin no more"* (See John 8:1-11). True grace always calls for a response by the believer who, while saved by grace and the cross of Christ alone, makes his calling and election sure by cooperating with God's plan to transform him or her into the image of Christ. Nowhere in Scripture so we find, "Come to Me and keep living like the Devil!" or "Come to Me and do whatever you want; I'll be fine with that." Somehow, we've developed the misunderstanding that 'grace' lacks discernment and holds no one accountable. Anyone who says, "I can treat you any way I want; and you have to be gracious and forgive me, even though I still intend to do it again," is spiritually and emotionally abusive. While it is true that God is love and that His grace is abundant, we cannot fall into the trap of believing that it is also blind. Sin, whether in those in the world or in the Church, is still an affront to God's holiness.

Such a view of 'grace' is inadequate, to say the least. Jesus DID say, *"Go and sin no more,"* calling the woman to a more godly life-style. Titus 2:11,12 says this, *"For the grace of God has been revealed, bringing salvation to all people. And we are instructed to turn from godless living and sinful pleasures. We should live in this evil world with wisdom, righteousness, and devotion to God."* Jesus' invitation, *"Come, follow Me,"* anticipates that the follower will become like Jesus and adopt a life-style that pleased Him. Any grace that does not is not true grace!

Matthew 18 also addresses the issue of grace and forgiveness. There, grace does not turn a blind eye to the transgressions and offences of others; it confronts them and calls the person forward to repentance and better behaviour. It does not teach us to just love and forgive one another and then ignore on-going mistreatment and sin.

By the way, in case you haven't already figured it out, let me give you some shocking news: Christians will fail you; they'll disappoint and hurt you. Sometimes, they can be downright rotten. God may be wonderful; but, on occasion, His kids can be absolutely bratty! You might as well get used to the idea.

Why is that? Because we're all still somewhere in the process of being conformed into the image of Christ – we're still not like Him – we should be, but we're not. Our transformation process is not yet complete. That's not an excuse; it's reality. We should be better than we are; we should be more loving, more holy, and more wise, but we're not. We should constantly be filled with Holy Spirit, but we're not. We should always obey His commands, but we do not. That's why we still need God's grace, not only from God, but also from and for each other. The transformation process is not yet complete.

Back to Matthew 18; the passage about confronting someone who has offended you. (Not just in your mind, but actually did something wrong against you). Once the person has been confronted privately (How ungracious, to point out someone's sin!) and then, of necessity, in front of witnesses (How embarrassing! Think of their feelings!), if they still do not repent – change their behaviour – they should be treated as an unbeliever and a tax collector. Unbelievers and tax collectors had no place in the early church. Usually, only true followers of Jesus were identified with, and regarded as part of, the first-century church. It was just too costly and dangerous for uncommitted believers or the unconverted to do so; persecution of the early church made sure of that! We know that some unbelievers would visit the meetings, but they weren't considered part of the church.

So how do we move forward in balance? We cannot afford a wishy-washy, gutless grace that says, "I'll forgive you regardless of how you keep treating me." To do so ignores the accountability that only true discipleship can provide. We're not called to turn a blind eye to our own sin or to that of another believer. By the way, granting forgiveness does not preclude accountability or correction. While it is true that Jesus told Peter that he was to forgive seventy times seven (490) times, Christ does not expect us to repeatedly expose ourselves to abuse or other destructive attacks. As my African friends so appreciate, you don't have to stick your left hand into a lion's mouth to prove to him that you've forgiven him for chewing off your right hand. Ignoring sin is dangerous, both to the offender and to their victims.

Nor can we to go the other extreme; self-righteously and legalistically condemning anyone and anything that doesn't meet our personal standards of righteousness. So what's the balance?

Jesus had it right! He said, *"Neither do I condemn you,"* (That's forgiveness!) AND, *"Go and sin no more!"* (That's correction!). Ephesians 4:15 puts it this way, *"Instead, we will speak the truth in love, growing in every way more and more like Christ, who is the head of His body, the church..."* Grace speaks in love when it speaks the truth and when it encourages us all to move on to maturity in Christ. It doesn't speak in love if it just criticizes, condemns and abandons. After all, "God loves us just the way we are and too much to let us stay that way."

I am reminded of a story – again one whose origin I do not know – about a sculptor who had carved a great statue. I forget what the statue portrayed, so let's just say it was a bear. The sculptor was asked how he knew what to do to create such a beautiful masterpiece. His reply went something like this, "I start with a block of stone, and then I take away everything that doesn't look like a bear."

Perhaps that's a good illustration of the discipleship process. A "disciple" (student) was one who was called to walk with a "Master" (teacher), to learn from Him, become like Him, and do all that the Master could do and then some. It's that transformative process to which every believer is called.

That's another reason why Christians cannot be 'an island.' We need each other to help us grow and to correct us when we go astray. Islands do not do well in the discipleship process; they have no one to help and no one to encourage them to remove anything that doesn't look like the Master. Lone wolf soldiers hardly ever win the war. But happy is the man who has such friends!

SOMETHING TO THINK ABOUT...

1. Can you identify your spiritual gifts? If so, what are they? If you can't, who could you ask to help you with that task?

2. Are you regularly participating in

    - a worship service?
    - a home/life/cell group where you are receiving teaching, encouragement and support?
    - An act of serving, teaching, or encouraging others?

3. Can you think of someone who has been a positive, spiritual influence in your life? Someone who has helped you become mature in your faith? If so, thank God for that person. If not, ask God to send someone to you who will be that kind of an influence in your life.

4. Is there anyone who you are intentionally and regularly helping to grow in his or her faith?

5. Are you open to be confronted or corrected? Or do you become defensive? Do you subscribe to the 'Everyone does what's right in his own eyes,' philosophy?

SOMETHING TO DO...

If you don't currently have a mentor – someone who regularly helps you grow in your faith, ask God to show you who that person might be. If you aren't helping someone else mature in their faith, ask God to show you the person to whom you could become a spiritual Big Brother or Big Sister.

CHAPTER 11

WALKING IN FREEDOM IN THE HERE AND NOW
(On duty)

John 8:36 *"So if the Son sets you free, you are truly free."*

By now you might be wondering, "So what's up with all this talk about discipleship and becoming like Jesus? Won't the whole transformation and discipleship thing really cramp my style? And the church attendance, I mean, come on; I've got better things to do than sit in some meeting on a beautiful Sunday morning. And the money deal; don't even go there! I need every nickel I can get. Is all of this really so important? Isn't it enough to have Jesus as my Saviour and go to Heaven when I die?"

I suppose it might be – if all you want is to get into Heaven to spend eternity with the God you never really got to know here on Earth. He has so much more for us than squeaking into Heaven by the skin of our teeth; and, quite frankly, I want everything He has for me!

Included in all that God has in mind for His children is the wonderful concept of freedom. He wants us to be free – free from sin and its devastating consequences, free from the on-going bondage that sin creates in our lives, and free to follow Him whole-heartedly into the destiny He has for our lives. While it is the Son who sets us free, it is up to us to walk in the freedom He gives to us. That kind of freedom only comes through the process known as 'discipleship.'

Let me suggest five powerful reasons that this whole 'discipleship thing' is important. Briefly, they are:

1. There is something wonderful about living free – free from the lies of the enemy, free from sin, and free from its painful consequences.

2. The Father wants us to have 'abundant life;' and we don't want to miss out on that, do we? We've been given an identity and a destiny. God wants us to experience a powerful, purposeful, and free life. How sad it would be to forfeit that, only to live a pointless life and never being the true you!

3. The rest of the church is relying on you to play your part. It will be permanently diminished if you do not make your own unique contribution.

4. Whether they recognize it or not, the people who do not yet follow Christ are waiting; their destiny and eternal state depends on the church doing her part and on you doing yours.

5. How (not where) you spend Eternity depends on it.

Those are pretty convincing arguments. Let me expand on them for a bit.

The Joy of Freedom:

As we've mentioned previously, Romans 6:16 tells us that we become the slave of the one we obey. The passage does not seem to differentiate between obedience that is a free-will choice and obedience that is the result of duress. The verse reads this way: *"Don't you realize that you become the slave of whatever you choose to obey? You can be a slave to sin, which leads to death, or you can choose to obey God, which leads to righteous living."*

This tells me that everything I do, if it has any moral value attached to it, is an act of obedience, either to Satan or to God ("Sin" vs. "Obedience") and is a demonstration of my loyalty to one kingdom or the other. Choosing to eat Corn Flakes instead of Bran Flakes is not a moral issue; so, we can't really say that we're either serving

God or serving Satan in that case. On the other hand, when there is a moral value to what we do, it will either be an act of obedience to God or to sin – and therefore to Satan.

When it comes to moral issues, we'd like to pretend that there is some kind of neutral ground – a moral 'no man's land, if you will – but, in reality, there is not. All of our thoughts, words, and actions either are in alignment with the Kingdom of Heaven or they're acts of obedience to the Kingdom of Darkness. Each one moves us either into freedom or into bondage.

We may call ourselves "Soldiers in the army of the King of Kings;" but, sometimes, we also participate in treasonous acts against His reign in our lives. In the natural world, treason may be punishable by death. Thankfully, God is a lot more patient than we are! Minimally, sin enslaves us under the tyranny of Satan.

No wonder Jesus taught the disciples to pray, "*May Your Kingdom come soon. May Your will be done on Earth, as it is in Heaven,*" (Matthew 6:10). Too often, we glibly repeat 'The Lord's Prayer' out of rote-level memory, without actually considering what we're supposed to be praying. Those lines actually mean, "God, let Your kingdom come in this World and in my life; and let Your will be done on Earth and in my life as it is in Heaven." It would be hypocritical to pray for God's will to be done in all the rest of the world but not in our own lives. How is God's will accomplished in Heaven? Might I suggest that His will is obeyed completely, joyfully and immediately? I can't imagine some angel responding to a command from the Lord by whining, "But I don't feel like it; I don't want to go there; can't I just stay home?" or "Get someone else to do it; I've got plans." Not a chance!

Here's the altruistic principle: "Disobedience to God ALWAYS results in a level of slavery to Satan." On the other hand, obedience to God, even though it might be costly, brings freedom and joy.

When we use our free will, as Adam and Eve did, to obey the enemy, we enslave ourselves, over and over again, to him. That's why the

Bible speaks of us as *"slaves to sin,"* before we came to Christ. Listen to what Romans 6:6 has to say, *"We know that our old sinful selves were crucified with Christ so that sin might lose its power in our lives. We are no longer **slaves to sin**..."*

Thankfully, that's the solution! Christ died (and spiritually, we also died with Him) so that our natural spirit could be redeemed and the accumulation of our sin could be done away with, all for the express purpose that we should no longer be slaves to sin. Christ died to free us from sin. His death freed us from the penalty of sin. Presently, He wants to free us from the power of sin in our lives through the transformation process. Eventually, in eternity, we will finally be freed from the very presence of sin! How wonderful that will be! All of that was provided for at the cross. Sadly, if we don't allow His death to be 'our' death, and if we don't look to Jesus as our Saviour, we are still under the penalty of sin. If we don't choose to live lives that are free, we're still stuck in slavery to the power of sin. Not only that, but we miss out on the joyful experience of walking with Christ and the fulfillment that His will can bring to our lives.

Can you comprehend such a thing? Imagine being a slave; captured, tormented, used by an evil and cruel master, and longing for freedom. Every slave wants to be free, after all. Imagine that someone came and bought you from the evil master, gave you your freedom, and made you a 'Free Man or Woman;' but you just kept living on the evil man's estate, living in fear and doing whatever he told you to do. Wouldn't that be a shame? It would be a waste of the purchase price that was paid, to say the least.

Years ago, when our son, Andrew, was a pre-schooler, we lived in a townhouse that had a very little back yard and an even smaller 'patio.' It was only a few patio stones, perhaps no larger than 2 metres square. He'd ride his little, red and white tricycle around and around in tiny circles. Eventually, we moved to a different townhouse where the back yard was four times as big and the patio was too. We looked out, only to see little Andrew circling around in the same tiny circles that he'd driven over and over and over again at the previous house. He could have gone in much larger circles and enjoyed his new freedom, but he automatically kept doing what he'd always done. It was a waste of the larger potential and robbed him of a greater experience.

In the same way, when Christians just keep living as they always had, not being discipled or changing their life-styles, it is a sad waste. They miss out on the freedom that Christ died to provide. Such freedom doesn't come naturally; young believers must realize that Christ wants them free – free from sin and free from legalistic thinking. Galatians 5:1 says, *"So Christ has truly set us free. Now make sure that you stay free, and don't get tied up again in slavery to the law."* As I said, that freedom doesn't come automatically; we have to fight for it. If we don't know that we need to fight, the battle is pretty much lost already.

Over the years, I've counselled a variety of people who want help with their 'drinking problem.' They are caught in a cycle of social drinking that turned into full-blown benders. Usually, such episodes have resulted in some devastating turn of events involving either family violence, car accidents, or other dealings with the police. In that sense, they've been 'forced' to seek help. These folks come in with one of two mind-sets. The first is that they want enough 'help' to enable them to keep drinking socially but stop getting 'plastered.' To these people the alcohol is still considered a 'friend,' - something that helps them relax, forget about their troubles, or become a more social person.

The other people come with a different mind-set; they intend to stop drinking completely. To them, booze has become an enemy that should have no place in their lives. Sometimes, they come wanting to be 'delivered' from the drinking; often they know that they're in for a difficult battle.

Can you guess which of these groups will experience 'success' and freedom? Obviously, it is the second cohort. This wasn't meant to be a full-blown diatribe against alcohol, but it is an example of how we should view any sin that's in our lives. As long as we think of some sin as a useful tool to help us on our way, we will never be free from its negative influences in our lives. i.e. How many of us have fallen into the trap of using our anger to get our own way? The problem with that is that our anger enslaves those around us to our will. And what does every slave want to be? Free!

On the other hand, if we see any and every sin as a place where Satan rules (and he does; Christ is certainly not the ruler over that area of our lives if sin is there!), chances are that we will take a more aggressive stance and be determined to free ourselves in that area.

I picture it this way: it is like guerilla warfare. The little devils lie in wait, looking for an opportunity to sneak up on us when we aren't looking, only to suddenly attack and take control of that place in our souls. Many men can testify that an innocent glance in the direction of a low neck-line or a high hem can lead to a captivating string of events if they're not on the alert. If we're happy and content to let the enemy rule in that area of our lives, we'll never get free. But if we want to be free, we're going to have to take a firm stand and fight back to win our freedom.

2 Corinthians 10:4,5 sheds some light on the subject: *"We use God's mighty weapons, not worldly weapons, to knock down the strongholds of human reasoning and to destroy false arguments. We destroy every proud obstacle that keeps people from knowing God. We capture their rebellious thoughts and teach them to obey Christ."*

As we can see, most of this battle for freedom takes place in the mind. This verse places the burden of responsibility on us. It says, "We use …we destroy… we capture…" We can't just sit back and assume that God is going to wave a magic wand somewhere up in Heaven and make all our issues go away. While that would be wonderful, it's usually not how it happens.

Paul told his young protégé, Timothy, *"Endure suffering along with me, as a good soldier of Christ Jesus. Soldiers don't get tied up in the affairs of civilian life, for then they cannot please the officer who enlisted them"* (2 Timothy 2:3,4). What happens when a soldier gets 'tied up'? He's caught in a trap and taken prisoner or killed. This verse isn't teaching us to have nothing to do with the every-day matters of life, but to avoid the things that will entangle us and make us captive prisoners. Did you notice the emphasis in Verse 4? The focus is on pleasing the One who enlisted us – Jesus!

Just imagine how wonderful your life could be if you were free – truly free from the habits and the consequences of sin. You'd be free to live without guilt, without shame, without fear of being caught red-handed, without the pain that sin always brings. What if our only focus was to please Jesus? Imagine the sweet fellowship you'd be free to enjoy with Him.

Yes, there would be repercussions, but they'd be worth it! Jesus told His disciples, *"I have told you all this so that you may have peace in Me. Here on Earth you will have many trials and sorrows. But take heart, because I have overcome the world"* (John 16:33). What had Jesus told the disciples? He told them many things as He was preparing these brothers for His departure. Among that long list of 'things,' we find this: *"If the world hates you, remember that it hated Me first. The world would love you as one of its own if you belonged to it, but you are no longer part of the world. I chose you to come out of the world, so it hates you"* (John 15:18,19). Thankfully, that's not the whole story, and Jesus ended the discourse with the fact that He had already overcome – conquered – the world! Yeah! We might lose a battle or two; but, in the end, Jesus' side – our side – wins! That's excellent news!

Living abundantly – rising above our circumstances:

Jesus also said that He came so we could have *"a rich and satisfying life"* (John 10:10). In spite of that, the sad reality is that many Christians have difficult times. Around the world today, believers are often persecuted, even to the point of torture and execution. After all, we've just read John 15! I get that. We're at war with the forces of darkness.

What is usually more subtle, or at least less extreme, is the conflict we find at home or within the church. Now, you'd expect that all these sanctified brothers and sisters in Christ would automatically congeal into one big, happy family. But that's just not the case. If you put a bunch of unhealthy, diseased, and wounded slaves in one room, what's going to happen? They'll infect each other; they'll bump into one another. What happens then? It's like poking an angry bear; the pain and anger come out, and sometimes it gets ugly. The slaves have their scabs torn off; broken limbs re-break, or new wounds are created. Before you know it, a riot has broken out in the church. This is a true embarrassment to the name of Christ; but, too frequently, this kind of thing is reality. Why? Because too many people aren't living in freedom from the power of sin in their lives.

By times, I've been asked to do 'marital counselling' to help bring a new level of peace and harmony into a marriage that is dysfunctional. Often, such counselling comes as a last-ditch effort; and it frequently comes too late in the history of the relationship. People expect me to sit down with the husband and wife and work out the issues between them. While some counsellors might have a technique that 'works' in that situation, I do not. My preference is to work with both parties individually to see each of them healed up to the point where their emotional 'buttons' – their wounds – are healed, and each person is free from the past. Once the buttons are gone, there's nothing left for the other partner to push; and a new level of harmony will come. Even if only one partner seeks help, the marriage will move toward improvement as the individual receives healing and has fewer emotional triggers for their spouse to set off.

Have you ever had a cut on the end of you finger? Sure, you have. Did you notice that, no matter what you were doing, it involved that finger and that every touch meant stinging pain? You could use all the other fingers with no problem, but that one with the cut; Ouch! Eventually, the cut would heal over; and you could go back to healthy function and never think twice about it.

CHAPTER 11 – WALKING IN FREEDOM...

It's the same way with wounded people in the church. As long as their wounds are relatively fresh or are still un-healed, everything causes pain; and pain produces an unpleasant reaction. Why are there 'issues' in the body of Christ? Because people come wounded and, too often, stay wounded. They haven't pursued their freedom successfully. What's really sad is that healing and freedom are available when we bring every thought into captivity and into the obedience to Christ.

Simply going to church doesn't automatically bring freedom. You can't expect to lock a bunch of ungodly people into a room and expect them to come out looking like Jesus. This explains why so many people get upset and run off to a different church and why ugly things known as 'church splits' and family break-ups happen. These are sad but true facts.

Fortunately, our relationship with God is not like that. Our relationship with God never changes according to our behaviour. Salvation is based on the cross – on what Christ did - not on what we did or do. But our fellowship with Him, the sharing of our lives and the freedom that He wants us to enjoy, will be greatly hampered if we choose to continue walking in sin.

Bottom line: Whatever sin we allow in our lives enslaves us to Satan, and whatever supposed benefit we get from it, just isn't worth our freedom. I like the saying, "Sanctification is its own reward." 'Sanctification,' comes from the Latin word, 'sanctus' which means 'holy.' – sinless and whole. Christians are deemed to be holy and righteous because of their position 'in Christ,' but their practical or experiential holiness – how spiritually whole we become and how much we live like Jesus, who was completely free from sin, – grows during the discipleship process. Perhaps the simplest explanation of what 'holy' means is this: Just be like Jesus; be free; be whole.

This is God's intent. Right at the beginning of this book we struck out on the theme that God intends for us to become like Jesus. I love how Romans 8:28, 29a puts it; *"And we know that God causes everything to work together for the good of those who love God and are called according to His purpose for them. For God knew His people in advance, and He chose them to become like His Son..."* Another way to say this verse might go like this, "God is at work in every situation for the good of those who love Him... to conform them into the image of His Son." In other words, in every situation you and I face, God is working on us, in us, and through us, for the express purpose of transforming us to be like Jesus. That's great news! It isn't just up to me to change myself; God is already at work; I just need to cooperate with Him.

Let me add a few more verses, just to drive this theme home; *"Even before He made the world, God loved us and chose us in Christ to be* **holy and without fault** *in His eyes"* (Ephesians 1:4) (Emphasis mine).

1 Peter 1:15,16 adds, *"But now you must be holy in everything you do, just as God who chose you is holy. For the Scriptures say, 'You must be holy because I am holy.'"*

As we can see, this is a cooperative effort. God does his part, and we must do ours. But what does that look like?

First, we need to recognize how completely dependent we need to be on God's Holy Spirit to lead and guide us. After all, He knows all truth and can teach us how to live in light of what is really true. By the way, one definition of wisdom is "knowing how to live in light of what is true." Do we really know what is true? At best, we have our perspective on truth; and we certainly don't know all truth. How can we possibly know how to live in light of the truth that we don't fully comprehend?

That is why we need to surrender our opinions and our desires, and exchange our will for God's. Only God knows all truth completely and accurately, and so we must give up our independence and rely on His leading – even when His ways don't seem to make a lot of sense to us.

Matthew 16:24,25 says, *"Then Jesus said to His disciples, 'If any of you wants to be My follower, you must give up your own way, take up your cross, and follow Me. If you try to hang on to your life, you will lose*

CHAPTER 11 - WALKING IN FREEDOM...

it. But if you give up your life for My sake, you will save it.'" The word that has been translated 'life' in these verses is actually the Greek word, 'pseuche' which means 'soul' and refers to our natural way of doing things – the parts of our personality, (composed of our mind, emotions, and will) that are independent from the Lord. This tells us that, the only way to really live in freedom is to exchange the way we'd do things naturally for the way God does them. It speaks of giving up, or saying, "No!" to what we'd naturally choose and let God to the choosing. It also mentions taking up our cross. Crosses were for one thing: execution. Hence we have the expression, 'dying to self.' While the world defines freedom as 'doing whatever you want,' godly freedom only comes when we lay down our desires and trade them for what God wants.

We might expect that, if we spend the rest of our days saying, "No," to our natural inclinations and dying to what we might feel like doing, our lives would become increasingly more miserable. Self-denial sounds so negative. Actually, that's a lie. Jesus said we'd find our lives – our true selves – and enjoy gain (See Verse 26).

Exodus 21 and Deuteronomy 15 tell us of a seemingly unimportant tid-bit of Jewish culture, but that law serves as an important illustration for us. In those days, people who could not pay their bills were sold into slavery for a certain period of time. During that season, they were 'slaves.' At the end of the time, usually after up to six years, they could go free – exactly what most slaves long for. But they also had a second option. If they had found their master to be good and kind – one with whom they had developed a loving relationship – they had the option to refuse to leave, and could choose to stay and serve the master for the rest of their lives. If that were the case, the master would take them to the doorpost of the house and pierce their ear with an awl as a public sign to all that the slave had chosen to remain in the service of his master. It also meant that he went from being a slave (one forced into service) to a 'servant' – someone who chose to serve out of love and respect.

What a great picture of the Christian life! We could not pay our own debt of sin and were slaves to sin, but we can choose to be servants of Jesus, because we love Him and want to serve Him. When I first heard this illustration several years ago, I actually considered getting my ear pierced, just as a reminder to myself that I now belong to Jesus. Part of me wishes I'd done that; maybe I still will!

Jesus, Himself, set an amazing example for us. He said, *"...I tell you the truth, the Son can do nothing by Himself. He does only what He sees the Father doing. Whatever the Father does, the Son also does"* (John 5:19). Jesus, in His earthly form, lived so dependently on His Father that He only did what God was doing, and He did those things in the same way the Father was doing them. I wonder what life would be like for us if we could say the same thing? I'm sure it would be amazing!

A few chapters later, in John 12:49, Jesus spoke about the powerful things He said, *"I don't speak on My own authority. The Father who sent Me has commanded Me what to say and how to say it."* Think of all the trouble we could avoid if we listened to God and only said what He said to say! Of course, that is much more easily said than done. But it is well worth the self-discipline! Maybe you're like me. As soon as some words have escaped my mouth, I find myself wishing that I could suck them back out of the air before anyone else hears them. Unfortunately, by then, it's too late. Thankfully, that is not always the case.

I remember one time, when I was serving a church as the Pastor of Administration, I'd unfortunately begun to butt heads with the Treasurer. The details of that aren't important; but, one night at an Elders' meeting, he proceeded to 'tear me to shreds' in front of the elders. Initially, everything within me wanted to defend myself and to lash out (i.e. punch him in the mouth! Ok, so I'm human; you shouldn't be too shocked!). For some reason – God's grace in my life, actually - I inwardly asked the Lord what was going on. He replied, "The fiery darts of the enemy." We know from Ephesians 6

CHAPTER 11 – WALKING IN FREEDOM...

that the only defense we have against such darts is the shield of faith. I had a vision of myself, kneeling down behind a large, glass shield, protected from all the little darts that were headed my direction but just bouncing off the shield in all directions. I was completely protected and not harmed by the barrage of accusations and insults. God gave me amazing peace; eventually, there seemed to be very little emotional reaction at all.

During the treasurer's tirade, I asked God what I should say or do about this. I was hoping to hear something about smiting a thousand Philistines with the jawbone of an ass (See the story of Samson); but what I heard was, *"...And as a lamb is silent before the shearers, He did not open His mouth"* (Acts 8:32). Apparently, when lambs are being shorn, they just give up the bleating and silently submit to shearer. I believed then, and still do, that God was telling me to say nothing. I don't know if God ever uses the expression, "Shut up!" but that was pretty much His message to me that night. Believe me, I had LOTS to say; but, out of sheer obedience, I chose to say nothing. When my assailant finally finished going up one side of me and down the other, he boldly asked, "So what do you have to say for yourself?" My reply shocked pretty much everyone, including me. "Not a thing," was all I had to say. I even smiled when I said it!

The follow up to that story came at another meeting, one with the entire board of the church. I was determined to say nothing – again, just out of sheer obedience. Towards the end of the meeting, a board member even said, "Well, everyone has made a lot of comments, except Don. I'd like to hear what he has to say." Boy, was that a test – I still had LOTS to say. Instead, I stood up, thanked the lady for caring about my perspective and only said this, "… at this time, I need to decline your invitation to make a comment," and then I sat down.

Later, another member of the Church Board confided something to this effect; "That was the smartest thing you could have said. If you'd complained and attacked the Treasurer, we'd have dismissed it as just a personality conflict. But when you refused to comment, we knew

213

that something deep, down, and dirty was going on and that we'd better get to the bottom of it."

Now, you must know, I'm just not smart enough to figure that out on my own. That was God's wisdom in action, and it was His grace in my life that enabled me to be obedient, to live in peace, and to be free. Listening to God really works!

Galatians 5 speaks to the same issue, but from a different perspective. There, Paul talks to us about being led by the Spirit of God. That means listening for what God has to say about things and then obeying His orders. That might sound pretty 'spiritual' and ethereal, but actually it is a basic practice of God's children. Taking orders from Headquarters is basic operating procedure in the army, isn't it? Servants wait for orders from the Master. Neither soldiers nor servants get a lot of credit for doing things that they weren't commissioned to do.

In that chapter, Paul outlines all the negative kinds of things that living in the flesh – living like a natural, unsaved person - will produce. Those are called the 'deeds of the flesh' or the 'works of the flesh.' In stark contrast, Galatians 5:22,23 lists what we refer to as the 'fruit' of the Spirit – the beautiful emotions or character qualities that the Spirit of God automatically produces in our lives as we learn to follow His leading. These include such wonderful emotions and character qualities as love, joy, peace, patience, kindness, goodness, faith (or faithfulness), gentleness, and self-control. Looking over that list, I'm pretty sure that we'd all love to be like that – to live that 'abundant life.' Isn't that what most people are searching for? Peace? Joy? Contentment? Freedom? Sure, it is!

I also notice that these things are called fruit. As far as we know, trees don't work hard to produce fruit; fruit just happens naturally. It isn't as if the tree decides one day, "OK, time to produce fruit," and then strains to force out an apple or a peach or whatever. No, fruit just grows naturally and automatically. As believers, we ought to be able to look back at what our lives were like a few years ago and compare that to what we see today. If there isn't more spiritual fruit – more of those great qualities – in our lives, something's wrong. Actually, we don't produce the fruit; the Holy Spirit super-naturally produces it in us. If our lives lack fruit, it could be that we haven't allowed the Spirit of God to work in us.

One term that we hear a lot these days is, 'quality of life.' It is true that modern medicine can help us live longer, but it can't always make us live better. We want, as the TV series said, to "live long and prosper," not just live a long, miserable life. Although dying to self and being led by the Spirit seems antithetical to 'looking out for number one' and 'grabbing all the gusto we can get,' it will bring a harvest of positive qualities that we can't obtain in any other way. And it will enhance our days.

Jesus wants us to experience that quality of life that He described as "abundant!" That doesn't promise us trouble-free, fun-filled lives; we know that in this world we will have trouble (John 16:33). God doesn't promise to keep us from challenges and difficulties; only to be with us in them. He might not change our circumstances as we think He ought to do, but He changes us in the midst of them.

Two factors of a 'rich and satisfying life' bear mentioning here. The first is our identity, and the second is our destiny. We've already talked about the identity that we have in Jesus Christ. 2 Corinthians 5:17 says, *"This means that anyone who belongs to Christ has become a new person. The old life is gone; a new life has begun!"* The 'all new' you has a spiritual identity, just as much as you have a natural identity.

We have a spiritual identity; so, what? Well, for one thing, God wants you to live in the identity that He has given to you. Believe me, He didn't do away with your old, damaged, sinful spirit, only to replace it with another old, damaged, and sinful one. When He made you a 'new creature,' He made you perfect. I believe that He restored your spirit and mine to be just as alive and holy and free as He originally created Adam's and Eve's; or, even better, like Jesus'. If the new, 'real you' is wonderful, why not learn to live out who you are? Wouldn't it be a good thing to become authentic to the new you? Absolutely!

The second factor is that God has made us new for a specific purpose – something He wants to accomplish in and through us. Perhaps we could label it our life's calling, or maybe we'd refer to it as our destiny. Soldiers are deployed on assignments or missions. Servants have specific jobs to do. Whatever name we give it, it is important, VERY important. As our Creator, God made us; and as our Redeemer, He remade us with a particular task or purpose in mind. That would be the cause that we're to live and die for – our 'raison d'être,' as the French would say. It's the reason we exist. I don't know about you, but I don't want to stand before the Lord and confess, "No, I missed it; I never figured out why I was made and never found out how to live passionately about what I was made to do. I just put in time, doing a lot of stuff; but I never actually did what You meant me to do." As the saying goes, "You only go around once;" and we rarely have opportunity to do 'do-overs.' Usually, we get it right the first time or we blow it forever.

Happily, some of us get around to answering that important question. It seems that all of us want to know who we are, where we came from, where we're going, who we can trust, and what we're supposed to do. i.e. "Why am I here?" Life in the Spirit will help to direct us to that supreme calling that God has for us. It will help us know what our assignment is.

Those working in the field of employment or Human Resources, mention something called 'working in your sweet spot.' In other words, you've found the perfect job for you. It is exactly suited to your personality and abilities. You love going to work, and it makes you feel satisfied and complete. It gives you energy. I've heard that if someone can make a living doing what he'd do for free or even for fun, they are very blessed. Following the Holy Spirit will direct us to our sweet spot. After all, it makes no sense that God would make a round peg and then drive it forcefully into a square hole – unless He reshapes either the peg, the hole, or both.

CHAPTER 11 - WALKING IN FREEDOM...

Discipleship – taking away anything that doesn't look like Jesus, also mysteriously reveals the real you and shows you what you've been made to do. Your life and your quality of life depend on you yielding to the Artist's hand. Amazingly, the new you and Jesus seem to look quite a bit alike!

That's all very well and fine, but what can we do about all that? How do we 'get discipled'? If it doesn't just happen naturally, and if we have a part to play, what do we need to do?

Have you noticed that 'discipleship,' 'disciple,' and 'discipline' all sound pretty much alike? In the cultural context, Jesus was recognized at the "Master," which simply indicates that He was the teacher. It would follow, then, that a disciple was simply a student. There was, however, more to the picture than that. In the Jewish culture of the day, a master would carefully select the finest students he could find; education was not considered the right that so many seem to believe is automatically theirs. In that day, if you wanted what we call higher education, you had to earn it by being the best potential student you could be – better than the rest of the candidates, hopefully. The masters chose their students based on one criteria: Did the student have proven potential to become like the master, to do what he would do and then grow in character, intellect and ability to do more than what the Master could do? In other words, the master was looking to invest his life into the next generation so that they could be and do more than the previous generation. All of the required preparation to even be considered to be a disciple took a great deal of work and discipline. No wonder we refer to the 'disciplines' of the faith! But what are they?

As you can probably guess, there are some regular routines that we need to practise if we want to grow up to be big, strong, soldiers or servants rather than slaves. Just like in the natural realm, there are certain things that we can do to grow up. In order to get healthy, we may need healing – help from a doctor. But beyond that, we need to eat right, exercise right, and sleep right. You'd never expect someone who eats junk food, never exercises except to lift the fork to

217

their face, and who stays up half the night to be healthy, let alone big and strong. You'd never catch a body-builder – or a soldier, for that matter – neglecting these basics of physical health.

For some reason, we tend to forget about all that when we come to the spiritual side of things. Perhaps we've forgotten to eat. How do we 'feed' our spirits? On the Word of God. Sometimes we eat alone, and sometimes we like to eat with a bunch of friends and make a party out of it. Whether we eat alone or in a group, common sense tells us that we can't go very long without food or we'll become weak and emaciated. It is possible to starve to death after all. When someone is sick, we might say that they're 'off their food,' indicating that they've lost their appetite.

The Bible is like spiritual food for our inner man. Somehow, it nourishes our spirits and feeds our souls in a way that you can almost feel as you read it and even afterward. There, we learn who God is and what His character is like. It builds us up and gives us insight into how we can live lives that are healthy and free and that honour Him. If we have no appetite for the Word, we have to admit that something is wrong.

Usually what robs us of our spiritual appetite is unhealthy or poisoned food; we've ingested something contaminated, maybe even rotten; and it has poisoned our system. What we 'eat' – whatever we fill our minds and hearts with – may be healthy, wholesome food or it may contain spiritual contamination. Can you think of a better way to disable soldiers, some more devious and effective way to weaken them so that they cannot fight well, than to poison their bodies with tainted food? Talk about sneaky – just add a bit of poison onto an otherwise healthy meal and that soldier is out of commission.

Our family used to have an old Bible that was given to one of the ancestors many years ago. On the presentation page, the donor had inscribed this truth, "Either this Book will keep you from sin, or sin will keep you from this Book." The first place to look when we're off our food is to look for food poisoning or unhealthy food.

CHAPTER 11 – WALKING IN FREEDOM...

Although the following passages are from the Old Testament and were originally intended for the nation of Israel, they still speak to us today.

Joshua 1:8 is God's covenant promise to Joshua, the warrior-leader who found himself at the controls for a nation of millions of people. (What a high calling! Talk about pressure!) What was God's word to him? *"Study this Book of Instruction continually. Meditate on it day and night so you will be sure to obey everything written in it. Only then will you prosper and succeed in all you do"* (Joshua 1:8). Right there, we have a sure-fire, 100% guaranteed promise of success. Read the Book! Obey it! Prosper! Powerful stuff – if we believe what God has said. If we did, wouldn't we be studying God's word all the time? Wouldn't we be thinking about it every day? Well, you'd think so, at least.

Psalm 1:2,3 affirms the same message: *"But they* (Those who are blessed) *delight in the law of the LORD, meditating on it day and night. They are like trees planted along the riverbank, bearing fruit each season. Their leaves never wither, and they prosper in all they do."* Notice the similarities: meditate on God's word, obey it, and prosper. Let's flip that coin over and see what it says, "Don't meditate; don't obey; and don't prosper." Hmmm.

So why aren't we more diligent in the read-mediate-obey-prosper cycle? As the man asked Jesus, *"I do believe, but help me overcome my unbelief!"* (Mark 9:24). Apparently, some things take more 'belief' than others.

The second important way to maintain spiritual health and strength is the discipline of prayer. Prayer, which is simply talking with God, whether in a natural language or in a spiritual one, nourishes and builds up our spiritual 'body.' So far, we've mentioned quite a bit about the wise practice of listening to God in prayer. That certainly builds us up and edifies our spirits.

We really don't know how this works, but we know from experience, that it does. Show me a Christian who does not have a consistent and passionate prayer life, and I'll show you a weak, anaemic believer.

If you were to scan the pages of Scripture, you'd find that, without exception, anyone who did great exploits for God had a vibrant prayer life. We know that Jesus prayed often and for extended periods of time. Daniel prayed regularly, even in the face of persecution.

Do a little research on the internet and you'll learn that it was Lord Alfred Tennyson who coined the phrase, "More things are wrought by prayer than this world dreams of."[1]

Jesus not only taught us to pray by personal example, He taught that we should pray in His name. "In Jesus' name," is not some magical incantation, tacked onto our shopping list of things we expect God to do for us; but, perhaps, we seem to slide it in at the end of a prayer, much the same way a magician might exclaim, "Hocus Pocus!" while performing some sleight of hand.

What we are actually saying, when we invoke the name of Jesus is essentially this: "I believe that this is what Jesus would ask or command." A policeman might command, "Stop in the name of the Law!" That means that he has the full authority of the law behind him, authorizing him to give that command. What the policeman can't do, and what he has no authority to do, is to order you to something that the law doesn't require. Why not? Because 'the law' hasn't given him the right to say that. Similarly, many people supposedly pray, "… in the name of Jesus," but have never checked with Jesus to see if He would authorize such a request. If we're asking for something that Jesus does not want, we can ask until we're blue in the face, but it might not produce the results we want.

In that sense, prayer is not so much about us bending the will of God into alignment with our own, but about us taking our cues from God and bringing our wills and our requests under the authority and leading of the Father. The only way for us to know what the Father wants is to find His will in His Word and to hear His voice, saying, "… *This is the way you should go, whether to the right or to the left"* (Isaiah 30:21). Did you notice how specific the instructions could be? "Ok, Father, which way should I go? Right or left?" "Left!" Amazing! The God of the universe wants to be that intimately involved in our lives.

CHAPTER 11 - WALKING IN FREEDOM...

Many people fall into discouragement when they appear to pray in Jesus' name, but then do not receive what they asked for. They may accept the enemy's deception that prayer doesn't work, or equally as bad, believe Satan's lie that God doesn't love them. Neither statement is true. What is true is that Jesus promised, *"You can ask for anything in my name, and I will do it, so that the Son can bring glory to the Father"* (John 14:13). That's a pretty wild claim! So why doesn't it work? Could it be that our concept of what Jesus should want is different that what He really does want? It isn't that prayer doesn't work; it's that prayer doesn't work if we don't work it properly.

I could decide that what I really need, and what Jesus really should want for me is a hot, new Ferrari. I could pray in faith, being careful to add on the 'right words,' 'in Jesus' name;' but I'll bet that this time next year I'll still be driving my Nissan!

In reality, that principle applies to everything pertaining to finding the 'abundant life' that Jesus promised. If we don't do our part, or we don't do it properly, we're not going to get the results we've been expecting. No soldier expects to win the battle by just doing whatever he feels like doing; he must obey orders if he's going to taste any victory. No servant can expect his master's accolades for doing something his master didn't want him to do.

There is a famous poem entitled, "The Charge of The Light Brigade," by Lord Alfred Tennyson. It is the story of an army unit that marched steadfastly in obedience to the orders of the commander, even though his orders would bring disaster. It led them all to their deaths. Of all the lines in that poem, these are the best known:

> "Theirs not to make reply,
> Theirs not to reason why,
> Theirs but to do and die:
> Into the Valley of Death
> Rode the six hundred." [2]

All that sounds really depressing – so many men marching needlessly to their deaths. It hardly seems fair. But their attitude appears to be correct; we march according to the commander's orders. Thankfully, we do not have a captain who makes mistakes or miscalculates battle strategy. He always sees things clearly and from a much greater perspective than we can. Obeying His orders, while not without much struggle and opposition sometimes, always guarantees success. I wonder what our lives would be like and how victorious they'd be if we had that same dogged determination, "Regardless of what the Master says, I'm going to obey!"

1 Corinthians 16:13 uses a great expression. While the KJV puts it this way, in more poetic language; *"Quit you like men;"* the NLT says it more plainly: *"Be on guard. Stand firm in the faith. Be courageous. Be strong."* I don't mean to be disrespectful to the Scripture, but in today's vernacular we might say, "Suck it up, Buttercup, and put your big boy pants on!" If we're going to endure and make it through some battles and into freedom and a *"rich and satisfying life,"* we need to be strong! That's the kind of attitude that will help us win the war, no matter where the battle takes place – in the church or in the world. As a good soldier, you might as well get used to the idea and prepare to 'Man up!' I am not sure how Paul would have expressed himself had he been writing to a woman instead of to Timothy. What we do know is that in both the Old and New Testaments we read of strong women who served the Lord: Deborah, Jael, Esther, Priscilla, Mary, and others. Without doubt, many of us could name spiritual sisters who are 'armed and dangerous' spiritually speaking. They're forces to be reckoned with, and it would be hard to imagine where many churches would be without them.

Maintaining our spiritual health is key to living in victory. Two other factors bear mentioning here: "baptism" and "communion." Both are illustrative plays or mimes that help us to stay focused on the cross. The first, baptism, is a silent play that depicts our death, burial and resurrection in Christ. It also depicts the washing away of our sins, which happened the moment we asked the Lord to forgive them. It is a one-time event that declares to the world and the church that, whatever we believed in and relied on before we came to Christ, we died to (so we were buried and plunged under the water – so much

CHAPTER 11 - WALKING IN FREEDOM...

more efficient and a lot less scary than using dirt!). It also shows that we have been raised to new life in Christ, when we come up out of the water and that we have embraced a new faith system – our faith in Jesus. Other religions also practised baptism, but Christians alone baptize in Jesus' name or in the name of the "Father, Son and Holy Spirit." It serves to proclaim that we have enlisted as soldiers in the army of the Lord – switched sides, so to speak or volunteered to serve our loving Master, Jesus.

Communion is also taken from the culture in which the Church was birthed. The Jewish people celebrate Passover every year. Part of their Seder meal involved the drinking of a variety of cups of wine and the eating of aphikomen, a special type of unleavened bread. Jesus claimed that He was the fulfillment of the prophetic meaning of the cup of redemption and the bread, when He said, *"This is My body...this is My blood."* He told the disciples to often eat and drink in order to remind ourselves of His sacrificial death for us. By reminding ourselves of the terrible price Jesus paid on our behalf, it calls us to renew or re-affirm that covenant relationship that we enter into with Him by faith.

While neither baptism nor communion has any saving power – they don't save us; faith does - they seem to bring a blessing into our lives and strengthen our spirits and our souls as they serve to strengthen our commitment to Christ. They may also bring some positive impact on us physically. I had a friend who has now gone to be with the Lord, but he claimed that once he started taking communion on a daily basis, both his hearing and his eyesight began to improve and his cholesterol levels went down. That might not prove anything, but it does give us something to ponder.

The bottom line is this; if we want to enjoy that 'abundant life' that Jesus offers to us, we need to be diligent and self-disciplined to do our part. I guess the real question is, "Is it worth it? Worth the sacrifice and self-denial?" As far as I know, I have never met anyone who said, "I wish I hadn't followed Jesus so closely," or, "I've wasted my life by walking with Him." In fact, just the opposite is true. Many of us look back and regret the wasted years we've spent either without Christ or by following Him at too great a distance.

Our Ministry in the Church:

We've already spoken at length about our place in the Body of Christ. Suffice it to say that, if we don't do our part, the whole body will be diminished. While it is not true that the spiritual health and vitality of our local assembly rests solely on my shoulders or yours, for that matter, we still have responsibility for the strength of our local fellowship. And, might I add, that it does not rest on the shoulders of your pastor. Ephesians 4:16 says that a church, as a body, can only be healthy and mature when the whole body and every joint does its part. Let's put it this way, "What if your church were totally dependent on your contribution – financially and spiritually? How strong would that fellowship be?" Do you go to church to 'get' something or to give? What are you 'adding' to that culture? How regularly do you 'serve' by taking responsibility for some ministry? What commission have you, as a soldier, received from the Commander? Are you 'on duty?' We all want strong, healthy and vibrant churches, but do we sacrifice to help make them that way? Enough said!

The World is Waiting:

As Jesus was about to leave this world in bodily form, He was giving major instructions to the disciples. You might think of it has His 'swan song,' or perhaps, in a less victorious scenario, someone's last words as they lie on their deathbed. What people talk about when they know that they're leaving this life is very important. Jesus proclaimed something of vital importance just before He was caught up in a cloud and taken to the Father's house. *"Jesus came and told His disciples, 'I have been given all authority in heaven and on earth. Therefore, go and make disciples of all the nations, baptizing them in the name of the Father and the Son and the Holy Spirit. Teach these new disciples to obey all the commands I have given you. And be sure of this: I am with you always, even to the end of the age'"* (Matthew 28: 18b, 19, 20).

CHAPTER 11 - WALKING IN FREEDOM...

The very last thing Jesus had to say to the church was both empowering and commissioning. He spoke of His authority and His abiding presence with the disciples; that's also our authority and our comfort. He also gave us a commission – a task – that He is expecting us to fulfill. You see, the Christian life isn't just about OUR freedom, but that of the whole world. His redemptive plan isn't just about a select 'Chosen Few' but encompasses those from every nation. After all, the whole world was lost under the control of Satan; and God wants His planet and His people back! So, what's the battle plan?

He left a small band of disciples – a 'Band of Brothers' and, without doubt, sisters – somewhere between twelve and five hundred of us, to spread out and reclaim that which was lost. We are to make disciples of Jesus in ALL nations. In that sense, every believer – every soldier – every disciple - has been commissioned and authorized to go and make disciples – new followers of Jesus. It isn't enough to just make converts; we're to make disciples – students and followers of Jesus who will become like Him. Sound familiar? What Jesus wants for your life, He wants for the nations.

John 15 is an extended metaphor, illustrating our need to always rely on Christ and to draw our life from Him. It uses the picture of a grape vine and its branches. If the branch is to survive, it needs to stay connected to the vine. Not only that, if the branch doesn't bear fruit because it has fallen down into the mud, the gardener will lift it up so that it can bear fruit.

There seems to be some discussion about what 'bearing fruit' looks like. Some say it means growing to be like Jesus. We certainly have that picture given to us in the fruit of the Spirit from Galatians 5. On the other hand, grape vines produce grapes; and grapes are just baby grape vines. Many sermons have declared that the fruit we are to bear is the harvest of new believers for which we're responsible. Jesus also said that the fields were white unto harvest and to pray to the Lord of the harvest to send labourers (Matthew 9:38 and Luke 10:2). Without exception, these verses are understood to be talking about evangelism that produces the fruit of many people coming to Christ. One way or the other, it is clear that we are to 'bear fruit.' Anyone would have a difficult time denying that this would include leading people to salvation in Christ.

As believers, we all share that "Great Commission" as part of our calling and destiny. Whether we call it 'evangelism' (literally sharing the "Good News" or the gospel of Jesus Christ), or 'soul winning' (a rather antiquated term) or 'sharing our faith,' we've been commissioned and sent to tell others, whether they're across the street or around the world, of God's love and His plan to free the captives from Satan's tyranny.

Our 'job' isn't finished until a) all the nations have been reached and b) the new believers have learned to do everything ("ALL") Jesus commanded the early disciples to do.

Doing evangelism or being a missionary (someone who was sent) is both costly and sometimes dangerous. As we speak, people are putting their necks on the line in order to share the gospel in lands where some don't want to hear it. Since Bible times, people have been persecuted or killed simply for sharing their faith. Obviously, Satan does not want to lose any ground, whether in people's lives or on the Earth, and will stop at pretty much nothing to prevent his kingdom from losing its influence. This doesn't change either our responsibility or our authority to go out and take the land.

Let's face it, everyone who is a believer today can trace their faith back to someone who shared the gospel with them and discipled them in the things of the Lord. Without those who shared with us, chances are we'd all still be lost in our sin and under Satan's control. But someone courageously shared their faith with us. Where would we be today if it weren't for their obedience and faithfulness to God's call on their lives?

Makes you wonder, doesn't it? Who's out there waiting for you to share your faith? Where might God's call on your life take you? Who is caught in slavery to sin that you could rescue?

CHAPTER 11 – WALKING IN FREEDOM...

Satan has us convinced that no one is waiting and that nobody wants to be 'preached at.' That just isn't true. There are countless stories of people waiting in spiritual darkness, ready to hear of God's love, and ripe for the harvest.

I remember hearing a medical missionary by the name of Dr. Helen Rosevere. This little bit of a woman had spent most of her life as a doctor in Africa. When I met her, she was speaking at a 'Missions Conference' at the Bible College I was attending. She told us of her life, of the struggles she'd survived, and of her arguments with God when He didn't do what she thought He should.

One story amazed us all. She told of being called to a distant village on some medical emergency and of having to drive alone across the savannah in the middle of the night in order to get home in time to do surgery the next morning. Apparently, no matter how much she prayed for the strength to stay awake, she'd fall asleep and drive around in circles until the jostling of the jeep would shake her awake. She was quite disappointed with God who was failing to keep her awake, so she pulled the jeep to a halt under one of those huge trees that dot the savannah landscape. She figured that she might as well get some actual sleep and stop wasting gasoline driving in circles. Somewhat angry about her unanswered prayers, she snuggled into the massive roots of the tree so she could nap. At that point she said the biggest African she'd ever met stepped out from behind the tree and stood between her and the jeep. Helen believed that he would kill her and steal the jeep. As she steeled herself for whatever was coming, she was amazed to hear the man simply ask, "Are you the one that the Creator sent to tell me about His son?" Amazing! True story! Don't let the enemy tell you no one wants to hear our message!

The world is waiting! God is waiting for us to obey His command. What are we doing about it?

Eternity Awaits:

Returning to a more self-focused emphasis, we need to understand that our future also will be greatly impacted by how we live here in this life. Let me be clear, where we spend eternity has already been settled by our faith in Christ. That makes sense. If God wants us to live WITH HIM in the here and now (and He does), He also wants us to do that forever. In John 14:1-3 we find these precious words, *"Don't let your hearts be troubled. Trust in God, and trust also in Me. There is more than enough room in My Father's home. If this were not so, would I have told you that I am going to prepare a place for you? When everything is ready, I will come and get you, so that you will always be with Me where I am."* God intends for us to spend eternity living with Him. Jesus is preparing that place. Why would He build us a place if we're not going to be there to enjoy it someday?

I remember being taught as a child that Christ was building mansions – huge, stately homes, full of grandeur and luxury for us. We were also taught that it was up to us to supply the building materials; that every time we did something good was like passing another brick up to Jesus so He could build us a larger mansion. I guess I don't really believe that any more. If the streets are made of gold and the gates of the city are made of huge pearls, it would appear that what we consider to be valuable here on Earth will have lost its importance by the time we get to Heaven. So, what's with the bigger and better mansions?

We know from Jewish culture, that when a young man got married, he and his wife would move into an addition on the father's house. This would preserve the inheritance according to how the land was originally divided up among the tribes, clans, and families. It would not be unusual for each son and his family to be housed in the larger estate of the father.

But I doubt that each time I do something positive here on Earth, my house in Heaven is expanded. If that were true, most of us would fall into a trap. The temptation would simply be to pre-purchase a better house in Heaven rather than serving our God just because He is worthy and we are thankful.

What I do believe, according to Matthew 25 and Luke 19, is that, according to our faithfulness as stewards of all that God has entrusted to us here, we will be given greater or lesser authority in this and the next life. Stewards were servants to whom the running of the master's household was entrusted. Essentially, they were the executive directors or CEO's of the business that the owner let them run. In this case, it was his house. The master was pre-occupied elsewhere, and so he left the running of the house up to the steward. Some stewards did well, ran the house properly, invested the entrusted funds wisely, and made a profit. None of the house, lands, or financial resources belonged to the steward; they were the master's. How well the stewards did determined what reward they received. Those rewards came in terms of greater opportunity to steward greater resources and responsibilities.

1 Corinthians 3 couches this concept in terms of building on God's foundation with common things like wood, hay and stubble (typical ordinary building materials of the day) or gold, silver, or precious stones (luxurious building materials). Both builders will have what they've built tested by a fire. One will survive the fire, but have nothing but ashes to show for his life's work. The other will have his work – built with non-combustible construction materials – tested, but it will survive. Some theologians see these materials as our 'works of service.' Others regard this passage as the quality of the theology we develop because Paul speaks of laying a foundation – Jesus, and we build on our faith in Jesus.

What we do know is that Jesus did teach about rewards that we might receive. In Matthew 5:12 and Luke 6:23, we find that suffering persecution because we pledge our allegiance to Jesus brings GREAT reward. This indicates that there will be levels or portions of rewards in Heaven – some greater and some lesser.

How you spend your time here in this life does not determine where you spend eternity; it determines how you spend it. Faith determines where; performance determines how!

SOMETHING TO THINK ABOUT...

1. If you picture your life as a war map, what areas are under the Spirit's control and what areas are under the enemy's? What do you think you might be able to do about that?

2. Assuming that the 'abundant like' does not mean a trouble-free one, how abundant, on a scale of 0 to 10, with 0 being completely miserable and 10 being mind-blowingly amazing, where would you score on the abundance scale? Why? What could be done?

3. What contribution of your time, talent and treasure are you making to your local church? Are you functioning like an island?

4. What is your plan to tell others – at home or abroad – about Christ? How will you fulfill your commission? If you don't have a specific plan, ask God for His strategies and develop a plan of action. Then go, do that!

5. If how you eternity, not where you spend it, were dependent on your service here, how would you judge your own 'performance' and stewardship? What changes might you need to make?

SOMETHING TO DO...

Everyone is on a spiritual journey. Share your story or your journey with someone. If you haven't yet made a commitment to Christ, talk with a friend about the things you're learning.

CHAPTER 12

FINALLY HOME
(After the war...)

***1 John 3:2** "Dear friends, we are already God's children, but He has not yet shown us what we will be like when Christ appears. But we do know that we will be like Him, for we will see Him as He really is."*

As we come to the final chapter, both in this book and eventually in our Earthly lives, we find that we have now come 'full-circle' and have arrived back where we began.

Remember Romans 8? God's plan is for our transformation and to conform us into the image of Jesus – so that we end up just like Him. In the process, God chooses to see us, not as we currently are experientially, but as what we can become experientially – the righteousness of Christ. If we are 'in Christ,' He has already granted us that "Complete in Christ" status, positionally, by faith (See Romans 4:18-22), and relates to us accordingly.

God looks past our current, natural reality to our true spiritual identity and future destiny. He takes that tarnished, twisted and destroyed image of God, restores our spirits to His original intent, and then treats us that way. Imagine what life would be like if we saw the 'buried treasure' in other people and began treating them appropriately. I know of one angry husband who was silenced by our Heavenly Father with these words, "Hey! That's my daughter you're talking about!"

When our time here on Earth is done, our struggle with sin and the battle against the principalities and powers will be complete, and we will be totally free! Then, the discipleship or transformation process will be accelerated to the point of completion.

As 1 John 3:2 tells us, when we see Jesus, we will automatically be made like Him. Somehow our human minds want to add an extra word, "more" into that sentence; but that's not what the Bible says. It doesn't say we'll become MORE like Him, but that we will be LIKE Him. Sometimes twins who look alike may elicit the comment, "Well, they couldn't be more alike!" because people have difficulty telling them apart. I know this all too well because I have an identical twin brother, and we're so much alike that we can fool people without even trying. Let's just say that we could probably switch places and, unless you knew us really well, you'd never know the difference. Regardless of how similar we are, Doug and I are not as much alike as Jesus Christ and all believers will be, once we see Him. Then we will all be exactly like Him.

Think of it, all the sin, all the personality foibles, and all the residual consequences of sin will be instantaneously washed away when we see Jesus. What a precious moment that will be! God's intention to conform us to be like Jesus will be finally and completely realized. Everything will be restored, and we will be totally free!

In Philippians 1:6 we have God's promise that He will complete the restoration process; *"And I am certain that God, who began the good work within you, will continue His work until it is finally finished on the day when Christ Jesus returns."* If that were true for the Philippians (and it was), it is also true for each and every one of us who believe in Jesus. We just need to learn to cooperate with God in the process and let Him do His work in us.

Jesus' words still echo in our ears and give hope to our hearts. *"If I go…I will come again…."* That is our hope.

The Apostle Paul spoke of this hope in Philippians, Chapter 3. There, he was 'giving his testimony' to the church at Philippi. In the first part of the chapter, Paul went into great detail about all his 'spiritual qualifications,' - the things he'd done in order to make himself

CHAPTER 12 – FINALLY HOME

'acceptable to God.' It was quite an impressive list of the spiritual attributes that the Jewish people believed would win God's favour.

After reviewing all his accomplishments, Paul made this startling statement; *"I once thought these things were valuable, but now I consider them worthless because of what Christ has done. Yes, everything else is worthless when compared with the infinite value of knowing Christ Jesus my Lord. For His sake, I have discarded everything else, counting it all as garbage, so that I could gain Christ and become one with Him. I no longer count on my own righteousness through obeying the law; rather, I become righteous through faith in Christ. For God's way of making us right with Himself depends on faith"* (Vs. 7-9). The King James reads it this way, *"I count them but dung...."*

To be blunt, comparing my own good works to the righteousness I have in Jesus, I now see them like … (Call it what you will… "dung," "poop," "excrement," or some other vernacular expression). However you put it, that's strong language and an even stronger message.

While Paul knew that his righteousness in Christ was real; he also realized that he was still in process – that more transformation was needed. Speaking of the resurrection of the dead, Paul confesses that he had not already obtained it and that he was not yet 'perfect' (Vs. 11-14). Instead he said, *"… so that one way or another I will experience the resurrection from the dead! I don't mean to say that I have already achieved these things or that I have already reached perfection. But I press on to possess that perfection for which Christ Jesus first possessed me. No, dear brothers and sisters, I have not achieved it, but I focus on this one thing: Forgetting the past and looking forward to what lies ahead, I press on to reach the end of the race and receive the heavenly prize for which God, through Christ Jesus, is calling us."*

While the NLT makes it clear that Paul is talking about striving for perfection, other versions sound like he's hoping to experience the resurrection. I used to think that Paul was saying he was still working his way to Heaven; and that, for all his striving, he still wasn't sure that he was saved or that he'd go to Heaven when he died. That cannot the case. It would be completely antithetical to everything Paul had been teaching. It also makes the central focus of Christianity a place or a destination. It would be all about getting into Heaven. I believe that what Paul was saying can be put this way: "I'm on my way to Heaven, but I'm still not completely transformed into the image of Jesus. That's my real calling and destiny." I think that's the real focus of our faith. God wants more for us than to just arrive at a destination. In the journey, He wants to transform us back into His image and into full Christ-likeness. Through the transformation process, God's kingdom is also established in our lives. Paul's destiny was sure; he was Heaven-bound. But he was not yet perfect. He was 'in Christ;' and, because of his faith, he was counted 'righteous.' But, in his experiential walk, he was still striving to become like Jesus. Positionally, (in Christ), Paul had already arrived; experientially, he was still on the journey.

Even at the end of his life, Paul had this testimony: *"I have fought the good fight, I have finished the race, and I have remained faithful. And now the prize awaits me—the crown of righteousness, which the Lord, the righteous Judge, will give me on the day of His return. And the prize is not just for me but for all who eagerly look forward to His appearing"* (2 Timothy 4:7,8). For all we know, Paul may very well have been laying on his death-bed as he penned those famous and much-loved, inspiring words. I believe it is the testimony of all believers; that there's something deep down in our spirits that identifies or resonates with that great assurance. What is the crown? Righteousness! When do we get it? On the day when we stand before Jesus and see Him face to face. What a day that will be!

1 Thessalonians 4:13-17 provides more detail about that 'appearing.' *"And now, dear brothers and sisters, we want you to know what will happen to the believers who have died so you will not grieve like people who have no hope. For since we believe that Jesus died and was raised to life again, we also believe that when Jesus returns, God will bring back with Him the believers who have died. We tell you this directly from the Lord: We who are still living when the Lord returns will not meet Him ahead of those who have died. For the Lord, Himself will come down from Heaven with a commanding shout, with the voice of*

CHAPTER 12 – FINALLY HOME

the archangel, and with the trumpet call of God. First, the believers who have died will rise from their graves. Then, together with them, we who are still alive and remain on the earth will be caught up in the clouds to meet the Lord in the air. Then we will be with the Lord forever."

In an even longer discourse, (1 Corinthians 15), Paul tells us that this immediate and critical transformation will even impact our physical bodies. *"But let me reveal to you a wonderful secret. We will not all die, but we will all be transformed! It will happen in a moment, in the blink of an eye, when the last trumpet is blown. For when the trumpet sounds, those who have died will be raised to live forever. And we who are living will also be transformed. For our dying bodies must be transformed into bodies that will never die; our mortal bodies must be transformed into immortal bodies. Then, when our dying bodies have been transformed into bodies that will never die, this Scripture will be fulfilled: 'Death is swallowed up in victory. O death, where is your victory? O death, where is your sting?' For sin is the sting that results in death, and the law gives sin its power. But thank God! He gives us victory over sin and death through our Lord Jesus Christ"* (Vs. 51-56).

This is our clear hope; it is our future - if we are in Christ. He will appear; we will meet Him in the air; and the transformation process will be complete. We sometimes hear people refer to 'body, soul, and spirit,' In the transformation process, it is just the opposite. First, our spirits are instantaneously transformed when we come to faith. Our souls are in process and are becoming like Jesus; and that process will continue until we see Christ. In that instant, our transformation process will be accelerated to completion. Lastly, our bodies will also be transformed into eternal and glorified form. Perhaps, rather than dying, we will live long enough to see the Lord's return. In that case, our souls and bodies will change at pretty much the same moment.

As enthusiastic preachers may proclaim, "Can somebody, anybody, shout 'Hallelujah'?" (Praise to You, God) or at least give a hearty, 'Amen!' (Let it be!)?"

Paul adds a comforting and yet frightening thought, *"But the day of the Lord will come as unexpectedly as a thief. Then the heavens will pass away with a terrible noise, and the very elements themselves will disappear in fire, and the Earth and everything on it will be found to deserve judgment. Since everything around us is going to be destroyed like this, what holy and godly lives you should live, looking forward to the day of God and hurrying it along. On that day, He will set the heavens on fire, and the elements will melt away in the flames. But we are looking forward to the new heavens and new Earth He has promised, a world filled with God's righteousness"* (2 Peter 3:10-13). Don't those new heavens and new Earth sound familiar? They sound like Eden and home!

As I said, by now we'll come full circle. My expectation is that the new Heavens and Earth will be pretty similar to how God originally created this world – without the divided loyalties, without sin, and without slavery. We can only imagine what it will be like. There is one major difference – other than the fact that we'll be there. Unlike the original Eden, our new world will be permanent. We will be with the Lord FOREVER (1 Thessalonians 4:17b). There will be no falling away this time; no deception and no treason; only confirmed righteousness.

Unfortunately, misinformed public opinion has provided us with a very inadequate and erroneous picture of what Heaven and Eternity will be like. Speculative imagination wants to paint a picture of chubby, naked, winged babies, floating around on fluffy, white clouds and strumming on miniature harps all day long. Good grief! How boring would that be!?! What about all that 'have dominion' and 'subdue' business? What about the Kingdom of Heaven being manifested on new Earth? Adam and Eve had tasks to do, work to accomplish, and a kingdom to establish. You must realize that they didn't do that by floating around strumming harps all day!

The Scriptures paint an amazing picture of Heaven – streets of gold, gates made of humungous pearls and fine jewels, etc. Whether one interprets these details literally or figuratively, one lesson seems clear; what we value so greatly here on Earth, will not hold the same importance there. After all, no-one really places a lot of value on a chunk of pavement!

CHAPTER 12 – FINALLY HOME

Whatever that world will be, we know that it will be glorious. We already find this Earth so beautiful. All we need to do is to observe a beautiful sunset or gaze in wonder at the majesty of the Rocky Mountains and we're in awe at the glory of creation. But we forget that what we see is a very different picture than what God created. If we're impressed by 'damaged goods,' think of how amazing the original must have been!

In the meantime, there is still one consistent theme in these passages. I John 3:3 adds, *"And all who have this eager expectation will keep themselves pure, just as He is pure."* The 1 Corinthians passage encourages us, *"So, my dear brothers and sisters, be strong and immovable. Always work enthusiastically for the Lord, for you know that nothing you do for the Lord is ever useless"* (15:58). 2 Peter is equally challenging as it asks, *"Since everything around us is going to be destroyed like this, what holy and godly lives you should live, looking forward to the day of God and hurrying it along...?"* and instructs us to *"...make every effort to be found living peaceful lives that are pure and blameless in His sight"* (2 Peter 3:11,12, 14b). What is that theme? We should live righteously and passionately as we wait to be with the Lord.

Paul told us the same type of thing in Ephesians 4:25-27, only he uses the metaphor of a bridegroom coming to take his bride. In Jewish culture, the couple would be formally engaged, and considered married. Then the groom would go away for between one and three years. During that time, he would build a home for his bride and himself. Often, that home was an extension on his father's house (Does this sound familiar? See John 14). During that time the bride would be living in constant expectation that, "This could be the day when my Beloved comes for me." With the assistance of her bridesmaids, she was always supposed to be ready for the groom to appear unannounced. Talk about waiting in hope. Sometimes, the groom would send jewels or other finery so that the bride could 'get all dolled up,' and ready for his return. Finally, the day would come; the groom would arrive without prior notice and take his bride home to the father's house.

Paul instructed the believing husbands to learn from Jesus' example with these words, *"For husbands, this means love your wives, just as Christ loved the church. He gave up His life for her to make her holy and clean, washed by the cleansing of God's word. He did this to present her to Himself as a glorious church without a spot or wrinkle or any other blemish. Instead,* **she will be holy and without fault.** *In the same way, husbands ought to love their wives..."* (Ephesians 5:25-28a). (Emphasis mine). The lesson stays the same; in order to be ready for Christ to come, all believers – the Church, the Bride of Christ – needs to prepare for His appearing. This involves embracing that transformative discipleship process so that we can be both positionally and experientially ready to meet Him.

Words fail us in our feeble and human expression of what it will be like to see Jesus and be finally and totally transformed into His image. In that day, we will be completely free from the penalty, power and presence of sin – both without and within. My 'inner cowboy' wants to shout, "Yee-haw!" at this point. The warrior in me replies, "Boo-yah!" Perhaps it is really my spirit crying out Martin Luther King's immortal words, "Free at last; free at last! Thank God almighty, I'm free at last!"

At this point, we really can only imagine what that day will bring. But in that day, what is now faith will become sight; and we won't have to wonder any longer. It will be the reality and the freedom to which Christ has called us. For now, though, let us always live in light of eternity. Let's give practical expression to our inner cry for freedom. Let's fight for it, if we have to!

CHAPTER 12 – FINALLY HOME

SOMETHING TO THINK ABOUT…

1. Why wait to fall at the feet of Jesus on that day? Can't we do it now? If so, what would that mean for your life?

2. Once we get to Heaven, many of our questions that remain unanswered in the here and now will fade into insignificance, and we won't even worry about them there. If you could ask Jesus one question, what would it be?

3. In light of Peter's exhortation that we should live so that, when Jesus comes, He might find us "in peace, spotless and blameless," what might need to change in your life, starting today?

4. What excites you the most about Heaven?

5. Write out a prayer telling Jesus how you're feeling about the prospect of meeting Him face to face.

SOMETHING TO DO…

Spend some time imagining what it would be like to see Jesus face to face. What might you do? What might you say?

CONCLUSION...

Let me close with some hopeful and comforting verses. They're a "doxology." That's an expression of worship and praise. It comes from the little book of Jude, Chapter 1 and Verses 24 and 25. Join with me in these great words; *"Now all glory to God, who is able to keep you from falling away and will bring you with great joy into His glorious presence without a single fault. All glory to Him who alone is God, our Saviour through Jesus Christ our Lord. All glory, majesty, power, and authority are His before all time, and in the present, and beyond all time! Amen."*

Did you catch that great truth? He is the one who can and will keep us from falling. We can't even do that for ourselves. He is the one who can bring us into His presence, without blame and with great joy. (Just imagine how wonderful that will be!) We can't do that, either! He is the one who will complete our transformation; all we can do is to co-operate with Him in that process. Thank God for that amazing truth! Amen? Amen!

If we were to continue reading in the saga of Gideon, we'd see how one encounter with a rhema word from God changed his life. He went from being a nobody, hiding from the enemy in a wine-press, to being a great and courageous warrior. Obediently acting on 'commands from headquarters,' he accomplished some amazing exploits – tore down pagan temples, sacrificed his father's prized breeding bulls, and fought many battles using some pretty unconventional forms of warfare. Ultimately, God used Gideon to overthrow the spiritual and natural enemies of His people and brought them into a freedom that they'd only dreamed of.

Your name probably isn't Gideon; it might be another; Jim or Nancy or whatever. Perhaps you've see yourself as somewhat of a nobody, hiding from the enemy. We tend to almost idolize these 'Great Heroes of the Faith' and imagine that God could never use us the way He used them. James 5 says that *"Elijah was as human as we are;"* but when he prayed, the environment responded, first by withholding rain for three years at his command, and then by pouring rain when he announced it was time. Sounds amazing, but let's remember, Elijah wasn't some super-human; he was just like the rest of us. If God could do the miraculous through him, He can also accomplish His amazing purposes through you. Who knows how God might want to transform your life and commission you to do great things for His kingdom?

So, let the warriors arise!

FOOTNOTES

CHAPTER 1

1. Richards, Lawrence O., Expository Dictionary of Bible Words, (Grand Rapids, Michigan; The Zondervan Corp., 1985). Pg. 350

2. Richards, Lawrence O., Expository Dictionary of Bible Words,(Grand Rapids, Michigan; The Zondervan Corp., 1985). Pg. 350

3. Brown, Francis (Ed), The New Brown, Driver, Briggs, and Gesenius Hebrew and Greek Lexicon, (LaFayette Indiana; Associated Publishers & Authors, Inc., 1978). Pg.350

4. Brown, Francis (Ed), The New Brown, Driver, Briggs, and Gesenius Hebrew and Greek Lexicon, (LaFayette Indiana; Associated Publishers & Authors, Inc., 1978). Pg. 921

5. Young, Robert, Analytical Concordance to the Holy Bible, (Guildford & London; United Society for Christian Literature, 1977). Pg. 488

6. Strong, James, A Concise Dictionary of the Words in The Hebrew Bible, (Chattanooga, TN; AMG Publishers, 1990) Pgs. 80 and 1735; included in Zodhiates, Spiros, (Ed), Hebrew-Greek Key Word Study Bible, New American Standard Bible, (Chattanooga, TN; AMG Publishers, 1990).

7. Strong, James, A Concise Dictionary of the Words in The Hebrew Bible, (Chattanooga, TN; AMG Publishers, 1990). Pg. 38; included in Zodhiates, Spiros, (Ed), Hebrew-Greek Key Word Study Bible, New American Standard Bible, (Chattanooga, TN; AMG Publishers, 1990).

8. Strong, James, A Concise Dictionary of the Words in The Hebrew Bible,(Chattanooga, TN; AMG Publishers, 1990). Pg. 15; included in Zodhiates, Spiros, (Ed), Hebrew-Greek Key Word Study Bible, New American Standard Bible, (Chattanooga, TN; AMG Publishers, 1990).

9. Strong, James, A Concise Dictionary of the Words in The Hebrew Bible, (Chattanooga, TN; AMG Publishers, 1990). Pg. 80; included in Zodhiates, Spiros, (Ed), Hebrew-Greek Key Word Study Bible, New American Standard Bible, (Chattanooga, TN; AMG Publishers, 1990).

10. Young, Robert, Analytical Concordance to the Holy Bible,(Guildford & London; United Society for Christian Literature, 1977). Pg. 367

11. Young, Robert, Analytical Concordance to the Holy Bible, (Guildford & London; United Society for Christian Literature, 1977). Pg. 1031

CHAPTER 2

1. Strong, James, A Concise Dictionary of the Words in The Hebrew Bible,(Chattanooga, TN; AMG Publishers, 1990). Pg. 91; included in Zodhiates, Spiros, (Ed), Hebrew-Greek Key Word Study Bible, New American Standard Bible, (Chattanooga, TN; AMG Publishers, 1990).

2. Young, Robert, Analytical Concordance to the Holy Bible,(Guildford & London; United Society for Christian Literature, 1977). Pg. 21

3. Young, Robert, Analytical Concordance to the Holy Bible, (Guildford & London; United Society for Christian Literature, 1977). Pg. 257

CHAPTER 3

1. Unpublished Class Notes, Ellel/Singing Waters Ministries, (Orangeville ON, 2002)

2. Vine, W. E., An Expository Dictionary of New Testament Words, (Old Tappan, New Jersey; Fleming H, 1966). Vol. III, Pg. 331

3. Vine, W. E., An Expository Dictionary of New Testament Words, (Old tappan, New Jersey; Fleming H, 1966). Vol. II, Pg. 10

CHAPTER 4

1. Young, William P., The Shack, (Newbury Park, CA; Windblown Media, 2007), Pg 188

CHAPTER 6

1. Young, Robert, Analytical Concordance to the Holy Bible, (Guildford & London; United Society for Christian Literature, 1977). Pg. 756

2. Young, Robert, Analytical Concordance to the Holy Bible, (Guildford & London; United Society for Christian Literature, 1977). Pg. 943

3. Young, Robert, Analytical Concordance to the Holy Bible, (Guildford & London; United Society for Christian Literature, 1977).Pg. 810

CHAPTER 9

1. Crabb, Lawrence J., Basic Principles of Biblical Counseling, (Grand Rapids, MI; Zondervan Publishing House, 1975) and Crabb, Lawrence J., Effective Biblical Counseling, (Grand Rapids, MI; Zondervan Publishing House, 1977)

CHAPTER 10

1. Quote from internet, website https;//web.cs.dial.ca/- Johnston/poetry/island/html

2. Hall, Elvine M., Jesus Paid It All Public Domain, 1865

CHAPTER 11

1. Tennyson, Alfred, Idylls of the King as quoted on the website goodreads.com, on the internet.

2. Tennyson, Alfred, The Charge of the Light Brigade as quoted on the website goodreads.com, the internet.

UNLESS OTHERWISE NOTED, ALL SCRIPTURE QUOTES ARE TAKEN FROM: NLT – NEW LIVING TRANSLATION
2nd Edition Tyndale Publishers, Inc., Carol Stream, Illinois, 1996, 2004, Tyndale Charitable Trust, Scripture quotations marked NLT are taken from the *Holy Bible,* New Living Translation. Copyright © 1996, 2004. Used by permission of Tyndale House Publishers, Inc., Carol Stream, Illinios. All rights reserved.

OTHER VERSIONS QUOTED:
KJV – KING JAMES VERSION
Public Domain

NASB – NEW AMERICAN STANDARD BIBLE
Zodhiates, Spiros, (ED.) Hebrew-Greek Key Word Study Bible – New American Standard Bible, (Chattanooga, TN; AMG Publishers, 1977)

Made in the USA
Columbia, SC
14 November 2017